GW00541047

A79448

# Against Citizenship

**DISSIDENT FEMINISMS**

Piya Chatterjee, Editor

*A list of books in the series appears at the end of this book.*

# Against Citizenship

## The Violence of the Normative

**AMY L. BRANDZEL**

**UNIVERSITY OF ILLINOIS PRESS**
Urbana, Chicago, and Springfield

© 2016 by the Board of Trustees
of the University of Illinois
All rights reserved

1 2 3 4 5 C P 5 4 3 2 1
∞ This book is printed on acid-free paper.

Printed and bound in Great Britain by
Marston Book Services Ltd, Oxfordshire

Library of Congress Cataloging-in-Publication Data
Brandzel, Amy L., 1970– author.
Against citizenship: the violence of the normative / Amy L.
Brandzel.
pages   cm. — (Dissident feminisms)
Includes bibliographical references and index.
ISBN 978-0-252-04003-0 (cloth : alk. paper)
ISBN 978-0-252-08150-7 (pbk: alk. paper)
ISBN 978-0-252-09823-9 (e-book)
1. Citizenship—United States—Cases. 2. Same-sex marriage—
Law and legislation—United States—Cases. 3. Hate crimes—
United States—Cases. 4. Race relations—United States—Cases.
I. Title.
KF4700.B73     2016
342.7308'3—dc23       2015035919

*To the teachers: the strangers and friends*
*who called me out and let me in.*

# Contents

# A Politics of Presence for the Present

So critique is risky. It can be a disruptive, disorienting, and at times
destructive enterprise of knowledge. It can be vertiginous knowledge,
knowledge that produces bouts of political inarticulateness and
uncertainty, knowledge that bears no immediate policy outcomes or
table of tactics. And it can include on its casualty list a number of
losses—discarded ways of thinking and operating—with no clear
replacements. But critique is risky in another sense as well, what
might be called an affirmative sense. For critique hazards the opening
of new modalities of thought and political possibility, and potentially
affords as well the possibility of enormous pleasure—political,
intellectual, and ethical.

—Wendy Brown and Janet Halley

In the introduction to *Left Legalism/Left Critique*, Wendy Brown and Janet Halley write in defense of critique.[1] Their agenda is to respond to various commentators that accuse and deride critical scholarship as merely negative and deconstructive practices that dismantle politics without offering any accessible alternatives. But in their/our defense, Brown and Halley argue that the value of critique stems from a commitment to "dissect our most established maxims and shibboleths, not only for scholastic purposes, but also for the deeply political ones of renewing perspective and opening up new possibility." This is why critique is risky, because critique cannot promise a programmatic or political blueprint to achieve justice; at its best, critique can promise only to shake up belief systems and contest epistemological frameworks. And as they state in the epigraph, critique is pleasurable. Critique is fun. Critique can be "a kind of euphoria in being released to think critically about something that one experiences as constraining, limited, or gagging."[2] I also think some of this fun comes from the pleasure of positioning ourselves on the right side of politics, of deeming ourselves uniquely qualified to expose operations of power. There is a joy and a pleasure in righteous critique. In the process, many critics, including myself, participate in bifurcating academic, political, and intellectual stances by deeming ourselves as the politically astute against those that are then marked as the unfortunate dupes of false consciousness. Therefore, before I embark on the critiques that are offered in this book, I want to take a moment in this preface to explore the pleasure and pain of critique. My goal is to situate this book within an accountable politics, or what I refer to as a politics of presence.

To be clear, the book you are about to read is full of righteousness and decimating critique. *Against Citizenship* joins other critical scholars who critique the ways in which aspirations for inclusion and recognition by the state are far from neutral. These critiques argue that seeking rights and inclusion within key institutions are not just private choices. Rather, these aspirations for inclusion re-create violence against vulnerable peoples. As a process, normative inclusion entrenches notions of proper versus improper, natural versus abnormal, and normative versus abject. There is no such thing as a movement for inclusion and citizenship for *some* that does not further the vulnerability and disenfranchisement of *others*. The goal of these critiques is to demonstrate how longing for inclusion and citizenship reinforce violence against abjected others. As this book argues, these kinds of radical critiques of the normative are most useful when they work to expose the intersectionality of normative belief systems and structures of thought, and offer suggestions as to how we might work against the reentrenchment of these processes.

And yet, it is not lost on me that I am participating in a form of epistemic violence myself when I call out political strategies and inclusionary gestures as violent. Therefore, this book's objects of critique (hate crime legislation, same-sex marriage, and the opposition of civil rights versus political rights for Indigenous nations) necessitate compassion toward the normative desires and aspirations for less vulnerability, more social belonging, and access to more life chances. Despite the turn to affect, many in academe remain impervious to the affective dimensions of the work that we do and the critiques that we offer. What does it mean to speak about victims and perpetrators of normative violence in such a way as to be accountable, or at the very least, *present* for the pain that this can cause? As much as I join critical left scholars and their critiques of inclusion-oriented politics, and as much as I believe that we cause violence to others when we participate in such a politics, I am also concerned with the ways in which scholars can remove themselves from being accountable for the pain and violence of our critiques. In what ways do we take pleasure in—perhaps even revel in—the joy of being able to call out, expose, and reveal power particularly when we can do so at the expense of those whose political alignments are close enough to our own that we can engage in politically savvy one-upmanship? How does the righteous indignation of radical critique refuse to witness the pain of normative exclusion?

Let me use queer theory and our critiques of assimilationist politics as an example. Perhaps no field can be (or should be) called out more for its band-wagon-like political agendas than queer studies, a field that is as culpable for creating monosystems of thought and action as it is for critiquing them.[3] In 2010, I attended an academic conference where most queer studies presenters could not help but make easy jabs at the "It Gets Better Project." Columnist Dan Savage initiated this antibullying campaign in September of 2010 in response to numerous suicides of queer youth.[4] The project consisted of thousands of short videos in which celebrities, politicians, and regular folks spoke earnestly to the presumed "gay" teenage viewer, who was marked as the normative subject of homophobic violence and bullying, about how life will just, undoubtedly and eventually, get better. The project does not address structural inequalities, nor does it have a political vision beyond mere hopefulness. For a field, such as queer studies, that desires to locate its political aspirations within the in-your-face political campaigns of ACT UP and Queer Nation, the "It Gets Better" campaign epitomizes docile acquiescence to heteronormativity and the violence that it empowers. Therefore, perhaps a bit predictably, many queer studies presenters criticized the campaign for its simplistic, assimilationist appeal.

While queer studies scholars are particularly known for their critical and cranky demeanors, their/our critiques of this project are part of a larger and much longer practice rampant within academe to deconstruct, and, at times, rhetorically decimate, the political strategies, campaigns, and projects that are initiated by political agencies in the name of change. And while the field of feminist studies has been interrogating its negotiations with theory, practice, and praxis for over a decade, *Against Citizenship* begins the important work of asking what a politics of responsibility and accountability would look like for queer studies. One of the central questions of this text is: how can we imagine a transformative politics for queer studies, one that creatively inhabits *both* a *skeptical demeanor* and a *reparative affiliation* with the political agencies and actors that we so often criticize in our work?

The political struggle, then, that arises from my own inhabited position within feminist and queer studies, is to try to practice a politics of presence alongside a radical and downright cranky disdain for normativity. I cannot help but wonder, what would the critiques or snarky asides have looked like had the presenters presumed the presence of a suicidal gay youth or the parents of a child who committed suicide in response to "bullying" and discrimination received in school? How can we create scholarship that is not only critical, but *accountable* to those actors and agencies whose political actions we so often find lacking, assimilationist, ethically bankrupt, or, even more painfully, culpable for re-creating violence against nonnormative peoples? This text tries to keep this tension alive, sometimes successfully I hope, between a queer politics of radical critique and a feminist politics of presence.

A politics of radical critique requires that we attend to and expose the violence of normative aspirations, while the politics of presence requires that we consider the ways in which our own critiques can (re)create pain, isolation, competition, and resentment. Hence, I want to discuss what is at stake when we consider the objects of this book within this framework. If this book centers the violence of "normative strivings" (to use Roderick Ferguson's eloquent phrasing), then perhaps we might be served by considering what is behind these longings for normativity and inclusion. While assimilationist tactics are deployed throughout the political and academic spectrum, I want to continue to use the example of queer critiques of gay and lesbian citizenship as a site to explore how to be accountable critics and scholars.

Queer theorists have been quite vocal calling out inclusionary gestures, whether it is through Lisa Duggan's "homonormativity," David Eng's "queer liberalism," Jasbir Puar's "homonationalism," or Roderick Ferguson's "normative strivings," but we have rarely acknowledged the trauma that motivates these gestures. In the early 2000s, Lisa Duggan initiated an investigation into how gay and lesbian political organizations prioritized neoliberalist ideals of privatization, individualism, and material comforts over issues such as redistributive and anti-assimilationist politics. Duggan argued that the mainstream "gay agenda" was successfully recoded into the "new homonormativity" because it was aligned with neoliberalist interests and conservative social mores.[5] Extending Duggan's insights, David Eng argues that the turn to what he names "queer liberalism" stems from a desire for "liberal inclusion of particularly gay and lesbian U.S. citizen-subjects petitioning for rights and recognition before the law," which colludes with the rhetoric of colorblindness in order to demand "the forgetting of race and the denial of racial difference." In fact, Eng argues that the timing is important in that "the advent of colorblindness in the U.S. nation-state thus becomes the condition of possibility for the historical emergence of queer freedom."[6] This desire for inclusion denotes not only the disavowal of racialized structures of power, but also represents a direct retreat from queer politics that opposed state-based legitimacy and recognition. In these narratives, then, we might see the ways in which gay, lesbian, and queer subjects are positioned as "selling out" or "giving in" to longings for recognition and the privileges this recognition affords.

In their article, "Intimate Investments: Homonormativity, Global Lockdown, and the Seductions of Empire," Anna M. Agathangelou, M. Daniel Bassichis, and Tamara L. Spira offer important insights into what they call the "affective economies" of bourgeois belonging and inclusion. Agathangelou et al. argue that there has been a "homonormative turn" in which gay and lesbian subjects have been seduced into collusion with violent operations of the U.S. nation-state and empire, including the "global lockdown" via the prison industrial complex, the war(s) on terror, and increased border militarization and surveillance technologies. As they state, "Stressing this politico-economic context, it becomes possible to read many of the contradictions of the homonormative moment *alongside* and *within* the recent intensification of the war on terror and of global lockdown."[7]

What they name as a process of being "seduced by empire," Jasbir Puar identifies as "homonationalism." For Puar, homonationalism is a biopolitical process, whereby the "emergence and sanctioning of queer subjecthood is a historical shift condoned only through a parallel process of demarcation from populations targeted for segregation, disposal, or death." Queer inclusion is produced through "a reintensification of racialization through queerness." As she astutely observes, "the cultivation of these homosexual subjects folded into life, enabled through a 'market virility' and 'regenerative reproductivity', is racially demarcated and paralleled by a rise in the targeting of queerly raced bodies for dying."[8] Importantly, Puar describes these homonationalist longings as stemming directly from a fantasy of a permanent inclusion into normative citizenship.

While seductions and fantasies no doubt play a large role in the various "bargains with the devil," can we consider these inclusionary gestures as also purposeful strategies of resistance? Roderick Ferguson's work has been extremely attentive to the ways African American familial and intimate formations have been extricated from the norms of citizenship and queered in the process. His book, *Aberrations in Black*, teases out the ways in which African American scholars and activists have both resisted and participated in normative logics at the intersections of racialization, sexualization, and citizenship. Ferguson shows how creative Black activists and scholars have deployed "nightmares of the heteronormative," that is, counterstrategies that have taken advantage of the abjection of nonheteronormative practices and affiliations as ways to counter racialization.[9] But sometimes these strategies also reveal "normative strivings," that is, the ways in which some African American intellectual and activist traditions have utilized "tactics" of "sexual and gender normativity."[10] These tactics counter racialization while also, inadvertently and advertently, reproduce heteronormative and imperialist logics.

Ferguson's analyses force a consideration of the complex ways normative strivings might also be, or might even primarily be, strategies of survival. While the homonormative, homonationalist, and queer liberalist might be imagined as participating in whitenormative, heteronormative citizenship, Ferguson reminds us to remain present to the types of violence and trauma that create the conditions for and precede the "normative strivings." The fantasies and seductions, then, are motivated in part by pain, and a desire to end the suffering and violence of exclusion. As Agathangelou et al. observe,

> seduction toward something better promises subjects an end to pain, marginalization, and violence in exchange for being recognized as legitimate subjects who can potentially participate in global capitalist relations and its futures—collusion becomes the cost of belonging. Lest we slip (back) into the realm of the hated, the despised, the killable, and the disposable (that is, if we ever had a chance to leave), we must actively support and often embody the threat of force that lies on the other side of this tenuous promise, or so the logic goes.[11]

Their explanation helps us see the ways in which the homonormative turn stems from "the traumas of state-sanctioned repression of queer communities," even while it also participates in furthering the pain and vulnerability of others.[12]

A politics of presence, then, requires a consideration of the ways in which experiences of trauma, pain, violence, and disposability might motivate the types of assimilationist gestures that are named throughout this book. It requires an acknowledgment, for example, of the ways in which the extensive energies driving the gay marriage movement in the United States stem from the experiences of disavowal, interpersonal violence, and isolations from intimacy that are manifest in heterosexual normativities of marriage. Here, the politics of presence requires not only understanding how heterosexual-only marriage laws produce material inequalities and familial separations, such as through health care and immigration policies, but also the ways in which the trauma of the AIDS epidemic on queer communities can been seen as one of the central forces driving the marriage movement.[13] Striving for marriage rights incorporates a desire for intimate recognition, a banishment of the pain and agony of nonrecognition for nonnormative kinship practices, and a means to respond to state practices ranging from benign neglect to outright dehumanization.

The politics of presence also demands a thoughtful appreciation of the experiences of trauma and victimization that stem from hate violence and the very real and rare opportunities for some disenfranchised people to require that the state at least claim to act "protectively" on their behalf. As Christina Hanhardt points out, violence has the ability to "undo a person," and the affective responses to that undoing can be profound.[14] This is not, then, about shaming activists for turning to the state for more hate crime legislation, even if and when that turn can replicate anti-intersectional strategies. In the rush to condemn hate crime legislation activists for appealing to the police apparatus of the state, critical scholars have often neglected the very important and critical work of being present for the violence and pain experienced by victims of hate crimes. Rather than admonishing hate crime activists for potentially being mired under any sort of "false consciousness," I want to follow the lead of Hanhardt and Katherine Whitlock. Whitlock critiques the effects of legislation while also offering a "call to love and justice," that is, "a loving and provocative challenge to friends and allies to consider the limitations and probable unintended consequences of many hate crime laws as they are currently formulated—consequences that compound rather than counteract the systemic violence of racism, misogyny, homophobia, poverty, and economic exploitation."[15]

And finally, the politics of presence requires a respectful analysis of how antiracist and decolonial scholars and activists negotiate the contours of anti-intersectionality within citizenship, sometimes by inadvertently or even consciously replicating those anti-intersectionalities as a means of survival. A politics of presence refuses to merely toss these actions aside through narratives of blame, culpability, or false consciousness; rather, these are moments whereby Indigenous peoples and people of color are navigating the visceral registers of pain, violence, and social death within the limiting structures of citizenship. This is a call, then, to reorient away from notions of personal failure toward an orientation that focuses our attention on the ways in which structures of U.S. settler colonialism and U.S. white supremacy collude to offer a predetermined opposition between raciality and Indigeneity.[16]

Violence initiates and drives normativities as much as it is the outcome of these aspirations. A politics of presence argues that activists and scholars can and must attend to both sides of the operation: to be present to the trauma that precedes, as well as the pain that follows, inclusionary gestures. Throughout this book, I am less invested in calling out normative strivings as problematic in and of themselves; I am more interested in demonstrating how anti-intersectional violence anticipates and unfolds through these gestures. *Against Citizenship* argues, alongside Lisa Marie Cacho, that anti-intersectional violence not only happens within the process of assimilationist strategies but also within any attempt to reconcile, recuperate, and recover the nonnormative. In her powerful essay on her family's negotiation of the very personal and social politics of her nephew's death, Cacho demonstrates that any attempt to expand the membership of the legible, the normative, and the valued results in a doubled violence. As she eloquently observes,

> Even if we had attempted to circumvent the devaluing processes of race and gender by citing other readily recognizable signs and signifiers of value, such as legality, heteronormativity, American citizenship, higher education, affluence, morality, or respectability, we still would not have had evidence to portray him as a productive, worthy, and responsible citizen. Ascribing (readily recognizable) value to the racialized devalued requires recuperating what registers as deviant and disreputable to reinterpret those devalued beliefs, behaviors, and bodies as misrecognized versions of normativity who deserve so much better. Value is ascribed through explicitly and implicitly disavowing relationships to the already devalued and disciplined categories of deviance and nonnormativity.[17]

Cacho's observations remind us that the mechanisms and desires for expanding the realm of the normative and the inclusion of the nonnormative are always-already acts of violence. This violence occurs not only on the bodies of those reified as the nonvalued, but also at the level of the (supposedly) newly valued.

These analyses remind us that violence is constitutive of and operationalized throughout normativities, antinormativities, and nonnormativities. There is no critique that can circumvent these operations, and there is no hope without critique. But there are modalities of differential responsibility and accountability for all of us.

# Acknowledgments

First and foremost, I want to offer my sincere gratitude for the University of Illinois Press editors that helped me grow this project. While I only worked with her for a few minutes, Larin McLaughlin was exceptionally helpful in giving my draft a full review and great pointers on how to improve it. After Larin left UIP, I was fortunate to be moved to the wonderful, kind, and gracious Dawn Durante, who has put up with my thousands of questions with generosity and humor. Dawn's engagement and enthusiasm for the project have been inspiring. I also want to thank Nancy Albright for the astute editing of this manuscript, Jennifer Clark for shepherding the book through production, and anonymous reviewers for their kind and careful engagement with the book. They were wonderful to work with.

Many, many years ago I found myself in the classrooms of some of the most thoughtful feminist intellectuals of our time. It was only later that I started to understand how lucky I was to learn from Bettina Aptheker, Wendy Brown, and Joan Scott. Later in life, I forged deep connections with brilliant scholars at the University of Minnesota, especially with Chani Marchiselli, Shirin Deylami, Sara Hottinger, Marwa Hassoun, Diane Detourney, and Margalit Chu. Danielle Bouchard was no doubt the best collaborator I can imagine. The Feminist Studies program was a vibrant intellectual space, where we debated about the racialized, gendered, and colonial politics of knowledge production, and I feel lucky to have started out my career in academia with those critical conversations that continue to inform my work. I learned so much from many faculty at the University of Minnesota, such as Erika Lee, Sara Evans, and Edén Torres, but owe the most to Jigna Desai, Richa Nagar, and Barbara Welke. With their help, generosity, and resilience, I was pushed in all of the ways I could hope for. My own teaching and mentoring is modeled on the three of them, and their wonderful combination of kindness, love, thoughtfulness, and the occasional-but-always-timely ass-kicking.

I've been extremely fortunate to be able to grow my relationships with Richa Nagar and Jigna Desai in ways that continue to warm my soul. Richa is a profound poet of life, and every moment I spend with her reminds me to find the potential poet inside myself. And I can't imagine writing or thinking without Jigna's infectious giggle and energizing mind. She is ridiculously fun, smart as hell, and totally and refreshingly unpretentious.

Although I had only a year with them, my colleagues at Oberlin College continue to warm my heart. Libby Murphy and Amy Margaris: we still have time to create our online university with matching smoking jackets. I was inspired by Lisa Kahaleole Hall's thoroughly intersectional pedagogy, and wanted to pick Meredith Raimondo's brain every single day. And I still can't believe I got to work with Wendy Kozol, who became the best mentor, reader, interlocutor, and friend I can imagine. I still pinch myself that a temporary gig at Oberlin College gave me Wendy.

My colleagues at the University of New Mexico have been lovely, and patient, as my medical tribulations started soon after I arrived (oh cancer, why can't you have better timing?) and sent my life, and my life's work, into a tailspin. But thank you David Correia, Janet Cramer, Jennifer Nez Denetdale, Alyosha Goldstein, Kathleen Holscher, Gabriel Meléndez, Sandy Rodrigue, Rebecca Schreiber, Antonio Tiongson, Michael Trujillo, and Irene Vásquez for your camaraderie throughout a very trying time in my life. And a very special thank you to Laura Gómez, Gail Houston, Alex Lubin, Bárbara Reyes, and Raji Valluri for supporting me as I manage my illness and my tenure track position at the same time.

Intellectual interlocutors have been harder to find than I expected, but Danielle Bouchard, Karma Chávez, Jigna Desai, Wendy Kozol, Chani Marchiselli, Scott Morgensen, and Sandra Soto have made the search worth every effort. I feel sorry for anyone around Karma and myself at the same time, as we are clearly soulmates of wickedness. Scott has made this a much better book and me a much better scholar. I am forever grateful for his engagement and his thorough, sustained, patient, and thought-provoking feedback that nourished my revisions. I hope this text shows at least some of what I have learned from him. And my graduate students have been wonderful interlocutors as well. I can't believe I get paid to work with them. Liza Minno Bloom, Gina Díaz, Jessica Harkins, Caroline Goodman, Fizz Perkal, Nicholas Sánchez, Kelley Sawyer, Eileen Shaugnessy, and many more to come (I hope): I am so grateful that we can be a part of each other's educational process. Special shout-outs to Santhosh Chandrashekar for his engagement with the book (Namaste!); to David Maile for the fun and inspiring conversations around Kanaka Maoli racialization, sovereignty, and resistance; and last, but not least, to Rachel Levitt for being willing to read every chapter and provide me with the most thoughtful and wonderful feedback an author could dream of. I'm so thankful I got them in the divorce (poor Karma)! And to my amazing GA's, especially Fizz, I can't express how thankful I am for all of their hard work.

And like any good queer, I am crushed-out on my friends for being wonderful, adorable, well-dressed, and even a little cranky when needed. Thank you Mel, Shay, Kellie, my f.c. Alex, and even my moody/adorable niece and nephew, for keeping my Minnesotan heart warm. Thank you to Naomers for being such a force in my life, and keeping me centered (and, to be clear, you dig). And thank you Molly, Jason, Erin, The Lesbian, Ronda, Mo, and Lindsay for giving me some much-needed sustenance in the desert.

My family of origin has had it hard, and if I were a nicer person I'd feel sorry for them. But, alas, you rolled the dice and got me. Thanks crazy cuzzins, supportive aunts and uncle, Mom, Bro, and Helen for being you and for asking if I'm done with this damn book yet. And yes, this attitude wouldn't look half as good without the important grooming tutorials I received from my grandmothers, Grey and Honey. Everything I do, even if—especially if—they wouldn't approve of it, is dedicated to them. And lastly, to my queer family for providing me with a place to come home to and all the improper love I could ever hope for: fuzzy butts forever!

# Against Citizenship

# The Violence of the Normative

In the early twenty-first century, the United States was in the midst of a violent, rampant, and thorough cultural defense of normative citizenship. While states across the United States attempted to delineate between deserving/desirable citizen-subjects and those undeserving of state protections through a diverse array of legal gymnastics, the State of Arizona became the national leader in mounting legislation that targeted nonnormative citizens and noncitizens.[1] Although leftist activists within Arizona pointed toward a much longer descent into reactionary politics, in 2010 the State earned an international reputation for its assault on undocumented migrants and people of color when the legislature passed Senate Bill (SB) 1070, an anti-immigration law, and House Bill (HB) 2281, a law targeting ethnic studies education.[2] In 2012, the U.S. Supreme Court upheld one of the most controversial parts of SB 1070, namely the "show me your papers" provision, which required police to determine the immigration paper status of any person they had a "reasonable suspicion" might be an undocumented migrant.[3] Arizona's anti-immigrant groups stirred up support for the legislation by deploying the rhetorical claim that the federal government was (supposedly) failing to secure national borders. However, despite such hostile rhetoric, states like Arizona were merely following the lead of the federal government's racialized, anti-immigrant profiling policies, such as Section 287g of the Immigration and Nationality Act (which worked to deputize local and state police as border patrol agents) and President Obama's "Secure Communities" program (which worked to track the immigration status of any person arrested or in custody).[4] Importantly, anti-immigration laws and rhetoric not only target racialized migrants, but they simultaneously reproduce the settler colonial project of (re)claiming Native territory.[5]

The movement toward banning ethnic studies education in Arizona mirrored efforts throughout the United States (and abroad) that worked to push back efforts to recognize and teach about privilege, subordination, and the various forms of difference and normativities that stem from and reproduce structural inequalities. HB 2281 banned any type of education within Arizona school districts that "promote[s] *resentment* towards a race or class of people," and "advocate[s] ethnic solidarity" (emphasis added).[6] With the Tucson School District's Mexican-American Studies program in their sights, conservative Arizona legislators, school administrators, and voters argued that ethnic studies programs are antithetical to the spirits of color/gender/sexuality-blind norms of citizenship.

The language of "resentment," as outlined within the anti-ethnic studies law, is merely another way of describing the fear of retaliation, a retaliation borne from being abjected—repeatedly and perpetually—into the space of nonnormative citizenship. These nonnormative citizen-subjects haunt the narrative of citizenship and its reliance upon the promises of democracy, equality, and inclusion; they are *the specters of citizenship*, the nonnormative subjects that are products of, and excuses for, the vicious, boundary machinations of citizenship. This book is about the operations of state violence that work to restrain the political and coalitional potential of these specters of citizenship by continuously producing anti-intersectional epistemologies and anti-intersectional citizenship practices, whereby the promises of citizenship are offered in exchange for the dissolution of coalitional politics with abject others.

Arizona was merely a staging ground for conservative lawmakers, as many states followed Arizona's lead with various copycat laws.[7] And these laws do not focus exclusively on resecuring the abjection of people of color and racialized immigrants. Rather, conservative lawmakers have mounted assaults on all types of nonnormative experiences, identities, and bodies. These laws range from the continuing criminalization of abortion providers and seekers, to policing transgender folks' use of bathrooms, to securing businesses' newly found "religious freedom" to deny benefits to employees or refuse to serve customers based on religious principles.[8] The range of laws exposes the ways in which normative citizen-subjects feel threatened by a diverse array of differences. As Sandra Soto and Miranda Joseph point out, laws such as SB 1070 and HB 2281 rely upon a "deliberately cultivated sense of vulnerability, a fear that any mention of race is reverse racism and race hatred, that our borders are being overrun with violent others, that our place and our future are now out of our control."[9] What they are naming is similar to what Jigna Desai and I named the "cultural defense of normative citizenship."[10] While focusing on conservative talk radio sensations like Don Imus, and their racist-sexist-homophobic rhetoric, we argued that their popularity marks a particularly discernible period in which wounded white masculinity becomes the vehicle for a "cultural defensiveness" that excuses and reignites modalities of brutality against nonnormative subjects. The concept of the cultural defense of normative citizenship builds on Lauren Berlant's brilliant analysis of the Reagan Era and the circulation of what she called the "scandal of ex-privilege," whereby "iconic citizens" (in this case, normative white/male/heterosexual citizen-subjects) relentlessly tell the stories of their loss. The loss includes nothing less than the ability *not* to have identities, "when it used to be just other people who had them."[11] Right-wing nostalgia continues to call for the return to a hypothetical past, one where their normative citizen-statuses were stable and secured.

When normative citizen-subjects are exposed *as normative*, as privileged, and as natural beneficiaries to the benefits of citizenship, they go on the defense. In order to restore themselves to normative citizen-status and the privilege of unaccountability, these subjects rehearse an argument for restoration, an argument that is premised upon recrafting normative subjectivities (based in whiteness, settler coloniality, heterosexuality, maleness, affluence, and able-bodiedness) into de-privileged, wounded subject statuses. Their goal is to restore the normativity and the idyllic past that have been—supposedly—lost to them. Hence, the narrative of sorrow and injury justifies the need for a "cultural defense" in which the violence against immigrants, Natives, queers, people of color, and gender-variant others is legitimated in the name of protection. While the cultural defense of normative citizenship was salient in the 1980s and 1990s as a reactionary politics against the variety of progressive, civil rights, and decolonial movements, the cultural defense of normative citizenship became an especially violent and hegemonic feature after September 11, 2001, which worked to consolidate and excuse military, police, and border violence against nonnormative others.[12] In the post–September 11th United States, cultural defenses are ubiquitous and deployed in numerous political campaigns in order to "protect the sanctity of marriage," "protect our borders," "protect women from regretful abortions," and, importantly, protect normative subjects from the "resentment" of abjected, nonnormative subjects.

The cultural defense of normative citizenship works for a few reasons. First, it succeeds because it utilizes and relies upon the premises of liberal democratic citizenship and its promise of soon-to-come-but-never-arrive inclusion, which undergirds the privileged access of normative citizen-subjects. And second, the cultural defense utilizes the fear that the violent machinations of citizenship and the privileges they afford the normative will create the conditions in which the nonnormative will rise in retaliation for their experience. This fear is rarely described directly, as if naming it would bring it into fruition; rather, this fear is redirected into supposedly racial-, sexual-, and gender-neutral discourses that instead serve to perpetuate racialized, sexualized, and gendered systems of control.[13] Couched in terms of tendencies (such as the tendency for criminality, the tendency for dependency on state resources, the tendency for border crossing, the tendency for sexual lasciviousness, and so forth), the fear of the resentment and retaliation of the oppressed is recoded into rationales for increased state surveillance and state-approved violence.

Rather than attempting to soothe the anxieties of the normative, or working tirelessly to assuage this fear of retaliatory justice, this book calls for a politics of alliance that makes these fears manifest. This book argues that the ever-lingering promise of citizenship has been one of the most resourceful tools for producing and maintaining anti-intersectional, anti-coalitional politics. And if there is one thing that is most threatening to privileged citizens and institutions of subordination and control, it is the potential of intersectional, coalitional politics. This book argues for a politics against citizenship as a political coalitional present to dismantle the heteronormative, whitenormative, and colonialnormative structures of U.S. culture and politics.

*Against Citizenship* argues that citizenship is not only the central structure for reifying the norms of whiteness, heterosexuality, consumerism, and settler colonialism within the United States, but that these norms are brutally enforced against nonnormative bodies, practices, behaviors, and forms of affiliation through oppositional, divide-and-conquer logics that set up nonnormative subjects to compete against each other in order to gain the privileged access to citizenship. This book examines the complex nature of the violence of normative citizenship by offering a comparative analysis of three case studies, namely same-sex marriage law, hate crime legislation, and Native Hawaiian sovereignty. Each of these case studies focuses on different aspects of normative citizenship, such as the heteronormativity of marriage law, the settler whitenormativity of the rights to bodily integrity, or the colonialnormativity of civil rights law. At the same time, by examining these different claims in relationship to each other, *Against Citizenship* works to expose how the intertwined norms of citizenship confound and obscure the mutual processes of settler colonialism, racism, sexism, and heterosexism. The book surveys how the U.S. nation-state requires *anti-intersectionality*—that is, the perpetual refusal to allow for, consider, or acknowledge the mutuality and contingency of these categories of difference—by the demand and expectation that challenges to the norms of citizenship be articulated in simple, single-axis formulations. Unfortunately, numerous progressive left organizations and academics fall prey to this demand by (re)producing anti-intersectional strategies themselves. Therefore, my agenda is to urge critical left scholars and activists to be mindful as to how anti-intersectional, identity-based claims inadvertently reinscribe the vicious norms of citizenship. But perhaps more to the point, this book is about configuring a politics for the intersectional present, a politics that works to *queer*—as in disrupt, denaturalize, and make strange—the racial, sexual, gender, colonial, and anti-intersectional normativities that are integral to the continuing oppression of nonnormative peoples in the United States, the violence of normative citizenship, and the cultural defenses of normativities that are all around us.

## Against Citizenship

To write a book "against citizenship" is not just about participating in an antinormative political and theoretical practice that is oppositional in nature. I am not just being difficult—although I am a strong supporter of the practice. If scholars and activists are to take queer, feminist, critical race, and decolonial politics seriously, as projects that work to expose and dismantle violent normativities, structures, and discourses, then scholars and activists must focus their critiques at those systems that naturalize and realign normative identities, normative knowledges, and normative practices—especially when they are used to frame and constrict the realm of the "political." Citizenship is one such discourse and an insidious one at best. This book argues, perhaps provocatively, that there is nothing redeemable about citizenship, nothing worth salvaging or sustaining in the name of "community," practice, or belonging. Citizenship is, inherently, a normativizing project—a project that regulates and disciplines the social body in order to produce model identities and hegemonic knowledge claims. Moreover, it is a violent exclusionary operation, one that relies upon and reproduces a multipronged, gatekeeping apparatus that works to create, retain, and imbue citizenship with meaning at the direct expense of the noncitizen. Citizenship will always claim to be aspirational—to include the excluded eventually, once they are marked as deserving or human enough. But this is nothing less than an illusion, because according to citizenship, there will always be, *there must be*, (an)Other who experiences the full force of the exclusionary technologies of citizenship. *Against Citizenship* argues that whenever we work on behalf of citizenship, whenever we strive to including more types of peoples under its reign, we inevitably reify the violence of citizenship against nonnormative others.

It is critical to offer some definitions, as there are, no doubt, some diverse framings of citizenship afoot in the academy and elsewhere. As many scholars have noted, there has been an explosion in the scholarship on citizenship in the last thirty years.[14] As an object of study, citizenship has been moved far afield from its previous location in political theorizing, and is now the quintessential interdisciplinary topic. Throughout this blossoming of scholarship, the types of citizenship have grown exponentially, from cultural citizenship,[15] multicultural citizenship,[16] Native citizenship,[17] differentiated citizenship,[18] sexual citizenship,[19] intimate citizenship,[20] infantile citizenship,[21] flexible citizenship,[22] postnational citizenship,[23] global citizenship,[24] cosmopolitan citizenship,[25] consumer citizenship,[26] corporate citizenship,[27] and most likely many more as these conversations continue. Citizenship has been found and documented by academics on scales as divergent as transnational, national, local/community-oriented, and even interpersonal practices. In this scholarship, citizenship has been defined, depending upon the disciplinary lens of the scholar, as a process of regulation and identification, as a mode of interpersonal, community, political, and even corporate interaction and agency, and as a practice of empowerment and disempowerment along various scales. To be more specific, while citizenship studies have primarily been dominated by accounts of citizenship as a legal status or a practice of civic engagement, scholars have also described citizenship as a practice of social responsibility and community-building, such as the activist-oriented projects of individuals, groups, organizations, governments, and corporations.

It is even more interesting to ask why: why has citizenship become such an important or primary object of analysis in the late twentieth and early twenty-first centuries? Some scholars argue that citizenship has become a critical site of negotiation due to the changing nature of economies, nation-states, and forms of sociality via neoliberal, globalized, and transnational commerce and communication, while others point toward the rise of international forms of governance and/or the demands of social movements.[28] Chantal Mouffe, along with other scholars, has argued that citizenship itself is a site of struggle, or what Mouffe describes as a battle over hegemony, and as such citizenship is a critical site of analysis for scholars and activists alike. In an earlier assessment of the rise of "citizenship studies" as a field, Will Kymlicka and Wayne Norman argued that citizenship became important due to the increasing challenges of difference, diversity, and "multiculturalism."[29] A more skeptical reading might interpret this observation a bit differently, in the sense that we might see the exponential growth of citizenship studies as a part of the governmentality of citizenship itself, whereby this scholarship can participate in the management of difference.

Of course, most citizenship studies scholars see their work as invested in social justice. They identify their projects as working to expose the falsities of what Iris Marion Young appropriately dubbed the "ideal of universal citizenship," and attempt to (re)imagine citizenship in such a way as to live up to its promises.[30] In this sense, then, citizenship studies is about injustice, lack, and exclusion as much as it is about the possibilities for a better, possibly more inclusive, future.[31] Feminists, radical democratic theorists, critical race scholars, and others have worked diligently to call out the failures of citizenship, but most of this scholarship argues that citizenship as a practice, ideal, or politics is actually recuperable for social justice projects, or at the very least remains an ambivalent project with potential benefits and pitfalls. Scholars are right to point out that citizenship has served as a powerful ideal for disenfranchised groups seeking to make claims for inclusion and rights.[32] Feminist scholar Ruth Lister, for example, argues that even though citizenship operates as an exclusionary and disciplining apparatus, it still has potential for resistance and "as an ideal it can provide a potent weapon in the hands of the disadvantaged and oppressed."[33] And several sexual citizenship scholars, namely Carl Stychin, David Bell and Jon Binnie, and Jeffrey Weeks, have argued that as dangerous as citizenship's normalizing and disciplining impulses can be, we must leave room for the way power produces and allows for contested spaces, identities, and modes of resistance.[34] As Bell and Binnie point out, the ambivalence of citizenship means that folks must make the "hard choices" to: (1) be enfolded into citizenship via demands for equality and inclusion that so violently normalize and discipline, or (2) continue to be discriminated against by remaining outside of citizenship and face the ostracisms and profound pain of exclusion.[35]

These scholars are attempting to name the ways in which power operates productively, as well as how disciplinary and exclusionary apparatuses such as citizenship still allow for agency, even for the noncitizen. Citizenship is certainly a site of struggle, and scholars have considered how nonnormative peoples and/or noncitizens work to transform operations of exclusion and normalization into possibilities for transformative, community-based political projects. These "acts of citizenship," according to Engin Isin and Greg Nielsen, are the "collective or individual deeds that rupture socio-historical patterns," and "create a sense of the possible and of a citizenship that is 'yet to come.'"[36] While I certainly do not deny agency, or the possibilities of tweaking citizenship (especially as an anticolonial gesture, as described later), I am concerned with how some of this scholarship works to cast a wide net in which to catch and locate practices, behaviors, and processes that are then identified as "acts of citizenship." Within such loose definitions, all forms of activism, community-making, and even dissidence get swept up within the net of citizenship.[37] As a few citizenship studies ethnographers have noted, some of their interviewees have rightfully balked at having their political actions described as acts of citizenship, thereby reminding us that scholarship can and does participate in reproducing the seductive modality of citizenship.[38] Scholars and activists alike should be careful of reproducing what I call "citizenspeak"—that is, discourses that realign behaviors, practices, and bodies under the name of citizenship. While most scholarship seems to subsume political acts into citizenship, other scholars understand that various actions, such as undocumented migrant protests or Indigenous resistance, are purposeful and willful acts of anticitizenship or noncitizenship.[39]

As much as the discourse of citizenship has provided opportunities for collective activism and critique, it has also distorted and severely restricted those critiques in ways that must be carefully interrogated. Citizenship is an authoritative discourse that works to delimit the possibilities of political debate in the United States. In its framing—as universal inclusion, equality, and an abstract citizen-subject that exists outside of (or beyond) power relations—citizenship warps arguments on subordination and injustice. And as this book demonstrates, under the setup of progressively inclusive citizenship, the intersectional and intertwined processes of sexism, racism, classism, heteronormativity, settler colonialism, and imperialism are contorted into separate, competing, *antiintersectional* epistemologies. It is critical, then, not to constrict political debate or absorb articulations of justice and resistance under the sign of, and faith in, citizenship.

Moreover, while scholars have tried to reimagine citizenship as beyond, outside of, or transgressive of the nation-state, these scholars have also admitted that cosmopolitan, postnational, and global citizenships are utopian at best—ideals for a future that has yet to come. In fact, as Linda Bosniak points out, one of the most important outcomes of this subfield of theorizations has been the ability to see how citizenship remains bound to the nation-state.[40] To be clear, I am not arguing that the nation-state determines the whole of citizenship, nor do I mean to deny individual or collective agency. However, it is a fantasy—and a dangerous one at that—to think we can wrest citizenship completely from the nation-state and remove the stains of its past and present exclusions. Put differently, while I certainly am not suggesting that citizenship is merely state-conferred or state-sanctioned, I believe that we cannot afford to downplay the role of the state, particularly when statelike interests can masquerade as celebratory calls for community.

Native citizenships, that is, citizenships within Indigenous nations and tribes, are, in my view, the most profound example of citizenships that challenge the nation-state's hegemony over citizenship.[41] Native citizenships are assertions of sovereignty that work to reimagine belonging, empowerment, kinship, and governance. They are also purposefully and provocatively anti-colonial and decolonial maneuvers.[42] And yet, it remains an open question as to whether Native citizenships can and will offer intersectional, coalitional, and nonnormative reimaginings of citizenship. These are the questions that are hotly contested within Native communities. Some Indigenous scholars, such as Taiaiake Alfred, consider citizenship to be an inherently settler project; some, such as Scott Lyons, argue that it is possible to reimagine citizenship through Native worldviews; and others, such as Elizabeth Cook-Lynn, argue that Natives do not have a choice, and that Indigenous sovereignty and survival depends on Native citizenship.[43] But as feminist and queer Indigenous scholars and activists point out, while Indigenous governance based in Native epistemologies can offer radical revisions of governance, they are also battlegrounds where privileges and subordinations play out. For example, Joanne Barker and Jennifer Denetdale have shown how the selective enforcement of "tradition" has been used in some Indigenous nations as mechanisms for embedding and naturalizing (U.S.-based) conservative ideologies into Native governance. As Barker bluntly observes, "it is not self-evident that a necessarily radical or oppositional form of Native governance will result if based on Native cultural traditions—at least not as those traditions are being articulated by many tribal officials and members through the kinds of racist, sexist, homophobic, and religiously fundamentalist discourses and ideologies that are dominant in U.S. national narrations."[44] Therefore, while Native citizenships are expressions of Indigenous sovereignty, and are being imagined in multiple ways, Indigenous communities debate about the ways in which Native citizenships are and are not impervious to reinforcing the violence of normativities.[45]

Native citizenships also expose the fact that citizenship is a primary mechanism for naturalizing settlement in settler colonial nation-states. Birthright citizenship, whereby citizenship is granted to persons born within the territory of a nation-state, is one avenue by which settlers continue the ongoing process of Indigenous land dispossession. In the United States, for example, citizenship relies upon and reproduces the extinguishing of Native land titles by continuing to convert Indigenous land into a U.S. possession that, through birthright citizenship, produces more and more settlers.[46] Another avenue for

Native dispossession is through what Philip Deloria so skillfully describes as the habitual and reoccurring practice of white settlers "playing Indian," whereby they mimic, appropriate, and perform Indianness in order to reimagine themselves as the natural beneficiaries and rightful heirs to the United States and the Native lands it occupies.[47] This is one of the reasons why Natives have had to do so much work to consistently and repeatedly point out the violent ironies of U.S. citizenship. For example, reacting to the absurdity of subjecting Natives to the WWI military draft without the legal access to U.S. citizenship, Carlos Montezuma (one of the founding members of the Society of American Indians) proclaimed, "this drafting of the Indians into the army is another wrong perpetuated upon the Indian without FIRST bestowing his just title—THE FIRST AMERICAN CITIZEN."[48] These analyses demonstrate that normative—that is, settler—citizenship is a colonial technology, whether through dispossessing Native land titles in order to make room for settlers (and migrants), or through settlers playing Indian in order to justify their claiming of Indigenous resources.

Citizenship is an external and internal system of sorting and distributing rights, resources, and most importantly, value, to various types of bodies throughout and across nation-states. Consider, for example, citizenship's role as a gatekeeping, exclusionary mechanism to demarcate citizens from noncitizens. Linda Bosniak argues that the great majority of abstract theorizations on citizenship willfully ignore the operations of exclusion at the borders of nation-states, whereby alienage and formal noncitizenship are left as excusable (if not necessary) forms of discrimination and exclusion.[49] Discriminatory treatment of noncitizens is often justified as a means to safeguard the rights and benefits of citizenship as the exclusive property of recognized citizens. As Donna Baines and Nandita Sharma observe, "citizenship is the glue that holds the nation-state together in a seemingly natural community authorized to exclude Others."[50] In the United States, where differentiation between citizens and noncitizens is racially loaded, noncitizens become "aliens" and "illegal aliens," identifications historically associated with and popularly coded as Asian and Latino migrants.[51] California's Proposition 187, the 1996 Welfare Reform Act, and, most critically, the events since September 11th are ample evidence of how citizenship gets mobilized to justify war on "aliens." As Kevin R. Johnson points out, "A war on noncitizens of color focusing on their immigration status, not race, as conscious or unconscious cover, serves to vent social frustration and hatred."[52] Importantly, the distinction between citizen and noncitizen is tenuous at best. As David Cole cautions, "the line between citizen and noncitizen is a fragile one, and government officials, while quick to cite the distinction when introducing new measures of surveillance and control, are also quick to elide the distinction as they grow accustomed to the powers they exercise over foreign nationals."[53] These analyses demonstrate the fungibility of noncitizenship, a fungibility that allows the construction of the alien-other to be readily available and deployable in the service of state surveillance, the circumscriptions of civil liberties, and the policing of bodies that these practices require.

Another way to understand the gatekeeping apparatus of citizenship is to focus on the ways in which citizenship operates as a mechanism to assure the securitization and monitoring of migration inside and across borders. Within borders, as Nicholas De Genova points out, citizenship functions as "the premier instrumentality for the particular subjection and historically specific subjugation of those whom states 'contain' within their juridical and spatial confines."[54] Across borders, as Barry Hindess observes, citizenship operates as a governance of (im)mobility, whereby it "serves to facilitate or promote certain kinds of movement and interaction between its members and inhibit or penalise others."[55] Moreover, citizenship works on a global scale, as an international system of population management that renders global populations governable by dividing them into discrete subpopulations of particular nation-states. But, of course, this global population management serves capital accumulation. As Baines and Sharma point out, within many nation-states, citizenship works to "maintain a pool of highly exploitable and socially excluded workers."[56]

But citizenship is not merely a system of have and have-nots; rather, it is a system whereby the ability to obtain and maintain the status, rights, privileges, and obligations of citizenship are fluid and constantly in flux. As much as there are external borders to citizenship, as Margaret Somers observes, there are also "internal borders of exclusion within the nation-state" that distribute various levels of access to rights, benefits, demands, and responsibilities of citizenship.[57] Therefore, we are not just speaking of noncitizens in the more obvious (though no less heinous) sense of refugees and undocumented migrants. Rather, we are speaking of the vast types of identities, performances, and presentations that mark people as outside of normative citizenship, or what citizenship studies tends to name "second-class citizens."

Numerous factors directly impact one's access to these various and fluctuating levels of citizenship, including legal mechanisms, cultural and social imaginations of national belonging, economic resources and access, physical barriers and structures, and bodily comportments, all of which work to create and mark normative and abject citizen-subjects. In one example, Leti Volpp explains that the historical as well as contemporaneous fixing of Asians as alien-others through U.S. orientalist discourses has made Asian Americans' access to citizenship tenuous at best. Volpp astutely argues:

Citizenship for Asian Americans in the form of legal status or rights has not guaranteed that Asian Americans will be understood as citizen-subjects or will be considered to subjectively stand in for the American citizenry. . . . While in the contemporary moment Asian Americans may be perceived as legitimate recipients of formal rights, there is discomfort associated with their being conceptualized as political subjects whose activity constitutes the American nation.[58]

In another example, Margrit Shildrick argues that the process of marking disabled people as dependent and abjected from the national imaginary has meant that they continue to experience exclusions from citizenship.[59] And while many sexual citizenship studies scholars have noted that nonheterosexual peoples and practices are disassociated from norms of citizenship, we are best served to remember the ways in which norms of sexuality are produced and maintained far beyond practices of heterosexuality.[60] Therefore, the intersections of racialized, gendered, classed, ablist, and colonial norms of sexuality reveal how various sexual practices are located outside of normative citizenship. And, of course, discourses of settlement, criminality, and terrorism have marked some types of racialized persons as the epitomes of noncitizens, if not anticitizens. While the list of nonnormative citizen-subjectivities is historically contingent, it is also purposefully endless; citizenship works to continuously mark Otherness because normative structures depend on the production of new kinds of difference.[61]

These examples illustrate how citizenship is a form of disciplinary and biopolitical power. As Aihwa Ong describes, citizenship is an operation of Foucauldian biopolitics, whereby the state regulates the conduct, comportment, and behavior of subjects "as a population (by age, ethnicity, occupation, and so on) and as individuals (sexual and reproductive behavior) so as to ensure security and prosperity for the nation as a whole."[62] For philosopher Michel Foucault, biopower is an extension and intensification of certain elements of disciplinary power and arose particularly in the eighteenth century through European colonial projects. While disciplinary power is especially invested in sculpting, controlling, and disciplining individuals, biopower works more at the level of mass populations, where individuals are mere members of a populace in which their "characteristics of birth, death, production, illness, and so on" are hierarchicalized to afford certain populations differential social value.[63] And if disciplinary power manifests through sovereign states claiming power "to take life and let live," biopower operates through the right to "make live and to let die."[64] But this distribution of life chances does not just operate within sovereign states; rather, international norms, systems, and governance extend operations of biopower across borders. The discourse of citizenship is one way in which biopolitical power is manifest as a globalized operation, thereby marking certain populations as worthy of citizenship and others as left out in anachronistic time and space.[65] As Barry Hindess observes, citizenship is a central element of imperialist imaginaries that offer to extend, grant, or force forms of (Western) democratic citizenship onto other nation-states (and, I would add, Indigenous tribes and nations). As he states, "To present a regime of population control in this way (as a matter of citizenship for the masses), is thus to suggest that they can now achieve the substance of citizenship through the modernization of their own states."[66] Citizenship works, then, to humanize and dehumanize across and within national borders and spaces, serving as a frequent alibi for empire expansion, war, and the theft of Indigenous lands and resources, as well as through the suppression of local forms of community and belonging.[67]

Foucault's insights on operations of disciplinary and biopolitical power are also helpful in understanding how citizenship operates to normalize, discipline, and regulate those incorporated within its grasp as much as those who are excluded. For Foucault, inclusion always comes with a cost, whereby recognition spawns regulation, and becoming a subject begets subjection. As he observed, subjection "applies itself to immediate everyday life which categorizes the individual, marks him by his own individuality, attaches him to his own identity, imposes a law of truth on him which he must recognize and which others have to recognize in him."[68] Subjects submit to subjection through processes of self-making and self-regulation in which societal norms and values are played out by and through the individual. Here, the governmentality of citizenship promotes and teaches self-governance through self-disciplining operations whereby subjects learn to see themselves as citizens through the material practices of citizen-like behaviors and attitudes. As Ong states, citizenship is "a cultural process of 'subjection,' in the Foucauldian sense of self-making and being made by power relations that produce consent through schemes of surveillance, discipline, control, and administration."[69]

In many ways, the biopolitical and disciplinary power of citizenship functions to create and mark citizens through encouraging conformity and affects of belonging. This is why the term *citizen* is often used as if it were synonymous with being a "good" or ethical participant in some form of social contract, therefore working to mark and reproduce proper—read, *normative*—behavior. The inclusion of gays and lesbians within citizenship, for example, has increasingly come with awareness as to how this inclusion is predicated upon the proximity to heteronormative behavior and practices. In fact, the most prevalent debate within sexual citizenship scholarship (as well as activism) has been the costs of "inclusion" within normative citizenship. This debate has also been described as a struggle over the potential benefits and burdens of recognition. As explained above, transformations in legal as well as cultural inclusions of gay and lesbian subjects into some of the normative realms of citizenship (marriage, military, property ownership, and so forth), has led some scholars (such as Bell and Binnie) to call for an awareness of the "hard choices" between the "push towards rights claims that make dissident sexualities fit into heterosexual culture, by demanding equality and recognition, versus the demand to reject settling for heteronormativity through, for example, sex-positive strategies of refusal—the kind of practices and identities enacted in queer counterpublics."[70] But this setup addresses only the individual costs and burdens of inclusion and recognition and negates the type of violence that recognition brings not only to an individual making such a "hard choice" but to those folks left without the ability to make any choices whatsoever.

Nations that are Indigenous to the territories that are claimed by the United States know all too well the violence of being "included" within citizenship. The 1887 Dawes Severalty Act (also referred to as the General Allotment Act), for instance, conferred U.S. citizenship on Native American men only when they emerged as property-owning (patriarchal) heads of households. The Dawes Act generated what Vine Deloria Jr. and David Wilkins call the "great social experiment" of enforcing private property ownership as part of the civilizing mission. Through the Act, the federal government divided up tribal lands, dispersed them to Native American men, and granted citizenship to those who "adopted the habits of civilized life."[71] While the United States "granted" or forced U.S. citizenship on certain Indigenous nations through treaties and specific laws, American Indians were not formally deemed U.S. citizens until 1924 under the Indian Citizenship Act.[72] And yet, even after the Indian Citizenship Act, courts continued to debate about whether Natives were worthy of U.S. citizenship.[73] According to Deloria and Wilkins, "Full citizenship rights under the Constitution would be distributed to Indians at the whim of Congress, partially, wholly, or in fluctuating segments. These same rights could also be withdrawn at any time by federal lawmakers. Until very recent times, this situation has been precisely the legal condition of Indians."[74]

Often, the "gift" of U.S. citizenship required the termination of tribal-nation statuses and the dissolution of Native citizenships.[75] This is why settler citizenship has been structured through, in Audra Simpson's eloquent phrasing, a "citizenship of grief."[76] While some Indigenous activists have advocated for and claimed U.S. citizenship, many others have called for Natives to refuse or decline the offer of U.S. citizenship.[77] As Kevin Bruyneel observes, for many Indigenous people, the bestowal of U.S. citizenship onto Native subjects is a "transparent colonial imposition of U.S. citizenship on their political identities" that threatens Indigenous sovereignty and tribal land holdings.[78] For example, in response to the 1924 Indian Citizenship Act, Jane Zane Gordon of the Wyandotte Nation eloquently warned: "It is not a matter of definite certainty that the Indian will accept the proffered benevolence or burden—whichever it may be—for the Indian must decide if 'the Greeks have come bearing gifts.'"[79] Gordon is among an extensive succession of Native activists and scholars that have pointed out that U.S. citizenship is no "gift."[80]

And yet, the violence of inclusion does not just impact Indigenous peoples. Rather, inclusion harms many different types of nonnormative citizen-subjects and noncitizen-subjects. The promise of inclusion into citizenship can create the conditions in which racialized and/or impoverished subjects are working themselves to the bone in an attempt to meet the demands of the "good life." This is what Lauren Berlant has named a "slow death," that is "the physical wearing out of a population and the deterioration of people in that population" which occurs "not in traumatic events, as discrete time-frame phenomena like military encounters" but in the drifting temporalities of everyday life.[81] For example, Elizabeth Lee and Geraldine Pratt utilize Berlant's "slow death" to consider how Filipino migrant workers are brought "even closer to their deaths" through the elusive, never-to-be-fully-achieved inclusion into citizenship.[82]

Inclusion is not just a bargained choice for the newly included; acts of inclusion always work to reify the boundaries and borders of exclusion. Therefore, when groups argue for their inclusion or social value they inadvertently and advertently capitalize on discourses that claim some people are legitimately excluded and devalued. Antiblackness and the specter of Black "criminality" constantly haunts discourses of citizenship, and, as such, is a readily available discourse for others to use to claim their righteous inclusion.[83] For example, Nicholas De Genova argues that some undocumented migrant movements have called for their inclusion into citizenship by claiming that they are not terrorists, not criminals, and not lazy nonworkers, thereby working to reinscribe racialized discourses that there are "others" who are legitimately unworthy of citizenship.[84] And in a different, yet related, register, Anna M. Agathangelou et al. argue that in the process of advocating for lesbian and gay marriage rights, "the privatization of the freedom of the queer subject enshrines a culture of loss of rights for non–U.S. citizens while naturalizing the backdrop of (specifically black) (non) subjects within the United States whose civically dead or dying status has rarely been assigned rights to lose."[85]

The point here is that citizenship is not merely normalizing or disciplining of those that are included, but the very process of demanding inclusion reproduces and extends the violent subjugations of exclusion. Citizenship is, in Ruth Wilson

Gilmore's brilliant phrasing, "the state-sanctioned or extralegal production and exploitation of group-differentiated vulnerability to premature death."[86] This is naming the intersectional and relational mechanism of social value/devaluing that Lisa Marie Cacho has described so eloquently in her book, *Social Death: Racialized Rightlessness and the Criminalization of the Unprotected*. It is worth quoting Cacho in full on this point:

> The production and ascription of human value are both violent and relational, both differential and contextual. Value is ascribed through explicitly or implicitly disavowing relationships to the already devalued and disciplined categories of deviance and nonnormativity. When we distinguish ourselves from unlawful and outlawed status categories, we implicitly insist that these socio-legal categories are not only necessary but should be reserved and preserved for the "genuinely" lazy (welfare recipients), "undoubtedly" immoral (marrying for citizenship), and "truly" dangerous (gang violence).... While these tactics may be politically strategic and even necessary at times, it is important to be cognizant of the fact that they work because a sympathetic public can register that some people are the wrong targets of legitimate laws. They work only if a sympathetic public already accepts that discrimination against not-valued others is legitimate and necessary.[87]

As Cacho and other scholars so wonderfully point out, the ascription of human value is violent and relational, and as this book argues, citizenship is a quintessential mechanism of such (de)valuing. Therefore, throughout this book, I consider citizenship to be a biopolitical and disciplinary mechanism of governmentality, as well as a moral and ethical value system. It is an internal and external system of sorting, distributing, and assigning rights, resources, and social value. It is not only normative and regulative of those inside and outside of its purview, but it is a violent dehumanizing mechanism that makes the devaluing of human lives seem commonsensical, logical, and even necessary. Being against citizenship, then, is not merely about being difficult or going against the tide; being against citizenship is the only ethical choice left to those of us that are identified with or allies to the undocumented migrant, the Indigenous sovereigns, or the criminalized of color. Being against citizenship is a prerequisite for refusing to participate in the further aggression against others, no matter how practical and immediately gratifying those political choices might seem.

## Intersectionality, Revisited

If one of the central arguments of this book is that citizenship discourses in the United States are hegemonically and violently anti-intersectional, then certainly more needs to be said about what intersectionality and anti-intersectionality entail. As understood within this text, intersectionality is an analytical frame and argument that categories of difference, identity, and subject formations are discursively produced and constituted in and against each other. It is an argument that categories of identity (such as those forged through racialized, sexualized, colonized, and gendered productions) and their comparative worth and meaning are articulated through each other. Intersectionality suggests that a (seemingly) racialized discourse is never just about race any more than a (seemingly) gendered discourse is just about gender. With an intersectional analysis, the goal is to examine how categories "articulate" (to use Anne McClintock's phrasing) each other, as in the racialization of sexuality, the gendering of Indigeneity, the sexualization of race, and so forth.[88] Intersectional analyses are efforts to tease out the ways in which discourses on race, sexuality, gender, class, ability, nation, and Indigeneity require and rely upon presumptive conceptual information about other categories of difference. In this way, intersectionality is as much an argument about how difference is produced, as it offers an analysis as to how systems and technologies of difference-production, such as citizenship, or nationalism, rely upon and reproduce these very same co-constitutive qualities.

Importantly, within this understanding, intersectionality is spatially and temporally contingent; intersectionality initiates an inquiry into a series of processes that are always contextual, situational, and fluid. Therefore, intersectionality *attempts to name* the messiness of identity, power, subordination, and privilege, but it can only approximate, rather than capture, this complexity. As I show in *Against Citizenship*, intersectionalities of identity and difference, value and worth, normative and deviant, are always in flux. *Against Citizenship* demonstrates that intersectionality is an operation that will never be fully understood, encapsulated, or resolved, but is an ongoing and active production that must be arduously and continuously traced in diverse and multiple locales, spaces, discourses, and periods.

As a dominant framework—in *name* at least—within the academic field of feminist studies, intersectionality has been used and deployed in a wide variety of ways. Critical race feminist Kimberlé Crenshaw first coined "intersectionality" as a metaphor to describe the ways systems of oppression overlap, and as an intervention into U.S. discrimination law that can only conceptualize harm as occurring through separate and containable categories of sexual discrimination, or racial discrimination, but certainly not both, and definitely not more.[89] Crenshaw pointed out that class action suits brought by women of color were consistently denied by a court system that needed the petitioners to choose which type of discrimination they were experiencing. Black feminists and women of color have a long history of refusing this request/requirement to choose, and many scholars have pointed out (including Crenshaw herself) that Crenshaw's call for an intersectional analysis connected to a vibrant lineage of African American women's scholarship. Maria Stewart called for an analysis of the combined effects of racial and gender-based oppression as early as 1832, and Sojourner Truth's infamous refrain, "Ain't I a woman?" from her 1851 Akron, Ohio, speech has been understood to be one of the most consistent and forceful calls for an intersectional analysis.[90] And at the time of Crenshaw's article, there were other similar concepts afloat throughout women of color and third-world feminist scholarship. So we can also turn to Patricia Hill Collins and her call for an analysis of "the matrix of oppression,"[91] the Combahee River Collective's call for analyzing "interlocking systems of oppression,"[92] or even various calls for understanding complex subjectivities,[93] all of which grounded their proposed analytical frameworks within avowedly antiracist feminist paradigms. As such, they exposed how antiracism and feminism refuse(d) to take responsibility for the ways in which they perpetuate malenormativity and whitenormativity. As Grace Hong and Roderick Ferguson astutely point out, an intersectional women of color framework offers "a rejection of the ways in which bourgeois and minority nationalisms create idealized identities."[94] This rejection of idealized, and I would add, *naturalized* identities, is central to any queer, feminist, and decolonial critique of citizenship.

While I use intersectionality to trace processes of citizen-subject productions, particularly as manifest in law and politics, other scholars have deployed intersectionality for different purposes. Some scholars use intersectionality as a method for considering how power and privilege operate on and/or are experienced by bodies, identities, and beings. In this way, then, intersectionality is deployed, as Sirma Bilge notes, as a "meta-theorisation of power and domination" that examines "the formation of subjectivities and agency within a nexus of social relations and structures (of race, class, gender) that work together to (re)produce power and privilege."[95] As such, intersectionality is used by scholars and activists to explore (inter)personal, situational positionings of identity within systems of oppression and privilege. It is here that we see the ways in which many feminist classrooms work to teach students to consider, take responsibility for, and confront the systemic mechanics of power that create and confound their own "intersectional identities." Moreover, social justice organizations and movements have increasingly taken on and deployed the framework of intersectionality as a means to create coalitional political visions as well as address the mechanisms of privilege and subordination among their constituencies.[96]

Although intersectionality has become increasingly important to social justice movements and organizations, it has also come under attack from feminist, queer, critical race, and poststructuralist scholars.[97] Some argue, for example, that intersectionality flattens and simplifies identity and subjectivity. By this they are referring to how—for example, in those classrooms I just mentioned—we teach students that their identity is merely an amalgamation of vectors of difference, thereby presenting identity and subjectivity as two-dimensional operations, as opposed to the much more complex multiple-dimensional projects that they are. Relatedly, critics are concerned about the ways in which intersectionality might reinforce the notion that categories of identity are separable and containable. Ironic as this might be, given the intentions behind intersectionality's founders, these critics are concerned that intersectionality has been understood as merely reciting normative, hegemonic, and multiculturalist framings for how identity operates.

Often, these seemingly disparate critiques are united by a shared objection to how intersectionality has been practiced. That is, critics are concerned with how folks claiming to be "practitioners" of intersectionality are "doing it." For example, some scholars might claim they are offering intersectional analysis, but do so in ways that are not attentive to the contextuality of identity formations and subjectivities, and/or are inattentive to the operations of power within these formations. Critics are also concerned with and often debate over which vectors of identity or difference must be included in order for it to be called "intersectional." Legal scholarship, in particular, tends to fixate on Crenshaw's original application of intersectionality to suggest the framework must be limited to the nexus of race and gender only.[98] Two points can easily address this concern, however. The first of which is to direct their attention back to the text, in which Crenshaw explicitly states that she offered intersectionality as a "provisional concept," and that the concept "can and should be expanded by factoring in issues such as class, sexual orientation, age, and color."[99] The second is to point out that the content and meaning of intersectionality, similar to any concept, is subject to transformation, expansion, and even contraction and elimination, across and through usages—or lack thereof—over time.

The most concerning criticism of intersectionality is that its origins in Black feminist theorizing actually hinders its theoretical potential. According to this logic, because it originated in Black feminist theorizing, African American women are the quintessential intersectional subjects. And if African American women are the models for intersectional analysis, then intersectional analysis must be limited to vectors of oppression or subordination, and, therefore, we will offer limited accounts for how power, identity, and subjectivity operate. But this reductionist reading of intersectionality exposes the ways in which racist and sexist epistemologies continue to impact how critics and scholars understand a concept that has its origins in women of color theorizing. As intersectional scholars point out, these willfully narrow readings of intersectionality demonstrate that there is "an undercurrent of anxiety around the continuing salience of Black women in a theory that reaches beyond their specific intersectional realities."[100] As Barbara Tomlinson shrewdly observes, this anxiety can also be found in the ways in which intersectionality is presumed to be a structural rather than poststructural project, whereby women of color are (again, still) figured as anti-poststructural in their accounts of identity and difference. This racialized framing is especially prevalent in European feminist debates around intersectionality. For example, consider Baukje Prins's setup of European versus U.S. deployments of intersectionality: "there are significant differences in how intersectionality is treated on either side of the Atlantic. The U.S. approach foregrounds the impact of system or structure upon the formation of identities, whereas British scholars focus on the dynamic and relational aspects of social identity."[101] As Tomlinson observes, framing "the black feminist scholars who originated intersectionality as 'unworthy'—parochial, 'race-bound,' incapable of 'theorizing'—justifies extracting from them the valuable tool of intersectionality" for their own projects.[102] Tomlinson and others rightfully remind scholars and practitioners to be especially wary of the ways in which "intersectionality" might be readily seen as simplistic, unvaried, and unnuanced through racialized epistemologies that mark women of color as always-already objects of analysis and not subjects of knowledge production.

The most common critique of intersectionality stems from a literal interpretation of the term as it conjures up a static metaphor (i.e., an "intersection") and a visual epistemology whereby one might assume they can easily trace separate lines of identity to the point of contact at a junction, or imagine that they can "picture" their "intersectional identity" by imaging a two-dimensional grid. Understood in these ways, intersectionality becomes easily positioned as an overly simplistic narrative of a fantastically complex and disordered process. Of course, I might remind these critics that the concept of intersectionality is not, necessarily, limited to or tied to any particular two-dimensional image. In other words, there is no reason why we cannot offer an optical representation of intersectionality that reflects the messier and more complex analysis as to how vectors of difference combine and collide in time and space.

As any quick scan of feminist studies reveals, intersectionality has certainly become a popular concept in the field, and some even suggest that it has become so dominant as to be mainstreamed and institutionalized.[103] Proof in point: there have been a number of anthologies and journal issues that have announced "Intersectionality Studies" as its own domain.[104] Several feminist journals and book series measure submissions on how intersectional the work is. Additionally, Women's Studies departments and programs throughout the country define their programs as expressly intersectional ones. The fear, then, is that intersectionality has become a "gold standard" that is either misconstruing how identity or subjectivity operates, or is requiring a methodological practice that is too firm to capture the complexities and varieties of feminist objects of analysis.[105]

Another concern is that through its mainstreaming, intersectionality has lost its critical edge as a critique of normativities. Critics are afraid that intersectionality has become so ubiquitous within feminist contexts that it has become emptied of significance. The ultimate impact of an intersectionality without teeth is that it can be/has been used as an alibi that lets scholars and activists off the hook for actually being attentive to the embodiments of power differentials. Anna Carastathis points out, for example, intersectionality's popularity "should be read through a white feminist desire to maintain racial innocence and assert feminism's arrival at a 'post-racial' moment."[106] But as critical intersectional scholars point out, the fact that intersectionality is a recurring refrain or request within feminist scholarship and activism is not the same as suggesting that it has become a central practice within these domains.[107]

While I am concerned that there is far more *claiming* of intersectional analysis than *doing* it, I remain hopeful that its deployment as a slogan in feminist studies announces a political gesture and commitment to continue the work of decentering whiteness as the central subject and object of the field. I am most concerned about the historical conditions in which these critiques of intersectionality are being lodged. By this I am referring to the repeated defensive gestures working to protect the whitenormativity of feminism, whereby intersectionality and women of color feminisms are accused of dividing an otherwise supposedly unified project of feminism and women's studies.[108] To put it another way, I am troubled by the way critiques of intersectionality are too readily taken up because they reify and reproduce the narratives of loss in feminism, narratives that implicitly, and sometimes explicitly, accuse women of color of being divisive and ruining the project of feminism for calling out privilege, subordination, and difference within feminist communities. As the work of feminist scholars Danielle Bouchard, Claire Hemmings, Robyn Wiegman, and others have pointed out, there is a reoccurring narrative of lament and a sentiment of loss in the stories that both feminism and women's studies tell of themselves.[109] It is a self-referential narrative in which the radical potential of feminism (as social activism, a branch of academia, and a unified movement) is thwarted by difference—difference of opinion, difference of strategy, and, most notably, difference of experience. It is only within these types of laments that Susan Moller Okin can ask, "Is Multiculturalism Bad for Women," or Naomi Zack can proffer a vision for an "inclusive feminism" that returns to a unitary—that is, white—feminist subject.[110] As I have argued elsewhere, feminist studies remains haunted by the historical telos of rights claims and citizenship aspirations of white women.[111] This is to suggest that, as far as I am concerned, intersectionality remains a radical critique and a hopeful practice that works to name and, perhaps one day, dislodge the white female subject of feminism.

Not all critiques of intersectionality are invested in re-centering a universal (read white) feminist subject. Queer feminist scholar Jasbir Puar has offered one of the most thorough critiques of intersectionality in an effort to push feminist and queer studies to be more accountable to critiques of racism, empire, and the logics of the normative. In her groundbreaking book, *Terrorist Assemblages: Homonationalism in Queer Times*, Puar argues that intersectionality is a limited framework for understanding identity and subject formation, and needs to be either replaced with or supplemented by a model of "assemblage." As she says, "assemblages allow us to attune to the movements, intensities, emotions, energies, affectivities, and textures as they inhabit events, spatiality, and corporealities. Intersectionality privileges naming, visuality, epistemology, representation, and meaning, while assemblage underscores feeling, tactility, ontology, affect, and information."[112] Here, Puar points our attention toward the visual epistemologies that are conjured up via the "intersection" that do not account for the spatial, embodied, affective, and temporal effects on difference. Puar's assemblage is not something that can be visualized, and this is very much her point; visuality does violence to, and reduces our account of, how power actually operates and is experienced. Puar's assemblage is also notoriously difficult to explain and understand. Therefore, Puar's critique of intersectionality and the alternative of assemblage help us consider the ways in which language itself hinders intersectionality. Language fails, like visuality, to properly grapple with processes of differentiation, power, identity, and subjectivity. Here we are, literally, at a loss for words.

In one of her follow-up articles on this issue, Puar clarifies that she is not asking us to choose assemblage over intersectionality as a theoretic framework. She explains, "There are different conceptual problems posed by each; intersectionality attempts to comprehend political institutions and their attendant forms of social normativity and disciplinary administration, while assemblages, in an effort to reintroduce politics into the political, asks what is prior to and beyond what gets established."[113] In this way, even critics of intersectionality consider it to be an appropriate framework for attempting to reveal the ways in which disciplinary and biopolitical power operates, particularly at the level of nation-state apparatuses such as citizenship.

Even though Puar clarifies that intersectionality and assemblage are not mutually exclusive, and that each framework has its time and place, I want to consider her most significant critique of intersectionality, namely that it serves and abets the nation-state's normalizing projects. According to Puar, "As a tool of diversity management and a mantra of liberal multiculturalism, intersectionality colludes with the disciplinary apparatus of the state—census, demography, racial profiling, surveillance—in that 'difference' is encased within a structural container that simply wishes the messiness of identity into a formulaic grid, producing analogies in its wake and engendering what Massumi names 'gridlock.'"[114] Apparently, while we are looking at the same process, we are coming up with opposite conclusions—what Puar names intersectional state practices, I describe as anti-intersectional ones. The nation-state does not practice intersectionality when it requires subjects to check preselected boxes to mark identity categories on a census, nor when it marks a subject as a potential terrorist due to their racially inflected affiliations or geographically marked surnames. Rather, these are anti-intersectional efforts by the nation-state, whereby categories of identity and difference are forged, segregated, and forced to exist in separate and hierarchicalized frames. The state's normativizing projects—projects that segregate categories of identity while simultaneously marking them as valuable or debased, legitimate or improper, human or inhuman, and worthy of life or abandoned for death—make intersectionality and the messiness of identity incomprehensible. Through my comparative case studies, I see normative citizenship maintained through the state-led practices of anti-intersectionality, whereby the state reproduces hegemonic epistemologies of identities that are normative, single-axis, and comparatively valued against other categories of identity. This book demonstrates that intersectionality is far from collusive with the nation-state; the nation-state's disciplinary apparatus works to actively refute the possibility of intersectional identities.

What, then, is at stake when we call nation-state practices "intersectional" or "anti-intersectional?" When we collapse hegemonic and systemic epistemologies with women of color theorizing and critique, we conflate processes with analyses. Calling nation-state processes of differentiation and separation "intersectional" negates the critical ways power, knowledge, and identity work to create normative belief systems, systems that are a matter of life and death. Such a conflation would proffer the nation-state as always-already intersectional and, as a result, would diminish the power and potential of the insights of women of color feminisms, queer critiques, and decolonial analyses that work to expose the normative, violent workings of the nation-state. Moreover, understanding a distinction between intersectional feminist frameworks and anti-intersectional hegemonic processes allows us to see how and when stakeholders, activists, academics, and others are complicit with the nation-state and the violence of citizenship. As this book demonstrates, far too often progressive as well as liberal political strategies follow the nation-state's lead by reproducing anti-intersectional political tactics that further cement the productions of normalcy and deviance in U.S. citizenship. Hegemonic anti-intersectionality renarrativizes the naturalness and idealization of normative categories and reenacts violence to nonnormative categories by renaturalizing their inhumanity. Therefore, understanding the ways in which hegemonic anti-intersectionality functions allows us to create methods in which we work to disrupt, queer, and make strange the naturalization of normative citizen-subjects.

## Queer Intersections and Interventions

As an interdisciplinary project, *Against Citizenship* intervenes in and merges at least five fields of study, namely citizenship studies, queer studies, Indigenous studies, critical race studies, and feminist studies. While there has been an explosion of scholarship on citizenship (as described above), my work most directly engages with the scholarship that has interrogated the nexus of legal and cultural negotiations of citizenship, specifically at the level of racial, sexual, colonial, imperial, and gendered identities. Some of the most formative work in this arena includes the work of feminist and queer scholars of citizenship, such as Lauren Berlant, Wendy Brown, Nancy Cott, Inderpal Grewal, Eithne Luibhéid, Aihwa Ong, Erica Rand, Siobhan Somerville, and Leti Volpp.[115] These scholars have investigated how the U.S. nation-state has historically, as well as contemporaneously, configured citizenship through productions of racial, gender, sexual, and national difference, and examined the ways in which the nation-state is invested in notions of proper sexual, racial, gender, and national behaviors, experiences, abilities, and identities. This book continues these lines of investigation, but uses intersectional, comparative case studies as a framework to explore how categories of normative and abject citizenship function in and against each other, differently, and contextually.

*Against Citizenship* also directly intervenes in current debates within queer studies about the proper objects and subjects of the field. Scholars such as Jigna Desai, David Eng, Lisa Duggan, Roderick Ferguson, Jack Halberstam, Jasbir Puar, Chandan Reddy, and Dean Spade, among others, have transformed the field by modeling queer diasporic, queer of color, and intersectional queer critiques.[116] This book builds on their insights in two significant ways. First, *Against Citizenship* responds to the call to focus queer analyses on the "wide field of normalization" that is the "site of violence," and, second, *Against Citizenship* moves queer critique away from a focus on queer, queerly racialized, and queerly Indianized bodies, and works more directly to analyze violent processes of the state.[117] Here, I aim queer theory's critiques at the hegemonic social structures and belief systems inherent in citizenspeak in an effort to queer the violent norms of citizenship.

My reading method has been greatly influenced by queer studies. I deploy what I consider to be a queer deconstructive method of discourse and narrative analysis in order to read for what is understood, assumed, left unspoken, or left in place, and the violence that comes with these productions. I offer symptomatic readings as a means to cull out these thematics, paying close attention to the structure and form of arguments as much as the content. Moreover, my own deployment of a queer method focuses not only on the production of norms, but reads for anxiety, angst, and fear in order to argue that these are productive moments of possibility. *Against Citizenship* argues that anxiety is one of the telltale signs of the fractures within the naturalization of categories of identity and their epistemological fortresses.

*Against Citizenship* follows the lead of Indigenous studies scholars such as Joanne Barker, Jodi Byrd, Jennifer Denetdale, and J. Kēhaulani Kauanui in order to investigate how practices of U.S. settler colonialism and imperialism are embedded in—that is, produced as norms of—U.S. citizenship, or what I describe as "colonialnormativity."[118] *Against Citizenship* investigates how this colonial-normativity is obscured by what Jodi Byrd calls the "cacophony of competing struggles," whereby attention to racism and raciality, in particular, has the tendency to direct attention away from Indigeneity and settler colonialism. Byrd's cacophony, and in my analysis, anti-intersectionality, is further entrenched by the U.S. nation-state's racialization of Indigeneity, whereby "the conflation of racialization into colonization and indigeneity into racial categories dependent upon blood logics underwrites the institution of settler colonialism when they proffer assimilation into the colonizing nation as reparation for genocide and theft of land and nations."[119] Moreover, by bringing together queer Indigenous studies and critical race theory, *Against Citizenship* works to consider the ways in which coalitional, intersectional politics can refuse the U.S. nation-state's setup of conflating, confusing, and disaggregating antiracist and anticolonial strategies.

While the previous section described some of the growing tensions and the potential of intersectionality within feminist studies, another intervention I make in this book is to demonstrate how an ardently feminist text does not have to focus on "women." This is not to say that work on women, similar to the work on queers of color, is not valuable. This is not a "postfeminist" or "postidentity" text, as much as the discourses of multiculturalism and the rhetoric of color/gender/sexual-blindness violently suggest. Rather, this is an engagement with branches within feminist studies that refuses to re-center, renaturalize, and renormativize an unqualified, undifferentiated "woman/women" as the quintessential subject and object of feminist studies. Moreover, as a wide variety of feminist scholarship demonstrates, one of its main targets of critique is the politics of knowledge production, especially as manifest within the academy and its radical constriction of possibilities. Hence, this book pays attention to academic scholarship, not merely as a form of "literature review" to situate my own work, but to position academic work as a key site of knowledge production that should be held accountable for the ways in which it (re)produces violent structures of thought. I offer to read academic discourses through and against legal and popular cultural discourses in order to flesh out how they collude and, in rare moments, diverge.

The following chapters explore the production of normative citizenship and the violence that these norms produce by examining different, yet interrelated sites of struggle. By examining how norms are produced and contested within three different political debates, namely same-sex marriage, hate crimes, and decolonial struggles in Hawai'i, I hope to offer insights and interventions for progressive political organizing and theoretical critiques. These case studies flesh out the contours of citizenship and expose how citizenship works to transform discourses of belonging into processes of violent dehumanization. Same-sex marriage, for example, illuminates citizenship as a form of affiliation deeply invested in articulations and practices of privacy, intimacy, family, and consumerism. It allows us to see the ways in which a seemingly private, personal affair is transformed through the nexus of marriage and citizenship into a gatekeeping process that works to mark some relationships, identities, behaviors, and practices as more worthy, more sustainable, more valuable, and more human than others. Hate crime legislation reveals citizenship as a form of state-forged, anti-intersectional boundary maintenance that is central to the expectation of safety and bodily integrity, or the lack thereof. A case study focusing on hate crimes allows us to consider the public machinations of citizenship and how it operates through marking some bodies as worthy of value, while others are marked as violable and expendable. Finally, the case study on racialization, Indigeneity, and sovereignty in Hawai'i provides an opportunity to see U.S. citizenship not only as a process that requires the perpetual and ongoing erasure of Native peoples but also works to reproduce them into racial subjects in order to resubjugate them over and over again. Through this case study we can see citizenship as a discourse of belonging that requires the elimination of Indigenous peoples. Together these diverse case studies offer to paint a more robust—yet far from complete—picture of the multiple ways in which citizenship is inherently violent.

Most importantly, by bringing together these seemingly diverse sites, I aim to demonstrate how we can work against hegemonic anti-intersectionality by not only drawing the connections across the violence of normativities, but also by working to queer the collective faith in citizenship, belonging, and inclusion—to make these faiths in and aspirations for citizenship, normalcy, and humanity odd, unnatural, and incompatible with political organizing and theoretical critique. This approach positions citizenspeak where it belongs: at the heart of boundary-producing, state-sanctioned violence and as one of the central excuses for the extension of U.S. empire.

## Outline of Chapters

In the following chapters, I focus on specific case studies in order to trace the productions of normative citizenship and the violence that comes from these processes. Each chapter contains a two-part argument. In Chapter One, "The Specters of Citizenship: Hate Crimes and the Fear of the Repressed," I examine the violent maintenance of citizenship through the police state, and the uses of hate crime legislation to both name and disallow any recognition of this violence. My intervention operates at two interconnected levels: the social level of identity categories and the structural level of the state. At the level of identity, hate crime legislation and the surrounding debates allow us to see how categories of difference and anti-intersectionality function—or to be more accurate, *dysfunction*—within the nation-state, producing different relationships to bodily integrity through racialized, gendered, and sexualized citizenships that are consistently set up against each other in order to compete for "protection" from the state. While recognizing the ways in which hate crime legislation emboldens the police state, this chapter intervenes into this debate to explain how and when certain identities are presumed to be the legitimate objects of violence. Here, I reveal how actors across the political spectrum consistently deploy what I refer to as "comparative anti-intersectional" analyses, which is a particular form of anti-intersectionality that works to control and/or deny the violence of citizenship for nonnormative identity categories. Through an intersectional analysis I flesh out the specific ways that race, Indigeneity, gender, gender identity, and sexuality are imagined as having quite different relationships to violence, citizenship, and the rights to bodily integrity.

At the structural level of the state, I add to left critiques of hate crime legislation by unpacking how these laws are used to create a dangerous discontinuum, in which hate crimes are marked as individualized errors, while police brutality is systemically assuaged. Hate crime legislation obscures and overshadows the possible understanding that violations to the bodily integrity of abjected subjects take place on a spectrum, from governmental actions, governmental inactions, organized groups, vigilantes, and individuals. By examining the machinations of hate crime legislation at these two levels, I argue that hate crime legislation works, simultaneously, to *recognize* and *deny*: (1) the violence of citizenship and (2) the fear that the oppressed will seek revenge and retaliate for this experience by using violence themselves. Hate crime legislation serves as an outlet for managing the specters of citizenship, their experiences of violence, and their possible retaliation for these experiences.

In Chapter Two, "Intersectionalities Lost and Found: Same-Sex Marriage Law and the Monstrosities of Alliance," I situate the struggle over same-sex marriage as a matter of anti-intersectional, normative citizenship, arguing that marriage has been used by the nation-state as one of the most effective means to produce a particularly racialized, gendered, heterosexualized, and colonized citizenry. I argue that the "fight" for same-sex marriage has exposed some cracks in normative citizenship, but not where one might expect. While most scholars of same-sex marriage rights debate whether same-sex marriage advocacy challenges norms of (hetero)sexuality, I suggest that it has exposed a somewhat surprising anxiety in that it points toward the intersectionality of gender, sex, and sexuality, thereby challenging the hegemonic anti-intersectional norm that these categories are separable and discrete. Gay marriage showcased a small space for disruption, whereby judges, legislators, activists, and citizens become particularly anxious about the constructed and nonessentialist natures of sex, gender, and sexuality. As much as anti-intersectionality has become second nature, the inability to completely ignore the intersectionality of sex, gender, and sexuality opened up the space for some "gender trouble." However, this trouble was mitigated quickly, whereby same-sex marriage advocacy relied on and utilized the anti-intersectionalities of sexuality, race, coloniality, and migration. In the second half of the chapter, I point out how same-sex marriage rights has completely altered the terrain for queer critique of normative citizenship. By reframing Jasbir Puar and Amit Rai's analyses of monstrosity, I argue that queerness has lost its power of *monstrous difference*, which has been the performative modality by which queers have been able to launch progressive left critiques of the nation-state.[120] Even more importantly, the disavowal of queer monstrosity works to delink abject sexualities from the racialized, colonized, and gendered monstrosities of U.S. empire. Here, I call for a monstrous alliance, one in which the monstrous specters of citizenship coalesce to strike fear into the hearts of normative citizen-subjects.

In Chapter Three, "Legal Detours of U.S. Empire: Locating Race and Indigeneity in Law, History, and Hawaiʻi," I use *Rice v. Cayetano* (2000), a Supreme Court case involving a white citizen's challenge to Native Hawaiian representation, as a springboard to explore how race and coloniality are set up as oppositional, anti-intersectional politics. Kanaka Maoli[121] and other Indigenous scholars and activists have been quite vocal in critiquing the ways in which the discourse of civil rights and racism serves to obscure and undermine sovereignty claims and critiques of colonialism. I add to these critiques by demonstrating how the combination of legal and historical discourses sets up a battle between the recognition of racism and the recognition of settler colonialism. In this chapter, I illuminate how discourses of citizenship, law, and history collude to (re)produce the misrecognition and disaggregation of anticolonialist and antiracist endeavors. Unfortunately, these anti-intersectional strategies can be replicated by anticolonial and antiracist activists and scholars who inadvertently participate in obscuring the relationship between racism and colonialism in the United States. In looking for alternatives to this hegemonic, anti-intersectional discourse whereby antiracism is always-already set in opposition to decolonialism, I turn to the district court version of the *Rice* case, which provides an example of a "queer merger" between Kanaka Maoli decolonial activists and Harold Rice. This strange merger between Harold Rice and sovereignty activists, and the incompatibility of their critiques of the sovereignty vote, provided a space whereby colonialism was marked as complicit with notions of racial difference and provided an opportunity to denaturalize U.S. colonialnormativity. Eradicating the violence of whitenormativity and colonialnormativity, and especially the violent outcomes of their alliance, will require nothing less than intersectional and comparative coalitional politics, one infused with a sense of queer critique.

In my last chapter, "In and Out of Time," I use the Supreme Court decisions that were announced in June of 2013 as a means to showcase the anti-intersectionalities of citizenship and the ways in which anti-intersectionality functions through temporality. While many gays, lesbians, and their allies celebrated two of the decisions (*United States v. Windsor* and *Hollingsworth v. Perry*) for upholding same-sex marriage rights, Indigenous and antiracist activists, scholars, and allies bemoaned the decisions that dismantled the Voting Rights Act (*Shelby County v. Holder*), delimited affirmative action programs (*Fisher v. University of Texas*), and eroded Indigenous sovereignty (*Adoptive Couple v. Baby Girl*). The cases elucidate the ways in which the temporality of racialized discrimination has been used to dismantle racial reparations and Indigenous rights, while simultaneously being used to grant gays and lesbians a limited form of membership into the exclusive rights of citizenship. In this way, these cases demonstrate how differently devalued and valued subjects are marked as in and out of time, and in the process, subjected to the temporal violence of normative citizenship. I end with an argument for a coalitional present that aims to dismantle the anti-intersectionalities of citizenship through a radical loss of faith in citizenship, law, and futurity as avenues for salvation and justice.

And I confess: in arguing for a politics that is avowedly intersectional and idealistically antinormative, I am being, unabashedly, impractical, and polemical. As far as I am concerned, the practical politics of piecemeal inclusion, or a "one-group-at-a-time, take-what-you-can" function as a liberalist alibi for mechanisms of violent, normative citizenship. *Against Citizenship* argues against practical politics, as pragmatic political gestures are other means for perpetuating anti-intersectional politics-as-usual. But being impractical is not apathetic; rather, it is a feminist, queer, decolonial, critical race practice, whereby we work against the grain, especially one so deeply grooved as anti-intersectional, inclusionary liberal politics. And within a politics of presence, one cannot wait for a better, less violent tomorrow. Rather, a politics of presence requires an assessment of the conditions of the present, in all of its violent machinations. And if the future is merely an intensification and accumulation of the present, then there is no time for a coalitional, intersectional, decolonial politics but now.[122]

# CHAPTER 1

# The Specters of Citizenship

## Hate Crimes and the Fear of the Repressed

We do not deride the fears of prospering white America. A nation of
violence and private property has every reason to dread the violated
and the deprived. Its history drives the violated into violence and, one of
these days, violence will literally signal the end of violence as a means.

—June Jordan (1981)

In the patriotic fervor that swept throughout U.S. national culture after the events of September 11, 2001, declarations of loyalty such as "United We Stand" and "God Bless America" became pervasive. Marking identifications on bodies via T-shirts and spaces such as houses and automobiles, there was a way in which U.S. nationalism had an almost desperate tone.[1] But as the space for left critique shriveled within the national public sphere, there was another bumper sticker pronouncement that allowed for a more complex reading: "These colors don't run." Most often this slogan was placed on top of an image of the American flag, suggesting that the reference to "colors" might correlate to the red, white, and blue of U.S. patriotism. However, the reference to "color" cannot help but bleed outside of these particular containers.[2] Considering the violence against people of color, especially in times of fervent U.S. nationalism, the reference to "color" directs our attention to the racialized violent border maintenance of normative citizenship.

The patriotic demand that "These Colors Don't Run" is complicated by the various forms of racial profiling that were institutionalized at both governmental and civilian levels on behalf of the "war on terror." These profiling techniques were aimed at, as well as productive of, the consolidation of Arabs, Muslims,

South Asians, and Middle Easterners into an amorphous racialized category of "Muslim-looking" people as potential terrorists.[3] For example, immediately after September 11, 2001, U.S. federal and state-level governments implemented several mechanisms to track, locate, and detain potential terrorists, including Homeland Security dragnets aimed at collecting "Muslim-looking" peoples for interrogation and indefinite detention, the reinstitutionalization of explicit racial profiling at various levels, and transformations in immigration and student visa policies.[4] Importantly, civilians operationalized racial profiling policies through a wave of violent physical and verbal attacks against "Muslim-looking" peoples in the days, weeks, and months after September 11, 2001. Reports vary, but some organizations suggest that there were over one thousand "hate crimes" against "Muslim-looking" peoples in the weeks immediately following the September 11th attack.[5] These ranged from verbal harassment, to violent physical assaults, to murder. Many incidents barely registered in the news, including a Pakistani store owner who was threatened by a "Caucasian" male in Norwich, Connecticut, to leave the country; an East Indian male who was stabbed in the arm by a group of white male perpetrators who accused him of being a "terrorist"; a South Asian woman who was spit on while riding the New York City subway; and a Sikh grocery store owner who was shot to death in Long Island.[6] One of the few stories that did make the national news was the murder of Balbir Singh Sodhi, a Sikh in Mesa, Arizona, who was shot five times by an assailant (Frank Roque) who declared "all Arabs had to be shot."[7] When we consider the long history of "patriotic" violence against people of color, alongside the post–September 11, 2001, consolidation of "Muslim-looking" peoples into "potential terrorists," we are forced to consider a wholly different reading as to which colors are *forced to run*—run to protect their bodily integrity, their communities, and their lives.

Violence against "others" has long been part of the boundary-marking apparatus of U.S. citizenship. As much as the discourse around hate crimes suggests that these are rare acts perpetrated by castigated (white, male, heterosexual) supremacists, many critical theorists have argued that hate crimes are extensions of state de facto and de jure discriminatory practices, with perpetrators acting as vigilantes in service of maintaining and enforcing the national imaginary of the normative body politic. These scholars have rightfully implicated the nation-state in maintaining—if not producing—the conditions for civilian hate crimes.[8] In his groundbreaking analysis of hate crimes after September 11, 2001, Muneer Ahmad argues that the U.S. nation-state has "projected violence against Arab, Muslim, and South Asians as a social norm" through government practices of racial profiling, immigration policies and detention programs, and

Homeland Security dragnets that detain and interrogate the loyalties of, literally, *countless* "Muslim-looking" citizens and noncitizens.[9] His analysis demonstrates that civilians who perpetrate hate crimes against "Muslim-looking" people are merely being "good citizens" and doing their part of enacting the violent boundary-maintenance work of citizenship.

Building on the idea that hate crimes are one of the enforcement mechanisms of normative citizenship, this chapter considers the violent maintenance of citizenship and the uses of hate crime legislation to both name and disallow any recognition of this violence. My intervention into how we understand citizenship to be violently organized functions at two interconnected levels, that is, at the structural level of state violence, and at the social level of identity categories. At the level of the state, hate crime legislation offers us important information as to how the violence of citizenship is managed, controlled, and directed. Many left scholars point to the ways in which hate crime legislation serves to give further license to state violence. In the name of "protecting" the nonnormative, the U.S. police state is given freer reign to violate vulnerable populations and continue the escalation of an already out-of-control prison industrial complex and border patrol.[10] Hate crime legislation perpetuates the erroneous understanding that civilian forms of violence are more common, and more heinous, than state-sanctioned forms of violence. Through the rhetoric of hate crimes legislation, hate crimes continue to be tied to the extraordinary, the heinous, and the past (most often, the organized vigilante white supremacy of the segregated South), while the ordinary, everyday violence of structural racism, especially as perpetuated via state and federal governance, is obscured. These are the connections that are deferred, if not denied: that hate crimes take place on a spectrum, from governmental actions, governmental inactions, organized groups, vigilantes, and individuals. There has been a dangerous discontinuum in which hate crimes and the violent operations of citizenship are individualized while state-sanctioned police violence is systemically assuaged. And yet, as much as hate crime legislation serves to distract people from seeing state-sanctioned violence as a "hate crime," there are also very important ways in which community groups have used hate crime legislation as a means to critique the state. Holding state actors accountable for the production of difference, hate crime legislation activists and community members use the language and laws of hate crimes to teach state actors (especially the police) about structural difference and the violations of bodily integrity from both state and nonstate actors.

Because politicians, activists, and scholars are increasingly debating as to which identity classifications should be included as "protectable," hate crime legislation is an especially ripe site for analyzing how identity categories function at the level of the social. As I demonstrate here, hate crime legislation and the surrounding debates allow us to see how categories of difference and intersectionality function—or to be more accurate, *dysfunction*—within the nation-state. Scholars rarely, if ever, apply an intersectional analysis to hate crime legislation. By deploying such a framework, I showcase how the debates on hate crime legislation are informed by, and contorted through, what I refer to as *the logics of comparative anti-intersectionality*, whereby the categories of race, Indigeneity, gender, and sexuality are segregated and set in opposition to each other. Individuals across the political spectrum consistently deploy comparative anti-intersectional ways of knowing. These epistemologies are used in order to safeguard normative citizenship by denying the possibility of intersectional identities and intersectional connectivities. Moreover, these epistemologies reflect and perpetuate the ways in which categories of race, Indigeneity, gender, and sexuality are understood as having very different relationships to violence, citizenship, and the right to bodily integrity.

Through combining an analysis of what hate crime legislation does, at the level of the state and at the level of social categories, this chapter argues that hate crime legislation exposes an ongoing and simultaneous *recognition and denial* of: (1) the violence of citizenship and (2) the fear that the oppressed will seek revenge and retaliate for this experience by using violence themselves. As the June Jordan epigraph that begins this chapter points out, "A nation of violence and private property has every reason to dread the violated and the deprived. Its history drives the violated into violence and, one of these days, violence will literally signal the end of violence as a means."[11] Therefore, hate crime legislation serves as an outlet for managing the specters of citizenship—the disenfranchised, the excluded, the Othered—their experience of violence, and their possible retaliation for this experience. My readings of hate crime legislation and the rhetoric surrounding it locates the state as the instigating conduit of normative violence and hate crime legislation as a *strategic pressure release valve* that keeps the violent mechanisms of citizenship operational.[12]

## The Evolution of Hate Crime Legislation

Hate crime legislation is a hotly contested site, whereby scholars, activists, and politicians argue over whether it protects or causes more harm to disenfranchised peoples and whether it works to excuse the state or hold it accountable for hate crimes. A liberal reading suggests that hate crime legislation is the successful manifestation of civil rights activism's goal to promote and protect the bodily integrity and rights of historically disenfranchised peoples. Meanwhile, conservatives rail against hate crime legislation, arguing that it is a form of "special rights," which works to mark certain kinds of victims (read: nonnormative citizen-subjects) as more worthy of protection than others (read: normative citizen-subjects). And many critical left scholars and activists have adamantly opposed hate crime legislation, mostly on the grounds that it bolsters the discriminatory criminal justice system and furthers the vulnerability of young men of color to police violence. This left critique suggests that hate crime legislation works to distract the populace from recognizing and confronting state violence and governmental practices of intimidation and harassment.

With this left critique in mind, we can conceptualize hate crime legislation as a complicated paradox; hate crime legislation is both a dangerous, yet valiant, response to the everyday experiences of violence for many people of color, Indigenous, LGBT folks, disabled communities, and women. Left activists and scholars certainly "cannot not want" (in Gayatri Spivak's famous phrasing) the right to bodily integrity and safety for the disenfranchised, the nonnormative, and the noncitizen. Yet at the same time, they cannot afford to support any legislation that reinforces the discriminatory and brutal police state. While I certainly delve into this quagmire, I hope to move the conversation away from the common pro/con setup, and, instead, use hate crime legislation to expose the state's investment in anti-intersectional epistemologies.

As the scholarship suggests, the exact definition of "hate crime" is a source of controversy amongst advocates and opponents of hate crime legislation. Most commonly, hate crimes are described as physical violence and/or physical intimidation that are motivated by the perpetrator's recognition of and hatred toward the victim's perceived *difference*. Tom Streissguth, for example, describes hate crimes as "selecting other humans for assault, injury, and murder on the basis of certain personal characteristics: different appearance, different color, different nationality, different language, different religion."[13] The reoccurring terms of hate crimes tend to emphasize an individual perpetrator's motivations (i.e., "hatred," "bias," or "prejudice") as well as their recognition and categorization of difference (i.e., "race," "color," "nationality," etc.). Importantly, these reoccurring definitions delimit hate crimes by individualizing them and obscuring societal contexts. And, of course, which differences matter is a central concern in the debates on hate crime. While most hate crime legislation readily recognizes hate crimes predicated upon perceived racial, ethnic, national origins, and religious grounds, the recognition of sexual orientation, gender, and gender identity have been much more contested. And as hate crime legislation has become increasingly commonplace in the U.S. political landscape, some activists have pushed for the inclusion of other categories, such as "the home-less," "the elderly," or "immigrants," or asked for more differentiation within the categories of inclusion, such as adding a specific subcategory for Sikhs, Arabs, and Hindus.[14]

The federal legislation on hate crimes tends to come in a few different forms. Some suggest that the earliest form of such legislation connects back to the Civil Rights Act of 1968, which criminalized the act of interfering with, intimidating, or threatening a person's performance of a civil right (such as serving on a jury or voting) on the basis of "race, color, religion, or national origin." One could, however, connect hate crime legislation to even earlier incarnations of civil rights legislation, particularly from the Reconstruction Era, such as the Civil Rights Act of 1871 (also referred to as the Ku Klux Klan Act), which aimed to provide civil remedies for African Americans who were intimidated or terror-ized by the Ku Klux Klan. The first official "hate crime" legislation focused on data collection and the search for "proof" of hate crimes.[15] For example, the first federal law using the language of "hate crimes" is the Hate Crime Statistics Act. Passed in 1990, the law requires that the federal government collect statistics on hate crimes involving "race, religion, sexual orientation, or ethnicity."[16] In 1994 it was modified to include counting acts aimed at people with disabilities, and in 2009 it was amended again to include data on gender and gender-identity–motivated hate crimes, as well as track the number of juveniles involved at either end of the incident.

These statistical acts follow the conservative impulse to, first, *count and prove* that hate crimes are an existing social problem before state and/or federal ac-tions will be considered.[17] When alleviation is deemed appropriate, it most often comes in the form of a "sentence enhancement" law, which increases the sentences of persons who are prosecuted for previously defined criminal activity (such as vandalism and/or assault) alongside what can be deemed as a hate crime. In 1994 Congress passed the Hate Crime Sentencing Enhancement Act as part of one of the most expansive crime bills in U.S. history.[18] The law directed the U.S. Sentencing Commission to create a three-tier guideline for sentence enhancements for hate crimes. Here, hate crimes were defined as, "a crime in which the defendant intentionally selects a victim, or in the case of a property crime, the property that is the object of the crime, because of the actual or perceived race, color, religion, national origin, ethnicity, gender, disability, or sexual orientation of any person."[19] These earlier incarnations of hate crime legislation laid the foundation for fixing *hate crime* within the national lexicon, and marked the transition from data collection to sentence enhancement.

The 2009 Matthew Shepard and James Byrd, Jr., Hate Crimes Prevention Act requires a bit more explanation. As a culmination of almost eleven years of delay in Congress, this hate crime legislation is the most elaborate in form and scope. First, it expands the types of identity groups to be "protected" under hate crime legislation, as well as what groups are counted within federal statistics on hate crimes. In particular, it adds gender, gender identity, and sexual orientation as protected categories, while adding gender and gender identity as categories for statistical tracking. To be clear, up until this law, race, color, religion, disability, and national origin were all both protected categories and statistical categories, while sexual orientation was merely included as a statistical category of importance. Even though the 2009 law added new categories to be protected, it also codified two different levels of protection and authority for the categories. Under this law, the federal government can step in to prosecute hate crimes solely as hate crimes (that is, without the requirement that another law be broken) in cases of race, color, religion, or national origin. However, the federal government can move to prosecute hate crimes involving these "newer" categories of gender, gender identity, sexual orientation, and disability only when the crime involves interstate and/or foreign commerce (for example, if the crime occurred during the course of travel across state lines or a national border).[20] Debates on hate crime legislation rarely, if ever, acknowledge this two-tiered system, a system that is premised upon a comparative anti-intersectional epistemology.

Hate crimes and hate crime legislation are often described in ways that suggest they have performative effects. Debates on hate crime legislation revolve around what types of "messages" are communicated by the hate crimes themselves and hate crime legislation. While often skirting the obvious connection to common definitions of "terrorism" (that is, a type of violence that works to create a state of fear for communities), proponents of hate crime legislation argue that hate crimes send a message of disposability and exclusion to whole communities. According to Stephen Sprinkle, author of *Unfinished Lives: Reviving the Memories of LGBTQ Hate Crimes Victims*, hate crimes are nothing less than "message killings."[21] Therefore, these scholars and activists suggest that legislation addressing hate crimes are a mechanism to send a *reverse* message—one of belonging, protection, and rights to citizenship.

Hate crime legislation is often seen as a pedagogical tool. Some defend hate crime legislation on the grounds that it can *teach* citizens to be better people; relatedly, those opposed to hate crime legislation argue that they are unfairly shamed and figured as supporters of "hate" through this same process. It also should be noted that hate crime legislation relies upon, as well as reproduces, particular claims about what it means to be a "good citizen." Collectively, the debates, laws, and organizing around hate crime legislation reveal how hate crimes have been incorporated into the practices of citizenship and popular notions of morality, goodness, and multicultural colorblindness—major cornerstones of the U.S. cultural imaginary surrounding citizenship's normative violence.

## The State of Violence

Hate crime legislation is not only a useful site to explore the ways in which the U.S. nation-state manages the violence of citizenship, but it is also one of the key mechanisms for controlling the terms by which one can understand and evaluate this violence. Through the discursive productions of hate crime legislation, hate crimes are marked as especially heinous acts perpetrated by especially heinous individuals. Therefore, state violence and everyday forms of discrimination (and the violence that accompanies discrimination) are actively obscured under the extraordinary imagery of hate crimes. And yet, hate crime legislation provides a platform and a vocabulary that can be used to police the state. Given this tension, hate crime legislation marks the states of violence and the ways in which this violence can be managed by, as well as used against, the state.

### THE CONNECTIONS DEFERRED

Two of the most important critiques against hate crime legislation are that it covers up the state's own violent acts against nonnormative peoples, and that it bolsters the prison industrial complex. But within these two critiques lies a set of more subtle issues that I want to explore. Scholars and activists suggest that hate crime legislation is, in Andrea Smith's words, "an apology for the racial and gender violence of the state" that works to appease and quiet the left.[22] And as AnnJanette Rosga's ethnographic work demonstrates, one of the reasons law enforcement officers pursue hate crime charges is to use these charges as a public relations strategy to smooth over public perceptions of police bigotry.[23] Therefore, one of the central concerns is that, as Susan Gelman and Frederick Lawrence put it, hate crime legislation tends to be "merely a symbolic gesture for the legislature that is then used as a cover for avoiding more difficult, and probably more expensive, action towards true equality."[24] While there are many distressing paradoxes when it comes to the issue of hate crimes, one of them is that hate crime legislation actually becomes part of a system that works against low-income people of color—those very same people that are the most common victims of hate crimes. For legal scholar Terry Maroney, hate crimes are often used as easy rationales for expanding government surveillance, particularly in inner cities. He points to the troubling irony that "government adoption of anti-hate measures reflects the fact that such measures fit easily into the values of the criminal justice system that remains weighted against hate crime victims and their communities."[25] As these critics point out, hate crime legislation bolsters the prison industrial complex, first through figuring the state as the (benevolent) arbitrator who will act to protect victim(s) and enact "justice" on the victim(s) behalf, and second by claiming that the cure for hate crimes is found in (most often an extended) jail sentence for the perpetrator(s). As many community organizers have argued, these are quite limited ways of structuring the responses to hate crimes.[26] But through this limited framing, and because the majority of hate crime victims are historically disenfranchised peoples, it is critical to consider the cruel paradox that hate crime legislation enhances the criminal justice system in the name of protecting those very same communities that they most actively criminalize and brutalize through racial profiling, police brutality, and other regulatory instruments of the criminal justice system.

The correlation between hate crime legislation and the insidious heightening of incarceration mechanisms makes a vulnerable population's investments in such legislation complicated. In the case of calls for inclusion of gender and gender identity, legal scholar and activist Dean Spade argues that trans folks are working against their own interests when they work on behalf of hate crime legislation. In his words, hate crime laws "do nothing to prevent violence against transgender people but instead focus on mobilizing resources for criminal punishment systems' response to such violence. Because trans people are frequent targets of criminal punishment systems and face severe violence at the hands of police and in prisons every day, investment in such a system for solving safety issues actually stands to increase harm and violence." This means that not only do hate crime laws fail to protect trans people, they actually *increase* their vulnerability to, in Spade's terms, "police punishment systems." Later, Spade goes even farther to argue that "the 'successful' lesbian and gay rights model to which we [trans] are assumed to aspire" offers only "the legitimization and expansion of systems that are killing us."[27] Importantly, Spade is offering what he refers to as a "critical trans politics," which works not only to critique more liberal efforts for recognition, inclusion, and incorporation, but actively succeeds in drawing intersectional connections between the "common causes of our time," such as immigration, prison abolition, and wealth redistribution.

Not only does hate crime legislation bolster police punishment systems, it also serves as an alibi to state violence. In the context of violence against gay and lesbian subjects, legal scholar Kendall Thomas argued years ago that these so-called "interpersonal" hate crimes are part of the nation-state's "constellation of diverse practices" to maintain social order. While his argument was articulated before *Lawrence v. Texas*, where the Supreme Court marked antisodomy laws as unconstitutional, Thomas astutely argued that sodomy laws were less invested in policing *private* sexual acts and much more directed at constricting the *public* performance of proper citizenship practices in which hate violence and government criminalization of sodomy work hand-in-hand. "In other words," Thomas observed, "private homophobic violence punishes what homosexual sodomy statutes prohibit."[28] In fact, he suggested that government inaction and/or indifference to violence against LGBT peoples provides license to hate crime perpetrators. In his words, "private citizens who commit acts of terrorist violence against gays and lesbians can be said to do so under *color*, or more precisely, under *cover of law*."[29] While he was describing a slightly different time, a time in which the U.S. had antisodomy laws on the books, I think our post-antisodomy law moment might not be as different as one might hope. Now, as then, the victimization of LGBT folks relies on the selective enforcement of the law, alongside the always-present government indifference to hate crimes against LGBT peoples. Therefore, Thomas's analysis pushes us to consider whether current hate crime legislation *provides even more cover for the state* and its representatives.

I want to return to Kendall Thomas's slippages of color/cover for a moment, as these slippages point out an important connection. When he argues that perpetrators of violence do so "under color, or more precisely, under cover of law," he points us to the oft-used metaphor "under color of law." While at one level one can imagine employing a critical race analysis with this metaphor (similar to how I started this chapter with an analysis of the post–September 11th refrain, "these colors don't run"), "under color of law" is also a legal metaphor to refer to the ways in which the state and state representatives use their positions of power for illegal or nefarious purposes. In legal parlance, "under color of law" refers to a misuse of power, "made possible only because the wrongdoer is clothed with the authority of state law."[30] But if I can point your attention back to the earlier discussion about the possible origin stories of hate crime legislation, recall that I mentioned that one might see the civil rights legislation of the Reconstruction Era as precursors to our current manifestation of hate crime laws. While the Civil Rights Act of 1871 focused on the violent operations of nongovernmental organizations, such as the Ku Klux Klan, other legislation at that time was directed at federal and state representatives for actively violating African Americans' civil rights. The Reconstruction Civil Rights laws each contain enforcement clauses that begin with the phrase, "That any person who, under color of any law, statute, ordinance, regulation, or custom." This phrasing highlights the ways in which the state and its representatives were marked as potential perpetrators of hate crimes during this era.

One of the most troubling outcomes of the current-day hate crime legislation is the ways in which there has been a bifurcation, whereby the term "hate crime" seems to point directly toward nongovernment actors. There is no legal rationale for this bifurcation; governmental actors, including police enforcement officers, can be held accountable to charges of hate crime violations. Given the sheer enormity of police brutality, the number of hate crimes charges would skyrocket if the violent mechanisms of law enforcement were actively included within the purview of hate crime legislation. Yet, police brutality is rarely, if ever, marked as a hate crime, whether in popular discourse, through legal apparatuses, newspaper accounts, or criminal charges. This is, no doubt, related to ways in which police violence is always-already marked as justifiable. For example, as of 2014, there are three systems for tracking homicide by police at the federal level; data on police killings is hidden or submerged in the Justice Department's Bureau of Justice Statistics report on "Arrest-Related Deaths," in the FBI's Uniform Crime Reports under "justifiable homicide," and by the Centers for Disease Control and Prevention's National Vital Statistics Report under "legal intervention" statistics.[31] At the FBI general information Web site, they suggest that issues involving "excessive force" with government and state actors can be described as "color of law" abuses, while the hate crime page is dominated with a black-and-white photo of KKK members burning crosses at night.[32] There is no such imagery related to color of law, no image of a police officer with hir/her/his hands in handcuffs or other stirring images. Rather, there is merely a stock image of a judge's gavel, a tame reference to an empty justice.

Of course, the problem is not that we lack stirring imagery on government Web sites; the problem is that this differentiation within the imagery of hate crimes reinforces the very mistaken notion that the state's violence is always-already ethical and just. In *Freedom with Violence*, Chandan Reddy demonstrates that hate crime legislation is symptomatic of the dominant liberal narrative of the U.S. multicultural state, whereby the "original violence" of racial difference is now the alibi by which the nation-state perpetuates its own (supposedly always) "legitimate" violence. But as Reddy observes, "the modern experience of race is neither an overcoming of violence by freedom, nor simply an extension of violence through freedom, but rather an ambiguous contemporary modernity as a racialized freedom with violence—every expression of contemporary racial transformation is at once conjoined with substantially modern forms of violence."[33] In this process, the state's violence is pardoned to the point of being seen as the equivalence to nonviolence.

Hate crime legislation, then, serves to (re)produce a dangerous dis-continuum. It binds hate crimes to the extraordinary, and to an especially horrific and violent past, thereby divorcing hate crimes from everyday acts, experiences, and structures of discrimination, as well as obscuring the (unfortunately) unexceptional violence of the state against nonnormative folks. When hate crimes are tied to the extraordinary, it reestablishes and normalizes the common state-led implementations of violent citizenship, such as police harassment and brutality and various forms of discrimination. Thus, hate crime legislation works to cordon off the violence of citizenship as if it is only manifest within especially horrific acts practiced by especially aberrant individuals. This legislation serves to delink that which must be seen as part of a continuum, whereby the violence of citizenship is practiced through governmental actions, governmental inactions, organized groups, and individuals. These are the connections that are deferred and denied within the discourses of hate crime legislation.

## (UN)DRESSING THE STATE

While the scholarship on hate crimes has made important and profound contributions, it has also sidestepped some of the complexities that undergird these debates. Hate crime legislation not only *actively disallows* the connection between the (supposedly legal and valid) violence of the state and the (supposedly illegal) violence of the individual, but, paradoxically, hate crime legislation also creates a space in which activists can critique the state for its role in violence, hate, and the productions of racialized, sexualized, colonial, and gendered difference. Throughout hate crime legislation debates, a wide array of activists, scholars, and even government officials describe the ways in which nonnormative peoples *should expect* to experience violence. Put differently, there is a reoccurring narrative throughout these debates that nonnormative peoples *cannot and should not expect* to experience safety and bodily integrity in their home, much less "on the streets." These discourses describe the state as a central perpetrator of violence, and, as such, create an opportunity to hold the state accountable for this violence.

Seeing hate crime legislation as able to both obscure the state's violence as well as create a space in which that violence is made visible is a very different reading than one that is most commonly celebrated by critical scholarship, especially work published within queer theory and prison abolition studies. I am concerned that the rush to critique creates a space in which we might offer simplistic readings of complex processes. Or, relatedly, we might question the ways in which scholars describe the proponents of hate crime legislation as under the false impression that the state can provide justice. I would suggest that these activists are being unfairly figured as having some type of fantastical notion that the state is neutral, liberal, and nonviolent. I am not arguing that there is no such thing as naïveté; I am arguing that this presumption of naïveté is being applied in ways that shut down possibilities for seeing the nuances and complexities that come with any type of political movement. The goal is to configure ways we can see these complexities, even if, in the end, we need to come down on the side of criticism. To suggest that the end result of hate crime legislation is to further violence against nonnormative peoples is different from suggesting that any proponent of hate crime legislation adheres to a false consciousness in state-based resolutions for this violence. In my reading of hate crime debates and the compilations of social science scholarship, I have found an abundance of sarcastic and biting critiques of state actors, whereby many activists involved in hate crime–related agendas have a very critical stance on the criminal justice system.

To be sure, proponents of hate crime legislation have inherited a mixed bag of civil rights activism. In one of the most astute analyses of hate crime legislation, forensic psychologist Karen Franklin argues that hate crime laws were originally designed by civil rights organizers as a form of redress for historically disenfranchised groups, but since these laws are executed by the criminal justice system "whose social values and practical priorities are frequently at odds with those in the civil rights movement," the *practice* of hate crime legislation has ended up "replicating the very power imbalances and inequalities they were designed to ameliorate."[34] Franklin takes great care to locate the problem in the *practice* of legislation without claiming that civil rights organizers have been duped by a misguided faith in the state. This is another way of recognizing the violent manifestations of trying to operationalize left critiques. The question is not whether the criminal justice system can be a source for justice. Rather, the question is whether hate crime legislation or the activism on its behalf provides some type of avenue to critique the violent mechanisms of the state and of the criminal policing system.

Some scholars provide a convincing argument that this is indeed the case. Barbara Perry, for example, argues that hate crime legislation, at the very least, provides a legitimated voice to articulate and demand that the state make good on the promises of equality and safety. As Perry points out, because hate crimes are not isolated incidents but part of systemic oppression in which the state is implicated, hate crime legislation provides at least a small avenue of critique for victims and their communities.[35] Karen Franklin argues that we might be able to deem hate crime legislation as at least partially successful in the sense that it has been a means to "sensitiz[e] police, prosecutors, and judges to the problems faced by minority crime victims."[36]

AnnJanette Rosga's ethnographic work on hate crime legislation makes a similar argument. Rosga argues that activists often utilize hate crime legislation as a means to not only critique incidents of violence, but also as a means to critique the state and police enforcement policies. In Rosga's framing, hate crime legislation allows for an opportunity to "police the state" as to how state actors do and do not confront issues of hate violence.[37] Activists often hold the state accountable, not as the neutral arbiter of difference, but as the primary producer of difference. It is worth quoting her in full to understand her argument:

> Certainly both activists and law enforcement officers are using the category hate crime to classify certain types of crime, to identify a (contested) selection of incidents deriving from, and/or enacting, social prejudices. However, social actors situated both within and outside of law enforcement are also mobilizing the category of hate crime in negotiations over police—and metonymically state—identity. In arguing for or against particular elements of hate crime's definition, in supporting or rejecting policies that will affect police procedure, interested advocates from across the political spectrum contribute to the ongoing construction of the function and roles of law enforcement officers.[38]

As Rosga incisively argues, hate crime legislation provides an opportunity for community members to negotiate with representatives of the state or state actors, thereby demonstrating the contestability of not only the functionality of hate crime law enforcement, but categories of identity and structures of hate as well.

Basia Spalek argues that community organizations use hate crime legislation as a means to critique local police practices and push for what she calls "representative democracy."[39] As a result of such efforts, local government offices tend to include community organizations in various efforts on hate crimes, such as participating in the creation of training manuals, as well as working to hire and "include" minorities within the ranks of the police and government agencies. Her point here is that as much as these efforts to include are always-already problematic, hate crime legislation does produce some forms of government responsiveness to local communities.

My own discursive analysis of hate crime legislation supports these ethnographic accounts. There is a plethora of literature that is geared toward "training" state employees about hate crimes, social and cultural "differences," and the regulations and processes of hate crime law. From guidelines on data collection to training guides and procedural manuals, the criminal justice system is inundated with instructions for understanding hate crimes. For example, since the Hate Crime Statistics Act was passed in 1990, the Department of Justice and FBI have published various iterations of the "Hate Crime Data Collection Guidelines," as well as a "Training Guide for Hate Crime Data Collection" that are directed at law enforcement personnel.[40] Each of these guidelines works to offer information on what hate crimes are, how they are to be recognized, how officers should treat victims, and a series of definitions of various identities and types of bias. The Training Guide in particular offers a set of "learning modules" and tutorials. While these materials are certainly problematic, especially in how identities are defined (to be discussed later), they are clearly written by social scientists as a means to educate and produce at least some political and social awareness for police enforcement officers.[41] For example, in the 1999 U.S. Department of Justice's "Training Guide for Hate Crime Data Collection," while learning module two focuses on "definitions and procedures," and module three offers various "case study exercises," the first module is a series of cognitive psychology lessons on "The Social Psychology of Prejudice." These are, no doubt, gentle and simplistic ways to describe how and why personal and individual forms of bias and discrimination lead to "hate," but they also do some labor to describe some of the historical and structural conditions that precede and follow these individualized mishaps. So, for example, while module one outlines topics such as "Prejudice: How It Affects the Way We Think and the Way We Act," "What Are the Emotional Bases of Prejudice?" and "What Are the Cognitive Consequences of Stereotypes?" it also offers a discussion about "The Social Sources of Prejudice" that provides an albeit succinct explanation as to how historical oppressions and stereotypes create "unequal treatment."[42]

It is worth noting that the 2012 incarnation of the guidelines is clearly focused on training police about how to be relatively good liberal multiculturalists when it comes to, especially, their treatment and interaction with gender and sexual variants. In response to the 2009 Shepard/Byrd Act, the guidelines have become inundated with various caveats and explanations about how to recognize, treat, and respond respectfully to the LGBT community as well as non–gender-conforming others. While most of these liberal tutorials are focused on offering extra information for the identity definitions (discussed later), there is a dedicated section (Section V) for "Understanding How to Distinguish Sexual Orientation, Gender Identity, Anti-Transgender, Anti-Gender Nonconforming Crimes."[43] This section, written in consultation with the "Hate Crime Coalition Working Group," offers lessons such as follows:

> Transgender and gender non-conforming people may be of any sexual orientation (gay, lesbian, bisexual, or heterosexual). Knowing about a person's gender

identity (as transgender or gender non-conforming) does not tell you anything about their sexual orientation. They are separate categories. . . .

Confusion in classifying the motive of a crime can occur when a perpetrator is motivated solely because of the victim's gender identity but uses an anti-gay term as well. They do this because they are often more familiar with anti-gay terms like "faggot," "dyke," and "queer," not because they are actually motivated by bias toward the victim's sexual orientation. Therefore, a perpetrator may use anti-gay epithets, even though they have targeted a person entirely because the victim is transgender or gender non-conforming. . . .

If you do not know if someone should be referred to with female or male pronouns, it is acceptable to ask that person their preferred pronoun. Disrespectful attitudes toward the victim or witness of a crime can add to their sense of trauma. By showing respect, officers can avoid a potential conflict with a victim or witness over misuse of proper names and pronouns and focus everyone's attention on solving the crime that occurred.[44]

Hate crime legislation, then, provides the opportunity to train the police and other state actors on processes of racialization and gender and sexual oppression, which is no small feat when we recognize that these same actors are, potentially, debating the merits of racial profiling, affirmative action policies, and community politics.[45] These guidelines, while far from satisfactory descriptions of the structures of (hate) violence and practices of subordination, at least offer various types of "teaching moments" that create openings for activists and communities to call out police and to hold them accountable. In these moments, hate crime legislation activists are not denying that the police are perpetuators of violence. Rather, they are performing shrewd negotiations within the conditions of state power and violence. As Rosga observes, "police are being asked to investigate and apprehend bigots by people who often enough refer to the police themselves as bigots."[46]

One of the most important contributions of community organizations involved in hate crimes and/or community violence is that they keep a statistical tally of hate crimes, and these numbers are always much higher than those kept by government officials. This gap—between community organizations' numbers and those of the government—is one of the most prevalent conversations within hate crime debates. Conservatives use the disjuncture to suggest that community organizations are padding the results, and that there is no such problem as hate crime.[47] In her written testimony, for example, former Commissioner of the U.S. Commission on Civil Rights Gail Heriot argues that hate crime incidents are "overstated" and some incidents turn out to be "hoaxes."[48] But more often than not, these community accounts are given much more credence than the government's. Honoring the legitimacy and accuracy of these higher numbers draws on and participates in the recurrent critique of state violence seen throughout the debates. As Michael Lieberman from the Anti-Defamation League testified to the U.S. Senate Judiciary Committee, it is commonly understood that "the most likely targets of hate violence are the least likely to report to the police," (here referencing specifically undocumented migrants and LGBT folks).[49] Scholars and legislators continuously ask why there is such a gap between these numbers, and the answer they point to—eventually and quite consistently—is that police enforcement agencies fail victims of hate crimes.

I have been fascinated to see the ways in which this critique of the state's underreporting of hate crimes is embedded within hate crime legislation and official materials. Even the U.S. Department of Justice (DOJ) is quick to acknowledge that there must be *some reason* as to why victims of hate crimes do not feel safe to report their experiences to local police. The DOJ's "Special Report" on the National Criminal Victimization Survey and Uniform Crime Reporting from 2005, for example, specifically acknowledges that only 44 percent of "hate crime victimizations" are reported to the police. The survey even poses the question as to why victims would not report to the police. In answering this question, the survey offers a few preordained possibilities (as would any survey), with options including the following: victims chose to "deal with it another way," it "was not important enough" to report, "the police would not help," or "police couldn't do anything."[50] Locating these last two options and their inherent critique of the police alongside the others certainly downplays its meaning, but when we understand that the majority of those interviewed somehow get classified within the impotent rationale of "dealt with another way," we can see that this, too, is a critique of a criminal justice system that is not accountable or responsive to nonnormative people.

The Hate Crime 2003–2009 Special Report, published in 2011, continues this line of thinking. Using the neutral language in bold type that states, "Approximately a third of hate crime victimizations not reported to the police was handled another way," admits finally that, "Approximately 15% of hate crime victims who did not report the crime believed that the police would not want to be bothered or to get involved, would be inefficient and ineffective, or would cause trouble for the victim."[51] A 2010 overview report published by the Congressional Research Service (aimed at informing Congress about the history and context of the hate crime legislation) states in a matter-of-fact tone that, "Despite improvements in collection and coverage, observers of the FBI data have long suspected that hate crime could be underreported."[52] But, interestingly, this report offers a few messier rationales than those offered by the statistical reports. Here, William Krouse (the author of the report) suggests that one reason might be that small or rural police enforcement units do not have enough "manpower" or "*inclination*" to document hate crimes (my emphasis).[53] Or perhaps this underreporting stems from a fear of what he calls "secondary victimization," which is quickly directed away from its most obvious reference to the possibility of enduring police brutality or harassment for reporting the hate crime, and, instead, associates it with gays and lesbians that might need to avoid "public disclosure of one's homosexuality." And last, the report suggests that perhaps government agencies avoid reporting (note the slippage here, as the question is why victims do not report to the agencies) in order to avoid admitting these types of problems exist within the community. The report suggests that agencies merely want to "keep the peace" rather than a more accurate understanding that they are actively working to retain and promote the violence of citizenship.[54]

One of the most interesting aspects of hate crime legislation is the way in which the state's role in hate violence is simultaneously concealed and acknowledged. Throughout hate crime debates, the state's violence is legitimated and reinforced through the rhetoric of exceptional, individualized vigilante hate crimes. And yet, within those very same debates, the U.S. nation-state is indirectly and implicitly understood as a perpetrator of hate violence, whether through inaccurate statistics, unresponsive agencies, or the structural maintenance of the bodily liabilities for nonnormative peoples. While these mechanisms might appear to be contradictory, they actually work together to control and contain public discourses and common knowledge about the violence of citizenship.

## Anti-intersectionality and the Order of Violability

One of the central questions for left legal thought has been whether it is possible to include disenfranchised and abjected identity categories into law without cementing those very same identities in their abjected forms.[55] Hate crime legislation is a particularly ripe site for considering this dilemma. Hate crime legislation relies upon defining various identity categories that should be "protected," but in this process, these identity categories are entrenched in law, and reinforced and naturalized as distinct, concrete entities rather than as situational and temporal productions. As AnnJanette Rosga states, a critical left analysis of hate crime legislation emphasizes "the ways in which the legal prohibition against hate crimes has had the paradoxical effect of reinforcing static identity boundaries and has contributed to the naturalization of difference."[56] Of course, while it is certainly true that hate crime legislation deploys and naturalizes categories of identity, these categories might be just as naturalized or reinforced within the event of the hate crime itself (if not before). Victor Hwang argues, for example, that hate crime incidents force victims to inhabit difference whereby they are marked, acutely and painfully, through the experience of violence.[57] This is why Rosga argues that it might be better to see the actual harm of hate crime not only through the framework of physical violence, but through discursive regimes as well. Hate crimes are most profoundly "violent inscription[s] of identity" that serve to perpetuate and naturalize identity categories in the service of the U.S. citizenship apparatus.[58]

However, by deploying an intersectional analysis, hate crime legislation offers a much more complex lesson as to how identities function through law. In this section, I have two interconnected arguments: first, through an intersectional analysis we can see that race, Indigeneity, sexuality, gender, and gender identity are talked about in very different ways, which points directly to the fact that these identity categories have *very different relationships to the violence of citizenship*. One of the most helpful elements of hate crime legislation is that it provides ample opportunities for the expression of presumptions and anxieties about the embodiments of difference and violability to U.S. citizenship apparatuses. While hate crime legislation has certainly not been easily consumed by conservatives, even liberals have had a hard time swallowing the claims that hate crimes occur and should be legislated against, particularly on behalf of LGBT folks and women. And while there appears to be more willingness to see race, ethnicity, and national origins as legitimate categories for protection, the absence of analysis and thoughtful negotiation with these categories actually works to further entrench and naturalize these categories, as well as segregate them in ways that deny their intersectionalities. Here, I juxtapose the easy incorporation of race, ethnicity, and national origin as hate crime categories, and the presumptions that come with these incorporations, against the antagonisms and resistance given to including sexuality and gender categories in order to expose how U.S. citizenship presumes and safeguards differing levels of bodily integrity, safety, and violability.

Second, beyond learning about how these different types of categories are understood as inherently and differentially violable, an intersectional analysis of hate crime legislation allows us to track the uses of anti-intersectionality as a common strategy of negation within these debates. Categories of difference are never standing on their own, but are always being formulated in and against other categories of difference. This is, of course, one of the main lessons of women of color feminist thought, as described in the Introduction. But throughout the conversations or debates on hate crimes, categories of identity are often compared and measured against each other through the continuous deployment of a discourse of limited resources (which is quite mistaken in this context, if not all contexts). Throughout hate crime debates, these categories of identity are forced to fight it out for which category is more worthy of protection. This is a very productive and useful rhetorical strategy that I call "comparative anti-intersectionality." While conservatives most often utilize this strategy, liberals seem to play along as well. Through this comparative anti-intersectional approach, one category of difference (usually race) is used to deny or demean another (usually sexuality or gender identity). Quite frankly, the rhetorical frameworks used for comparative anti-intersectional analyses often sound like setups for bad jokes (akin to the "two gays walk into a bar . . ." storytelling approach). These "silly" frameworks are then used to completely negate the horrific, painful experiences of violence for many people. But first, let me explain how identities are defined in hate crime legislation in the order of violability.

## TAXONOMIES OF VIOLATION

If we are concerned that identity categories are cemented and fixed into law, we should be even more concerned when the legal mandates go out of their way to offer specific definitions of the identity categories in question. But as much as definitions simplify and contort how identity operates, I would suggest it might be even more telling to trace which categories are seen as needing a definition and which categories are presumed to be normative, shared knowledge. Throughout the hate crime guideline materials produced by the DOJ, definitions of identity and bias crimes abound. In the 1999 "Hate Crime Data Collection Guidelines," the second page is dedicated to laying out hate crime terminology and definitions, including "Bias" and its various forms: "Disability Bias," "Ethnicity/National Origin Bias," "Racial Bias," "Religious Bias," and "Sexual Orientation Bias," as well as certain identities, including "Bisexual," "Disabled,"[59] "Gay," "Heterosexual," "Homosexual," and "Lesbian." These definitions, then, serve to potentially fix these categories into a very limited rubric, whereby a lesbian becomes, for example:

> **Lesbian**—(adjective) Of or relating to females who experience a sexual attraction toward and responsiveness to other females; (noun) a homosexual female.[60]

But if one looks for the terms that are present and absent from an intersectional viewpoint, one can see the ways these categories take on different meanings in relationship to violence. For example, in the guidelines, while "Ethnicity/

National Bias" and "Racial Bias" are defined, the referents "race," "ethnicity," and "national origin" are omitted, thereby suggesting that they do not require further explanation. Left without definitions, these terms move to the arena of presumptive knowledge, suggesting that they are always-already known terms and concepts. This is notably different than categories of sexuality; the 1999 guidelines' definitions are focused primarily on outlining the various types of sexuality and what they might mean.

Throughout these definitions or lack thereof, each type of difference is afforded different levels of violability. Race seems to be understood as the quintessential category of hate crimes, and in many ways it is described as so integral to the experience of violable citizenship that it does not need to be defined. The lack of definition or elaboration on race works to negate systemic racism and its multitude forms of violence and provides an opportunity for the U.S. nation-state to subsume Indigeneity under race (literally). The refusal or inability to give an account of the meaning(s) of race stands in direct opposition to the ways in which sexual orientation and gender identity are seen as needing definition, or confinement, and questionably comprehensible as categories that should be included within legislation. To include sexual orientation or gender identity is to offer, as the argument goes, access to rights discourses that these categories do not deserve. And then there is the category of gender (apparently meaning "men" and "women"), which is possibly the most hotly contested category in some respects. According to anxious narratives, to include this category as a protected hate crime category is to potentially overwhelm the system and create chaos. Put differently, gender-based violence is so integral to citizenship that to include it as a protected category would destabilize American democracy as we know it.

It is critical to consider the various ways that the presumptive knowability of race functions within hate crime legislation. Consider, for example, that while "race" itself does not warrant a definition, there is a definition of "racial bias" that appears to describe and define elements that are marked as "racial." In other words, if race does not warrant a definition, but "racial bias" does, the juxtaposition of absence, presence, and referral works to solidify, fix, and naturalize "race" even further. The definition of racial bias is "A preformed negative opinion or attitude toward a group of persons who possess common physical characteristics, e.g., color of skin, eyes, and/or hair; facial features; etc., genetically transmitted by descent and heredity which distinguish them as a distinct division of humankind, e.g., Asians, blacks, whites."[61] There are numerous problematics at work here, but for the sake of brevity, I want to point to only two. First, this definition infers that raciality is *the* fundamental division of humanity, and, therefore, marks other identity categories as somehow less divisive and less integral to systemic classifications of difference. Second, this definition relies upon and reproduces the Western white supremacist epistemological and ontological understanding of race (i.e., a physically locatable, biological, and fundamental division of humankind), but here it is without a history and potentially without an end in sight.

Because race does not warrant more explanation, one needs to delve further, and the Hate Crime Incident Report Form, as produced by the FBI, offers more information as to what might be seen as included under the purview of "race." This is the form that the FBI provides to local and state police departments to report hate crimes. The form requires that the reporting officer designate the type of "bias crime." Notably, under the general category of "race" and racially biased crimes, a reporting officer will find the "Anti-American Indian or Alaska Native" and "Anti-Native Hawaiian or Other Pacific Islander" boxes alongside "Anti-White," "Anti-Black or African American," "Anti-Asian," and "Anti-Multiple Group."[62] While "American Indian or Alaska Native" are categories that have been subsumed under "Race" in hate crime forms for quite some time, "Native Hawaiian" is a "newer" category that was part of the changes made via the Office of Management and Budget (OMB) in 1997 when they decided to separate the categories of Asian from Pacific Islander, and Ethnicity from National Origin.[63] Importantly, in the process of situating Indigenous nations as merely subgroups of a "race," rather than placing Indigenous nations under a much more appropriate category such as "national origin," hate crime legislation participates in the settler colonial project of disappearing Native governance. But it gets worse. It is important to juxtapose this incorporation of Indigeneity under "race" alongside the guidelines' definition of "Racial Bias," as described earlier. If race is something akin to a group of people merely marked by similar physical features and genetics, then certainly there is no room for considering how kinship, political structures, and ties to land bind Native nations and Indigenous communities. The point here is that while "race" does not warrant definition or explanation, subsuming Indigenous nations under "race" speaks volumes.

A few more points on the lack of engagement with Indigeneity in hate crime legislation are in order. The bare and surface inclusion of Natives in hate crime data coheres to what Eve Tuck and K. Wayne Yang describe as a common social science technique, whereby Natives are marked as especially "at risk and asterisk peoples."[64] Within social science schemas, Natives are considered especially vulnerable ("at risk"), but they are also deemed to be too few for a sample size ("asterisk peoples") to actually be included within social science studies.

Throughout my research on federal hate crime legislation and social science literature on the topic, there was scant, if any, inclusion of Indigenous communities, despite the fact that police brutality and hate violence against Natives is quite clearly one of the most profound mechanisms for perpetuating settler colonialism and state surveillance of Native communities. Sociologist Barbara Perry's works stands out against this lacuna in hate crime literature, as she has dedicated a large body of work to hate crime and police violence against Native Americans. She argues that hate crimes against Natives is so endemic and regularized that the Native communities she interviewed barely registered their occurrence.[65] Any quick survey of news media offers a small glimpse into the regularity and consistency of violence perpetuated against Natives, especially in border towns. But Natives were rarely, if ever, mentioned in the debates, federal government reports, social science literature (Perry is the rare exception), and various testimonies before Congress. And even though the federal government consistently publishes statistics that attest to the vulnerability of Natives, this data somehow avoids using the language of hate crimes. Moreover, this data and the information around Indigenous peoples' vulnerability to violent crime quickly slip into very familiar victim-blaming rhetoric.

For example, in a ten-year review by the Bureau of Justice Statistics on "American Indians and Crime" from 1992–2002, the foreword offers the following synopsis:

> The findings reveal a disturbing picture of the victimization of American Indians and Alaska Natives. . . . American Indians are more likely than people of other races to experience violence at the hands of someone of a different race, and the criminal victimizer is more likely to have consumed alcohol preceding the offense. In three recent BJS-sponsored tribal level criminal victimization surveys, victims reported that alcohol use by the offender was a factor in more than 40% of the incidents of overall violence, and more specifically, domestic violence.[66]

The "disturbing picture," painted in broad strokes, creates a series of leaps: from Native vulnerability to victimizers who are "different races" to the overwhelming presence of alcohol. Despite sounding eerily similar to the conditions of hate crimes, as described in other federal reports, this ten-year review avoids and evades the obvious connection and does not mention hate crime even once. And since the leaps continue to make the most obvious stereotypical jump possible in relationship to Indigenous communities (i.e., alcoholism), it does not take long for a report that is supposedly dedicated to outlining the extreme vulnerabilities of Native populations to actually end up inferring the oft-used settler colonial lesson plan: if Natives want to avoid being victims, they should avoid alcohol altogether. And as one delves further into the document, passing the data on the various statistics on murder, rape, and aggravated assault, one will find a lengthy discussion on Natives as criminals. In fact, the majority of this report narrates, at length, the various statistics on Native criminal recidivism, capital punishment, and how Native and Indigenous criminal punishment systems function alongside the U.S. federal system.[67] The point here is that while Natives might be included within the categories of hate crime legislation, their extreme vulnerability, violability, and colonized status is renewed through the combined processes of submerging Indigeneity under the sign of "race," the refusal to use the rhetoric of hate crime, and, lastly, the persistent narratives of abject Native criminalities and alcoholism.

The centrality of race as well as its underdevelopment, alongside the settler incorporation and indifference to Indigeneity, becomes all the more interesting when juxtaposed against the detailed definitions of, and outright obsession with, sexuality. Returning to the 1999 "Hate Crime Data Collection Guidelines," among the fifteen definitions of identity terms, more than half are dedicated to sexuality. Needing to define terms such as "gay," "lesbian," "homosexual," "heterosexual," and "bisexual" suggests that sexuality remains in the realm of the unknown, unmarked, and needing further explanation. In the process of juxtaposing the treatment of sexuality and race within the definitions, then, we can also see the ways in which race becomes presumed normative knowledge, always-already understood by all, in and against the potential unknowability of sexuality.

In my first round of analysis of hate crime legislation (2005–2007), I was struck by a reoccurring thematic: that lawmakers, scholars, and activists were quick to argue that we needed to have firm definitions around the terms of sexuality, but would not make this same request for the other categories such as race or ethnicity. This need to define the sexual appeared almost fetishistic, in that these definitions needed to do much more than merely specify or explain sexuality; rather, they were being asked to soothe a frightened public as to what was seen as the dangerous flexibility of sexuality. It is this same fear of contagion that has been, as argued in Chapter Two, increasingly abated by the same-sex marriage movement.

The story of the inclusion of sexual orientation as a category to be "counted" within the 1990 Hate Crime Statistics Act is a very telling example of this anxiety around sexuality.[68] At the time, liberals were arguing that sexual orientation should be included as a category within hate crime statistics, merely as a means to investigate whether people were victimized on account of "sexual orientation." But the Christian Right quickly responded that this inclusion was part of the "radical gay agenda," which might start with something so seemingly innocuous as "counting" hate crimes against gay and lesbian folks but would clearly just be the beginning of more and more protections for gays and lesbians. As Senator Helms explained to his colleagues:

> Mr. President, the Hate Crime Statistics Act admittedly has a catchy name, as is so often the case around this place. Catchy and deceptive names hide dangerous legislation to preclude many Senators from reading the fine print. . . . In this case let the Senate understand that this bill is the flagship of the homosexual, lesbian legislative agenda. They have said that over and over again.[69]

Senators Jesse Helms and Orrin Hatch both proposed amendments to the bill that would provide for the proper containment for sexual orientation due to its supposedly inherently different status. Senator Helms's amendment included disclaimers such as, "The homosexual movement threatens the strength and the survival of the American family as the basic unit of society" and, "the federal government should not provide discrimination protections on the basis of 'sexual orientation.'"[70] Senator Hatch proposed a much more direct series of statements, which Congress actually approved. Importantly, these gay caveats are particularly redundant when the Act itself already states the stipulation that the law should not be seen as "including an action based on discrimination due to sexual orientation."[71] The need to clarify ad nauseam stages the sheer anxiety over sexual identities. In the end, the Hate Crime Statistics Act contained the following heterosexual manifesto:

> Sec. 2 (a) Congress finds that—
> The American family life is the foundation of American society;
> Federal policy should encourage the well-being, financial security and health of the American family;
> Schools should not de-emphasize the critical value of American family life.
> Nothing in this Act shall be construed, nor shall any funds appropriated to carry out the purpose of the Act be used, to promote or encourage homosexuality.[72]

Interestingly, observers rarely comment on the oddity of the manifesto within the statistics act. Clearly, acknowledging that hate crimes against gays and lesbians should *count* turns out to be extremely threatening, so threatening that folks needed to reestablish the heteronormativity of U.S. society.

By the time the Matthew Shepard and James Byrd Jr. Act went to Congress for the third and final time (2009), the need to define the sexual seemed to be at least somewhat contested. In his written testimony before the Senate Judiciary Committee, Senators Sessions and Hatch asked Attorney General Holder on

numerous occasions as to whether it was safe to leave the term "sexual orientation" undefined. Each time Holder responded that there was no need for a
definition because the term was defined elsewhere in law; Holder claimed that
"the terms used in the bill are not unclear" and, most notably, that "the Department believes that 'sexual orientation' is a commonly understood term."[73]

However, actions by the House Republicans called into question the need
to define the sexual and used the occasion to offer frightening tales of abject
sexual practices. According to Rep. Gohmert (TX):

> But when we discuss sexual orientation—we brought that up in committee, and
> we were told, Why wouldn't you define sexual orientation? You should. . . . Be-
> cause the Diagnostic and Statistical Manual IV tells us the names of different
> conditions. It talks about all the types of sexual orientation people have. There
> are all kinds of sexual orientations. Some are weird. Some are sick. Some will
> get you put in prison. But if you don't define it, they're included.[74]

In order to perform this point, Rep. Barrett (SC) read parts of the DSM Manual
on the House floor, starting with the alphabet, describing "asphyxophilia," "au-
togynephilia," "bisexuality," and so on.[75] All of these titillating performances
were used to drum up support for the various amendments that were offered
by Rep. King (IA) to define sexual orientation as akin to pedophilia or any other
"scary" sexual proclivity they could find in a psychology handbook. Definitions
were necessary because, according to King,

> This [law] is a bald-faced effort to enforce public affirmation for behaviors that
> have been considered to be historically aberrant behaviors by the American
> Psychological Association, Mr. Speaker. There is a long list of them. The list that
> I have is 547 of them long. As near as I can determine, they're all specially pro-
> tected activities or thought processes that are protected under this hate crimes
> legislation, Mr. Speaker.[76]

Hence, King proposed a number of amendments (six in all, none passed), which
offered to explicitly exclude "pedophilias" from being included under "sexual
orientation," to replace the term "gender" with "sex" throughout the bill, and
to replace the title of the bill with the clever "Thought Crimes Prevention Act."
So even if there was less angst around whether sexual identities needed to be
defined/confined in this later incarnation of hate crime legislation, clearly these
moments expose the reoccurring anxieties around the inclusion of sexuality as
proffering normative citizenship for nonheterosexuals.

Importantly, the inclusion of "gender identity" within the later editions of
the Shepard/Byrd Act did some of the work to displace the anxieties of this

potentially contagious abject sexuality onto transgender people. While Attorney General Holder might confidently report that "we all know" what we mean by "sexual orientation," he did not make this claim when it came to "gender identity." Rather, he merely recited the definition of "gender identity" that was explicitly offered in the law, as "actual or perceived gender-related characteristics." However, House Republicans characteristically used the occasion to make fun of their own confusion around gender, since somehow their confusion correlates with the notion that transgender people are undeserving of protection. Rep. King offered the following belittling analogy:

> Now, if I would define a fence post as "actual or perceived characteristics of a fence post," you get the idea what the definition of gender identity is when it is the actual or perceived gender-related characteristics. It is no definition at all.[77]

By repeatedly claiming that gender identity was incomprehensible, House Republicans as well as other conservatives worked to turn the violence against gender-nonconforming people into a shared joke. But it was a joke that they were called out on by Rep. Barney Frank (NY), who offered a biting analogy of his own:

> And the assertion that there is no basis for protecting transgender people against violence, that's Marxist in ideology. And I mean by that, of course, Chico Marx, who said at one notable point when Groucho caught him red-handed, 'Who are you going to believe—me or your own eyes?'[78]

These heated exchanges might explain why the 2012 revised hate crime data guidelines are so extensive in their liberal tutorials about gender nonconforming people and LGBT identities. Not only is there a section (Section V) dedicated toward explaining how to be a kinder, gentler, more respectful police officer to transgender and gender nonconforming people, there are also new extra notations splattered throughout the identity definitions. For example, after defining the following terms, the guidelines offer the following tips:

> Homosexual . . . Note: This is an outdated clinical term considered derogatory and offensive by many people; current journalistic standards restrict usage of the term; "lesbian" and/or "gay" accurately describes those who are attracted to people of the same sex.
>
> Sexual orientation . . . Note: Avoid the offensive terms "sexual preference" or "lifestyle."
>
> Transgender . . . Note: The person may also identify himself or herself as "transsexual." Additional information is provided in Section V ["Understanding How to Distinguish Sexual Orientation, Gender Identity, Anti-Transgender,

Anti-Gender Nonconforming Crimes"]. Note: A transgender person may outwardly express his or her gender identity all of the time, part of the time, or none of the time; a transgender person may decide to change his or her body to medically conform to his or her gender identity. Note: Avoid the following terms: "he-she," "she-male," "tranny," "it," "shim," "drag queen," "transvestite," and "cross-dresser."[79]

These 2012 guidelines are remarkably different than the earlier versions, not just because they offer many more terms, but because they go out of their way to offer lessons in liberal multicultural terminology. These language lessons become even more elaborate and extensive, depending on how difficult it might be to teach law enforcement officers how to be good liberals when faced with negotiating nonnormative genders.

But I do not want to suggest that the inclusion of gender identity did all the work of distracting public debate away from homophobic reactions to the inclusion of sexual orientation protections. Rather, as I argue in the next chapter on gay marriage, the changing levels of anxiety regarding sexuality are directly impacted by a movement for marriage rights that has served to move lesbian and gay identities away from the realm of the monstrous and has reworked them into what Jasbir Puar has called "homonationalist" categories of identity.[80] Within the anti-intersectional comparative framework of hate crime legislation, sexual orientation was marked as threatening, but far less so than "gender identity" and "gender."

Those that have attempted to maintain and promote feminist critiques within the late twentieth and early twenty-first centuries will not be surprised to learn that the category that served to be the most threatening to folks from across the political spectrum was the inclusion of "gender," here seeming to mean the violence against "women," and sometimes, "men." As mentioned earlier, the first federal legislation deploying the category "hate crime" was the Hate Crime Statistics Act (HCSA) of 1990. Similar to many bills, the path to the HCSA's final formulation was a convoluted one. The bill's origins have been linked to the Coalition on Hate Crimes Prevention, which represents the merger of numerous civil rights organizations. As Valerie Jenness and Kendal Broad note, the Coalition included sexual orientation as a viable category, but had a much more difficult time including gender. The Coalition determined, in the end, that gender should not be included because: (1) it would delay passage of the bill; (2) it would "open the door" for other groups and issues such as age and disability (again, deploying a false "scarcity of resources" discourse); (3) it would make the legislation "too cumbersome," if not impossible, since violent crimes against women are so pervasive; (4) and finally, violence against women did not fit the mold of hate crimes because they are often perpetrated by acquaintances rather than strangers.[81] Importantly, the "too muchness" of the violence against women repeats throughout hate crime legislation debates and continues to this day. Clearly, by suggesting that violence against women is too cumbersome, too pervasive, too intimate, and too common to fit within traditional notions of hate crimes highlights not only the acceptance of misogyny in U.S. culture, but even tells us a bit about the presumptions of other systems of subordination. An intersectional analysis reveals that violence via gender operates to produce anxieties about its pervasiveness, which inadvertently exposes the prevailing false logic that hate violence against other identity categories is rare. Thus, in the process of deeming gender "too much," hate crimes based on race, national origin, ethnicity, religion, disability, and even sexual orientation are crafted into infrequent, discrete, and containable events.

Although the Violence Against Women Act (VAWA) of 1994 explicitly argued women had a "right to be free from crimes of violence motivated by gender," gender was not included within federal hate crimes law until the Shepard/Byrd Act.[82] While there are certainly scholars that trace this progression from exclusion to inclusion for the category of "gender," what interests me here are the ways in which the fear and anxieties around the sheer frequency of gender violence are still very much part of hate crime debates.[83] For example, Brian Walsh, from the Heritage Foundation, offers the observation that "virtually every sexual assault resulting in bodily injury . . . is committed 'because of' the gender of the victim," which would, he implies, overload the system.[84]

Throughout the legislative debates on the Shepard/Byrd Act, as well as some of the scholarship on hate crime legislation, various people express the concern that if gender is included, all forms of sexual violence—especially rape—will count as hate crimes. This becomes the (particularly callous) "what about rape?" refrain that is littered throughout the debates, as various legislators anxiously ask whether all rapes would be included under the law. Gail Heriot, speaking as the Commissioner of the U.S. Commission on Civil Rights, argued that "rapists are seldom indifferent to the gender of their victims. They are virtually chosen because of their gender, among other things."[85] Quite frankly, it took me a while to realize that this was an argument *against* including gender as a category, until I saw the testimony of various left-leaning organizations who answered the anxious refrain "Does this include rape?" with an emphatic "Do not worry, rape is not included" refrain of their own. For example, in the written testimony offered by a coalition of over forty-five women's and gender rights groups (including NOW, YWCA, Feminist Majority, and GenderPac), almost two pages of testimony attempts to respond to the "floodgate" narrative, assuring legislators that the floodgates will remain closed. They argue that if the limited applications of gender hate crime laws at the state level are any indication, we can see that these laws are applied in only limited, "targeted" ways. Put differently, and more directly, the indifference as modeled by state-level governmental officials offers the evidence that federal-level inaction will follow suit. They also (correctly) point out that gender-based prosecutions can occur only when the case involves interstate or foreign commerce, something that rarely gets mentioned within all of the hyperbole of hate crime legislation.[86]

It is critical to ask, why is there all of this emotional and intellectual labor spent assuring people that gender will not be taken seriously as a category of hate crimes? What is at stake in the actual acknowledgment that "women" experience hate violence on a regular basis, most often manifested in the form of sexual violation? Why would it be a problem to prosecute these cases under the category of "hate crimes?" It is quite telling that the horrific violence of rape is used in such a way as to silence the discourse on violence against women. In this way, sexual violence becomes preserved as normatively benign.

Reading hate crime legislation and the debates around which categories of identity to include or not include exposes the anxieties about categories of difference and the elusiveness of equal citizenship. It reveals the ways in which the violence of citizenship is normatively understood as operating differently through racialized, colonial, gendered, and sexualized epistemologies. And it allows us to see the ways in which taxonomies of violence and bodily integrity undergird normative citizenship. Importantly, this framing is perpetuated through the deployment of history as well.

In a hearing on the Hate Crime Prevention Act of 1997 before the Committee on the Judiciary, civil rights activist and State Representative John Conyers Jr. (MI) (an ardent sponsor of the hate crime legislation) initiated the hearings with a description of how recent events had recalled the history of civil rights activism as well as the history of vigilante body politics of the racialized U.S. state:

> In effect, the genesis of this bill tracks back to the '40's when the NAACP and others were trying to pass a federal anti-lynch statute. And for years and years that legislation was introduced and did not go very far. The impetus for this measure that brings us here today is the terrible tragedy that occurred recently in Jasper, Texas, in which the Nation, Texans in particular, and Members of Congress in both Houses and both parties made public their outrage that a lynching can still go on. So it is my intention, if this measure succeeds, and I feel that it will, that this bill be also named in honor of the late James Byrd, who was brutally murdered and is the causative force behind this measure.[87]

Representative Conyers's choice of words is particularly telling; while the term "genesis" marks an origin, it simultaneously suggests a manifestation of events that have been evolving since the moment of origin. Conyers implies that the 1997 legislation would be, then, a follow-through on civil rights efforts to dismantle segregation. Simultaneously, Conyers connects the brutal murder of James Byrd to the practice of silently sanctioned white supremacist lynching. But as soon as Conyers summons the history of racialized violence, this history is actively averted. Conyers continues:

> The history of violence, racial violence in this country is *too well known* by all of us to have to, to need to review it here. But it is a critical element in moving this country forward. I see this as an all important measure, and I am pleased that we have such a distinguished group of witnesses.[88]

In these passages, Conyers works to link present-day hate crimes to a history of racialized violence that is "too well known" to need to publicize and occupy space within public discourse. The history of white supremacist violence is vanished into the space of common knowledge—too common to rehearse today. In this way, race becomes both marked as the quintessential category of violent citizenship as well as a category that does not deserve or need further elaboration.

Yet in hearings on the same law almost a decade later, Congresswoman Maxine Waters pointedly returns to Representative Conyers and the normative knowledge and experiences of racialized violence in citizenship. In her questioning of a conservative witness before the subcommittee, Waters struggles to have the witness explain the argument that there is no evidence that local police do not respond to hate crime complaints. But the witness (Timothy Lynch from the Cato Institute) refuses to agree that, even in the case of Emmett Till, the government failed to appropriately prosecute the case. In her frustration, Waters offers her own testimony:

> The findings may not be particularly identified as set forth in this legislation, but the Chairman of the Judiciary Committee [Rep. John Conyers], who just cited his tenure here in Congress, this African-American man, does not need to have anyone tell him that there are no findings that such things happen. He knows from experience.[89]

It is worth asking why Rep. Waters would turn to Conyers, or perhaps African American masculinity in general, in this moment in which she clearly is arguing that the U.S. government has failed to protect people of color. Perhaps she was trying to honor Conyers's commitment to hate crime legislation, or his strenuous civil rights activism. Or perhaps she was referencing the fact that African American men are particularly marked and victimized by the prison industrial complex. Regardless of her intent, her exasperation speaks volumes and is clearly her way of reaffirming the normative knowledge and experience of racialized citizenship as an experience of state-sanctioned violence within the United States. Her exasperation also reminds us of the need to elaborate on and find the language and space for serious discussions about the violability and vulnerability of African Americans.

Throughout the debates on hate crime legislation, history becomes a battleground that either exposes or denies the relevance of current-day hate crimes. While the uses of history as a source for basing a political claim is one of the central themes of this book, in the arena of hate crimes the discourses of history serve to showcase national anxieties about the violence of colonial, racialized, sexualized, and gendered citizenship. Here, the history of violence against people of color is known—perhaps "too well known"—in that it haunts the discourses and debates on hate crime legislation. It is a haunting, however, of a *particular extraordinary sort*; the history of racialized violence is circumscribed via representations of organized white supremacists in the U.S. South. The historical residue of this particular type of violence, then, works to suggest that hate crime against people of color functions in a limited way, one that is projected back into a particular historical moment in the U.S. past and one that functions through white supremacists against African Americans. The lack of articulation and further elaboration on the current practices of violence against people of color, and the presumptive knowledge around race and raciality, serve to sanction the discourse that racialized violence is, for the most part, historical.

Importantly, histories of gender, gender identity, and sexuality-based violence, as well as the historical violence against Native Americans, rarely surface in these debates. These histories do not haunt hate crimes and are not easily deployable, but, in fact, take work and efforts to execute. This suggests a particularly interesting aspect as to how history works within hate crime debates: while on the one hand it is not well known enough to provide the proof that gender-based and sexuality-based violence should be recognized, it can also be deemed as so well known as to negate active articulations as to how racial violence currently operates in the United States. In many ways, then, history works to negate the violence of citizenship at one level or another; because sexualized- and gendered-based violence are left without a remarkable history, they are more easily denied, but since we refuse to articulate the details or circumstances of hate crimes against people of color and Native Americans, racialized violence in the present moment is willfully ignored.

## COMPARATIVE ANTI-INTERSECTIONALITY

One of the most dominant rhetorical features of the hate crime debate is the purposeful deployment of comparative anti-intersectional analysis in order to deny the experience of hate violence. Comparative anti-intersectionality is a rhetorical maneuver by which a person selectively compares two or more (single-axis) categories of identity in order to argue, in this case, that one of the categories is more worthy of inclusion within hate crime legislation than another. Rhetorical gestures aimed at belittling political alliances and left political actions is not new, and comparative anti-intersectionality will sound eerily familiar to anyone attempting to organize or think long-term about what an intersectional left politics could and should look like. Comparative anti-intersectionality is the flip side of the coin to what I describe in the next chapter as the political analogies that are common throughout liberal politics (i.e., "gay marriage now is like interracial marriage back then"). And like the political analogies, history once again rears its head, mostly to offer superficial attention to race in order to completely negate the other categories. But comparative anti-intersectional arguments are also offered in facetious tones and even jokelike scenario formats. The agenda is simple: either this device is used in order to argue against including sexual orientation or gender identity as hate crime categories, or it is used to belittle all categories and mark hate crime legislation itself as silly and a form of "special rights."

In the case of comparative anti-intersectionality, history is deployed selectively and with a political purpose. Most commonly, anti-hate crime legislation political actors attempt to teach us the "real" lessons of the 1950s and 1960s civil rights movements. In 1997, Senator Sessions, for example, argues that the Civil Rights Acts were justified because back then "we had a real problem. I am not sure we have that same problem here. There are no water fountains prohibiting homosexuals from drinking from them. We don't require homosexuals to sit in the back of the bus or to stand on the metro."[90] A few months later, on the Senate floor, Sessions goes even farther to argue that the current hate crime legislation "cheapens the Civil Rights Movement"; as he insinuates, race discrimination "back then" was a legitimate problem, but women, sexual minorities, and transgender folks do not experience anything on par.[91]

Another form of the comparative anti-intersectional move does not rely on history, but deploys a similar incredulous tone. Within this rhetorical gesture, various anti-hate crime legislation actors produce comparative setups that border on the absurd. Senator Sessions, for example, asks Attorney General Holder, if it is true that "a grandma" who is mugged while using an ATM machine will have less protection than a man who is attacked after "walking out of a 'gay' bar?"[92] In another example, Representative Gohmert argues that this law "says to the world that in the priorities of the majority of the United States Congress, a transvestite [*sic*] with gender identity issues will now be more important to protect than a heterosexual, than college or school students, or even senior citizens and widows with no gender identity issues."[93] And last, Civil Rights Commissioner Gail Heriot offers the strange comparative logic "Why, for example, should Matthew Shepard's killers be treated differently from Jeffrey Dahmer or Ted Kaczynski?"[94]

The jokelike scenarios are more challenging to describe since they tend to be quite long-winded, and often confuse the person they are questioning at the time. Representative Michelle Bachmann argues, for example, that the Shepard/Byrd Act would deny "equal protection" by using the following scenario involving "a gay in the crosswalk":

> So if the person is gay, and that is the status that is being protected, and the person driving the car is straight, would it be a hate crime if the person driving the car who is straight hit the person who is gay in the crosswalk? So does it say, then, that that life that was hit in the crosswalk is more valuable because it was a gay life versus if the person who was in the car, who is gay, who hits the person in the crosswalk, who is straight, does that mean that the straight person in the crosswalk doesn't have a cause of action against the person who is gay who is driving that car?[95]

And lest the reader think that this is just a matter of Representative Michelle Bachman being Michelle Bachman, here is another example from an exchange between Senator Sessions and Gail Heriot, who are usually on the same page when it comes to hate crime legislation:

> SENATOR SESSIONS: Let me ask you, Ms. Heriot. An individual, perhaps, let's say hypothetically, is angry that the husband left his sister alone with a bunch of children and he takes up a homosexual lifestyle which he thinks is bad and he attacks this former brother-in-law. Would that—
>
> MS. HERIOT: I'm getting confused over the theory of relativity here.
>
> SENATOR SESSIONS: Well, the question would be, would that cover the circumstances?
>
> MS. HERIOT: You're going to have to run the facts by me again there.
>
> SENATOR SESSIONS: Okay. The facts would be that, let's say that a man left his wife and children.
>
> MS. HERIOT: Okay.
>
> SENATOR SESSIONS: And the brother of the wife, former wife, doesn't like this and attacks the man and states that he didn't like his lifestyle when he attacked him. Would that meet the basic standards of this case?

**MS. HERIOT:** That's actually a good, good hypothetical. I like that hypothetical. The answer is, I think probably a Federal prosecutor could look at that case and say, yes, it's covered.

**SENATOR SESSIONS:** Now, if the man ran off with another woman and he had the same anger in his system and he has a confrontation and attacks him, would that cover it?

**MS. HERIOT:** Run it by me again.[96]

There are a few critical points to be made about this practice of comparative anti-intersectionality. First, these are just a few of the many possible examples in which rhetoric demonstrates that categories of identity are always understood in and against each other. Identities do not exist as lone categories, but are always produced, understood, and reinforced intersectionally. While comparative anti-intersectionality tends to be more explicit about this practice, the previous section on the taxonomies of bodily integrity and violability also showcase how anti-intersectionality is always functioning throughout these debates. In this way, anti-intersectionality is not something we can merely ignore. Instead, we must vigilantly attend to the ways in which it serves as an effective mechanism for devaluing, negation, belittling, and denial. Second, as much as we might debate whether nonnormative identities are being enshrined in law as always-already injured (or never to be normative), these reflections on hate crime legislation debates demonstrate the danger of the ways in which anti-intersectionality is being cemented into law. And last, these reflections demonstrate the ways in which categories of identity and their relationships to the violence of citizenship are not at all analogous. Rather, the violent practices of citizenship are colonial, racialized, gendered, and sexualized in ways that rely upon both anti-intersectionality as well as our continuous deployments of history to call up and deny this violence over and over again.

## The Specters of Citizenship

One of the most important ways in which the violence of citizenship is acknowledged is through the rare moments in which people describe hate crime legislation as a means to keep the potential retaliation of the oppressed at bay. Sociologists are particularly helpful in this regard. Kelina Craig, for example, in her article "Retaliation, Fear, or Rage: An Investigation of African American and White Reactions to Racist Hate Crimes," argues that, "At least part of the rationale for sentencing in hate crime cases is based on the legislative intuition about the likelihood that members of hate crime victims' groups *will want and seek revenge.*"[97] But, as a careful reading of this scholar's work demonstrates, the potential for revenge is attached directly to African American bodies. As Craig passively notes, "Among African Americans (who some contend are the most frequent victims of racist hate crimes), retaliation may appear to be an especially practical option."[98] Basia Spalek in *Communities, Identities and Crime* argues that hate crimes might serve to "reawaken dormant identities;" that is, according to Spalek's logic, the experience might engage a part of a person's identity that they were not previously relating to, or they might even adopt a more politicized stance through a process of "radicalization of identity," which "may have positive or negative outcomes."[99] One of these (supposedly) negative outcomes includes, according to Spalek, joining an extremist group or an organization involved in defending the community from hate crime. In fact, Spalek seems to consider retaliation as a process that can be "re-awakened" such as when the author offers the not-so-subtle U.S. orientalist narrative whereby "Muslims" are "re-awakened" in response to antiterror legislation.[100] This telling example points to an awareness that governmental actions such as legislation for the "war on terror" are forms of hate crimes. But it also points toward the ways in which hate crime legislation is used to control an expected retaliatory response to this violence.

Hate crime legislation coincides with white, settler, heterosexual, middle-class anxieties that the disenfranchised will rise up in anger and retaliate for their subordination.[101] This anxiety surfaces over and over throughout appeals for hate crime legislation, whereby proponents remind the audience they need not worry because normatively privileged subject positions are protected too. For example, in one of the most impassioned (and polemic) arguments on behalf of hate crime legislation, Jack Levin and Jack McDevitt remind their readers that hate crime legislation benefits everyone, "Thus Christians who are attacked are as likely as Jews and Muslims to be protected by law. Whites are as likely to be protected as Blacks, Asians, and Latinos. Straights are as likely as gays and lesbians. Of all the racially motivated incidents reported to the FBI in a year, some 20 percent involve White victims targeted by members of another racial group."[102] In this way, hate crime legislation coheres to the logics of colorblindness, gender-blindness, sexual-blindness, and settler colonial–blindness in order to assuage anxieties and neutralize the danger that hate crime legislation admits to the existence of privilege and subordination via categories of identity.

This "don't worry" refrain is used in service of maintaining rhetorics of blindness and privilege as well as attempting to assuage these publics' anxiety, assuring them that if the oppressed do retaliate, certainly hate crime legislation will work to protect the normatively privileged as well. Note, for example, when Senator Sessions asked Attorney General Holder to speak to the potential "hate crime" incident when a Proposition 8 (the 2008 statewide proposition and constitutional amendment to ban same-sex marriage in California) supporter was "bruised and bloodied by an opponent of Proposition 8" for distributing yard signs.[103] Importantly, Senator Sessions merges this incident with a Bash Back! protest in Lansing, Michigan, against Mount Hope Church, in order to ask, "If we assume the first attack resulted from direct opposition to a gender identity or sexual orientation issue and the second resulted from hating the specific beliefs of the church, can you explain in detail why or why not these crimes would qualify under S. 909 [the Shepard/Byrd Act]?"[104] By combining these two "incidents," Sessions's question exposes the anxiety that repressed folks such as LGBT peoples might, in fact, "bash back" as promised. Holder responds by pointing out that the Bash Back! demonstration was not violent and therefore would not qualify for hate crime, but quickly returns to the "don't worry" refrain when he states, "if evidence were developed that a gay, lesbian, or transgendered individual committed a violent act against a heterosexual because the assailant had a bias against heterosexuals, that assault could indeed be prosecuted under this statute. In other words, the bill would protect heterosexuals as well as LGBT community members, just as the bill would protect people of all races, not merely groups traditionally viewed as minorities."[105] While it is disturbing to note the ways in which the privileges of normativity are consistently obscured throughout hate crime debates, and that citizenship is always-already a protective mechanism for normative bodies, I think it is worth considering the possibilities of taking advantage of the fears and anxieties of the specters of violent citizenship that are consistently exposed throughout these debates.

AnnJanette Rosga argues that hate crime legislation works "in the service of a historically-cleansed United States, an imagined nation-state of benevolent tolerance."[106] But I would argue that as the anxieties throughout hate crime debates demonstrate, the cleansing is *never fully complete*; the stains of discriminatory violence and the violent operations integral to U.S. citizenship are never completely washed away. The mark of racialized and settler colonial violence is too well known to ever fully disappear and the practices of gendered and sexualized violence are too unpredictable and far-reaching to contain. If hate crime legislation debates offer a staging for the (albeit slight) recognition of this violence, I would suggest disenfranchised peoples might be better served to capitalize on the anxieties that circulate underneath this recognition—that the oppressed can and will retaliate.

An intersectional analysis of hate crime legislation reveals the various levels of anxiety about the recognition of violence and citizenship: anxieties that the historical residues of hate crimes against people of color are a part of the citizenship apparatus; anxieties that settler colonial violence against Natives in the present recognizes the endurance of Native sovereignty; anxieties that gender violence is too prevalent and that recognizing it would, therefore, tear apart the American polity; and anxieties that sexual and gender identities are unrecognizable and that, perhaps, the homosociality of citizenship might easily slip into homosexuality without careful and deliberate circumscription of queerness and gender nonconformity. Read collectively and against each other, these anxieties reveal the ways in which hate crime legislation exhumes the specters of citizenship, that is, the embodiments of difference that contest the narrative of universal settler citizenship and the role of the state in safeguarding the bodily integrity of "citizens." Hate crime legislation is used as a mechanism to control the anxiety that these specters of citizenship will seek revenge for their experiences of racialized, colonial, gendered, sexualized citizenship.

Moreover, hate crime legislation reveals how these specters operate. Here, racialized subjects are marked as inherently, comprehensibly, victims to violence. Yet, while racialized citizenship does not include the right to bodily integrity, racialized violence looms over the American landscape as a historical remnant that might be avenged in the present. Hate crime legislation attempts to hold back the tide of revenge against whitenormative citizenship by attempting to name and circumscribe racialized violence as extreme, random, and, for the most part, historical. Hate crime legislation coheres to the logic of settler colonial elimination of Natives, here by continuing the project of racializing Indigeneity in order to dismantle sovereignty. Moreover, within hate crime legislation, settler colonial violence is naturalized as a product of Native criminality and substance use. Female-gendered subjects are also inherently victimized, but only within (supposedly) domestic and sexual relations. The recognition, then, of the public face of the privatized experiences of female citizenship would work to unravel the heteronormative, patriarchal systems of relations integral to citizenship. And the queer subject also works to threaten to undermine heteronormative citizenship, but only so much as it eludes capture and remains unnamed and outside the realm of comprehensibility. By working to drag it into recognition, hate crime legislation reveals the compulsive need to name, locate, and circumscribe queerness as a means to safeguard heterosexuality and the homosociality of citizenship.

Through this analysis, perhaps we can begin to see the ways in which strategies such as comparative anti-intersectionality are used as mechanisms to "divide and conquer," thereby keeping the diverse array of specters from forming coalitional strategies of resistance. Anti-intersectional strategies perpetuate inaccurate notions that justice is a scarce resource, and promote competition for recognition that seeks small-sighted gains rather than radical transformation. Anti-intersectional strategies also further the violability of the specters of citizenship. But if we move differently, against the grain of comparative anti-intersectionality and toward a coalition of resistance among the specters of citizenship, then we might be able to strike genuine fear and create actual disruption of the U.S. social order.

# CHAPTER 2

# Intersectionalities Lost and Found

## Same-Sex Marriage Law and the Monstrosities of Alliance

What if we said that no one, not a single one of us, would get traded for socioeconomic access or the achievement of short-term legal goals? What if we began to really talk *queer*—beyond identity categories? What if we decided to build and lead a movement to transform this nation—a movement to make this country a global partner instead of a bully? What if we began to help build hope? What if we said to everyone: here is what *this* queer movement is doing next: We are queering Living Wages and Affordable Healthcare and Transgender Justice and Getting Old Queerly and Total Immigration Access and HIV Activism and Ending Incarceration and the Possibility of Dangerous Sexual Desires. We need to create a movement that says: *Join us. Dream with us. Dare with us. Go for broke. Change the world.* What if that was our queer vision, for what we do next?

—Amber Hollibaugh (2013)

How do you explain to your friends, family, loved ones, and allies that when they advocate on behalf of same-sex marriage rights, they are advocating for violence against others? How do you articulate and explain that what might feel like a victory for some gay and lesbian couples coincides with the deepening of the discrimination against many others? In the days after the U.S. Supreme Court offered their decisions on same-sex marriage in late June of 2013 (in *United States v. Windsor* and *Hollingsworth v. Perry*), the majority of my friends and family were absolutely gleeful.[1] Gay and lesbian couples and their straight allies celebrated in the streets, and countless numbers fell to one knee in order to "pop the question" to their romantic partners. On Facebook and other social media, folks like myself—folks invested in queer, feminist, anticolonial, and critical race critiques of marriage—tried desperately to find ways to articulate our arguments against marriage. But as I struggled to configure a way to formulate my critique, I realized how very difficult it would be to rain on their parade, so to speak. It is one thing to declare that I, personally, do not want to be married, or that I find marriage to be a conservative "family value," or that the fight for so-called "marriage equality" is a waste of resources from other, more distributable political efforts. But my argument is somewhat different, and much more painful to admit: the fight for same-sex marriage has caused extreme harm to already vulnerable populations and is a violent enforcement of colonialnormative and whitenormative citizenship.

But how could I tell folks that I love and admire that their recognition comes at the cost of causing violence against others? I was hungry for examples, scanning social, print, and online media to see if anyone who shares my point of view could find a way to articulate this painful conclusion. But what I noticed is that there was limited-to-negligible space in which people could articulate any left-leaning critiques of marriage without also simultaneously offering a series of concessions. Most left critics of marriage offered what seemed like the requisite caveat: the Supreme Court decisions marked a move toward equality and away from gay, lesbian, and bisexual persecution, and that was worth celebrating. Many offered the suggestion that this was a matter of individual choice, and while they were not interested in marriage, others were welcome to the practice. Some paid homage to the celebrations, but quickly followed up with a series of arguments against same-sex marriage, such as: that it is a conservative goal, that not everyone is included within its purview, that perpetuating the transference of resources like health care through romantic dyads is a far cry from distributive justice, and that queer and feminist critiques of marriage have been increasingly silenced through same-sex marriage advocacy.[2]

Some pundits drew readers' attention to the other U.S. Supreme Court decisions of late June 2013 to point out that the Court's support for some same-sex couples stood in stark contrast to its gutting of the Voting Rights Act (*Shelby County v. Holder*), its continued dismantling of Native American sovereignty and kinship (*Adoptive Couple v. Baby Girl*), and the increasing decimation of affirmative action policies (*Fisher v. University of Texas*).[3] Intersectional analyses are hard work, but become much more palatable if one can use disparate case studies to make one's point. By contrasting the Supreme Court cases of June 2013, these authors were able to call our attention to the ways in which the gates of normative citizenship might be opening up for certain types of gay and lesbian subjects, but those same gates continue to foreclose the opportunities for other types of (racialized and Indigenous) bodies. For example, as Kai Green and Treva Ellison eloquently propose, "We need to ask, what does the expansion of sexual citizenship, embodied in the DOMA/Prop 8 rulings, mean in the context of the attacks on and planned abandonment of programs and policies, like universal suffrage and public education, that were fought for and won by Black social movements alongside the expansion of death-dealing institutions and relations like debt, imprisonment, and homelessness."[4]

While I use these other Supreme Court decisions in the final chapter to explore how certain bodies, identities, and performances are given more legitimacy, rights, and access to bodily integrity and livability compared to others, I would also argue that one can focus exclusively on the governmentality of marriage itself as a means to showcase these disparities. Put differently, we do not need to look outside of the Supreme Court's decisions on same-sex marriage to see the ways in which the anti-intersectionalities of marriage law creates, perpetuates, and exacerbates violence against the vulnerable. This chapter offers to explain this story, especially through contextualizing the advocacy for same-sex marriage within the trajectories of the U.S. nation-state's legal and cultural regulations of marriage, intimacy, civility, and kinship practices.

As of 2015, same-sex marriage law continues to be a moving target. I have little doubt that, just as the normative discourse of liberal citizenship attests, same-sex marriages will soon be widely legalized and included within normative citizenship.[5] But this inclusion marks an opportunity to see the ways in which same-sex marriage advocacy brought to light some intersectionalities, while disappearing others. As I demonstrate in this chapter, early incarnations of same-sex marriage advocacy exposed the intersectionalities of sex, gender, and sexuality, and this exposure facilitated a series of anxieties about the dangers posed by the constructedness of sex, gender, and sexuality. But, unfortunately, this moment was fleeting, as the anti-intersectional politics of marriage advocacy, particularly the anti-intersectionalities of race, sexuality, settler colonialism, and imperialism, took sway and assisted in the eventual legalization of same-sex marriage.

Therefore, the 2013 Supreme Court decisions *United States v. Windsor* and *Hollingsworth v. Perry* provide a perfect venue for reflection on what has been lost and gained through the inevitable "success" of same-sex marriage advocacy. The "marriage fever" that has swept across the United States after the Supreme Court "victories" for same-sex marriage offers a critical opportunity to see the shrinking space for radical queer politics. As I argue in the second half of this chapter, same-sex marriage advocacy has worked to undermine the monstrous difference that has been central to queer activism and radical intersectional political visions. Queer activists have been able to offer important critiques of normativities, including normative citizenship, by embracing and capitalizing on the fears and anxieties of perverse sexualities; that is, they have been able to use queer monstrosity as a productive, performative modality for political activism. But the embrace of sameness, normativity, and assimilation of same-sex marriage has worked to move queerness away from monstrosity, in dangerous and unsettling ways. As noted here, if queer monstrosity is one of the central mechanisms for exposing and critiquing the violence of normative citizenship, then we must find ways to reanimate the monstrosities of queerness to forge an alliance with the monsters of U.S. settler colonialism and U.S. empire.

## Marriage, Civilization, and Their Discontents

When President George W. Bush finally came out in favor of a Federal Marriage Amendment "protecting marriage" in a press conference on February 24, 2004, he claimed, "After more than two centuries of American jurisprudence and millennia of human experience, a few judges and local authorities are presuming to change the most fundamental institution of civilization. Their actions have created confusion on an issue that requires clarity."[6] Interestingly, when the Federal Marriage Amendment was first proposed in 2001, only the most conservative, fundamentalist politicians would touch it. The Federal Marriage Amendment was originally designed by the *supposedly* intersectional, self-identified "multicultural" Alliance for Marriage, an organization that excels at the practice of claiming multiracial politics in the service of heterosexism.[7] The Federal Marriage Amendment's warm reception and President George W. Bush's endorsement in 2004 suggests that something dramatic happened in the homophobic landscape during those intervening years.

Conservatives blamed gay and lesbian rights activists, and claimed that these activists forced the issue with the assistance of "activist judges" who had the audacity to suggest that basing marriage rights on the participants' gender was discrimination. Liberals argued that conservative and right-wing political organizations made marriage a wedge issue for over a decade, particularly with their emphasis on "family values," welfare reform, and tax benefits. While it is certainly true that same-sex marriage started gaining traction in state courts (as described later in this chapter), perhaps it is more useful to consider same-sex marriage in light of the increasing struggles over racialized citizenship in the United States after September 11, 2001. At a time when terrorism loomed within and beyond the U.S. nation-state's borders, the maintenance, surveillance, and recalibration of the racial, gender, colonial, and sexual configuration of the U.S. citizenry became central, and marriage is one of the primary mechanisms to do this work. As a site of citizenship production and a particularly successful form of governmentality, marriage is critical to the formation and tracking of a properly gendered, properly racialized, properly normative settler citizen.

The historiography on marriage law in the United States gives us plenty of evidence. In my earlier work on same-sex marriage I offered a thorough history of marriage law, but for my purposes here, a broad overview will suffice.[8] Historian Nancy Cott's brilliant work on the history of marriage in the United States reveals that although marriage has been commonly thought of as a "private" affair, it is very much a public institution and "a configuration of state power." Giving a historical edge to a long-standing feminist argument, Cott asserts that marriage has been a tool of "cultural regulation" and is not only a "vehicle for public policy" but *the* vehicle by which the state shapes the public order into a "gendered order."[9] An intersectional history of marriage law in the United States demonstrates that this order is not just gendered, but racialized, sexualized, and imbricated in settler colonialism as well.

While marriage was primarily informal in the colonial era, states began to assume authority over it by instituting laws outlining whom one could marry, which marriages were invalid, how to dissolve marriages, and the financial repercussions of these actions. Importantly, the state became immersed in these supposedly private marriage matters as a means to control and direct wealth; marriage was used as a means to track capital accumulation, control the acquisition and distribution of private property, and position patriarchs as responsible for their dependents so the state was not financially liable. After the Civil War, the federal government was increasingly involved in marriage law, which had generally been considered the states' domain; eventually the federal government used marriage law to assert national unity and national identity, particularly after the crisis in whitenormative nationhood after the Civil War. Through marriage law, the federal government persecuted Mormons, policed and enforced proper marriage of emancipated slaves, and denied women's rights (such as the vote), the free exercise of which, it was argued, would cause conflict in the home. Throughout these operations, the government instituted a uniform standard of marriage in order to create the "American family" as heterosexual, monogamous, patriarchal, private-propertied, settler, and intraracial.

Nineteenth century court decisions were especially helpful for showcasing how marriage law is a state apparatus to cultivate an enlightened—as in civilized—citizenry. In *Adams v. Palmer* (1863), the court declared that marriage was "the first step from barbarism to incipient civilization, the purest tie of social life, and the true basis of human progress."[10] And in *Maynard v. Hill* (1888), the Supreme Court claimed that marriage was "the most important relation in life, as having more to do with the morals and civilization of a people than any other institution."[11] These discourses of morality, civility, and teleological progress are the coded discourses of white supremacist colonialism.

In the early moments of nation building in the United States, heteromonogamous conjugality became a key technology of settler colonialism. Indigenous studies scholars have shown how the forceful assimilation into heteropatriarchal marriage norms was one of the most successful mechanisms for chipping away at Native sovereignty, governance, and kinship structures.[12] Settler norms of heteropatriarchal marriage were central elements in the Dawes Act of 1887. As described in the Introduction, the Dawes Act not only severed collective ownership of land via the promotion of private ownership, but this privatization focused on authorizing male power as heads of monogamous households. The Dawes Act was explicitly aimed at cultivating and "civilizing" Natives into proper U.S. citizens by dissolving Native women's authority, rooting out polygamous relationships among Indigenous peoples, and foreclosing collective Native ownership of land, all in one package. And just to make the assault on Native women more complete, the federal government passed a law in 1888 that ensured Native women who married U.S. citizens would lose their tribal citizenship while being granted the "gift" of U.S. citizenship.[13] This law continued the settler colonial project of shrinking Native membership, and, therefore, Native sovereignty and land rights.

While heteromasculine marriage was a useful tool to usher in profound land dispossession, violent dislocations, and the targeted denial of tribal membership to Native women, it was also essential to the project of privatizing the dependency of (mostly white) middle- and upper-class women. Carole Pateman points out that white men's citizenship and participation in the public sphere depended on the assumption that a man would have a wife and children enjoying their nominal citizenship in the private sphere. This is why Pateman argues that the social contract was founded on "the sexual contract."[14] The practice of coverture, which transferred a woman's property to her husband at the time of marriage, also had the effect of transferring a woman's own self and personhood to her husband. Since eighteenth- and nineteenth-century perceptions of citizenship relied on notions of independence (perceived as ownership in oneself and one's labor power), a white woman's dependency positioned her as a noncitizen.[15] In fact, throughout the nineteenth and twentieth centuries, U.S. courts were unsure as to whether (white) women should be considered citizens, especially since they were so often held accountable to the burdens of the status without the benefits.[16]

Historically, many women's ability to immigrate, emigrate, and naturalize was linked to their marital status and, importantly, to their partners' racial identity. Whether a woman automatically held the citizenship status of her husband was ambiguous before the mid–nineteenth century, but in the Citizenship Act of 1855 Congress passed legislation declaring that only male citizens could bestow U.S. citizenship on their white wives.[17] This male citizen privilege was extended in the 1888 law described above, whereby (mostly white) men extended their U.S. citizenship onto their Native wives. At the turn of the twentieth century, Congress declared that American women who married foreigners would take the nationality of their husbands. This law, the Expatriation Act of 1907, de-naturalized thousands of American women who had married noncitizens.[18] According to this logic, women were so dependent on their husbands that their loyalty to nation-states must follow the men. As Candice Lewis Bredbenner demonstrates, the 1907 statute sparked a women's rights campaign directed toward abolishing women's derivative citizenship. This movement achieved some success with the passage of the 1922 Cable Act, but it was not until the 1934 Equal Nationality Bill that women's legal citizenship was finally dislodged from their marital status.[19]

Given that marriage law has been a vehicle by which the state has engaged in the racialized gendering of the American polity, it is critical to examine how this racialized gendering was motivated by a desire to ensure a properly *intraracial* settler society. So-called "antimiscegenation" laws worked to (re)produce and solidify discourses of white settler purity by outlawing marriage across various color lines. While many states had interracial marriage bans before the Civil War, these laws became increasingly critical mechanisms for marking and pro-ducing white superiority and nationhood after emancipation as the conflation of blackness and servitude started to be undone. And even though a majority of interracial marriage bans fixated on the potential for "miscegenation" between African Americans and whites, other states were also anxious about whites intermarrying with Asians, Latinos, Native Americans, and Pacific Islanders.[20]

As feminist historians have pointed out, white women's sexual intima-cies were far more policed than that of white men. Antimiscegenation laws, like the Expatriation Act discussed earlier, made clear that white women who "introduced foreign elements into the body politic" would be punished.[21] And while the history of antimiscegenation laws that focused on white and Native American marriages is far more complex, national policy makers selectively promoted marriage between white men and Native women as another means for assimilating and eradicating Native existence. Throughout various periods in U.S. history, settler rhetoric encouraged the "intermarriage" of white men and Native women in the hope that Indigeneity would be absorbed into the great white race. As Thomas Jefferson offered (as in threatened) "mix with us by marriage, your blood will run in our veins, and will spread over this great island."[22] This spread of "intermarried" blood, of course, was another means for white settlers to claim Native land and Indigeneity as their own.

Marriage law has also been a very pliable and useful instrument to police racialized subjects. For example, in her study of the Freedmen's Bureau's promotion of marriage for newly emancipated slaves, Katherine Franke argues that African Americans' familial and intimacy practices were heavily policed by the federal government. Prior to emancipation, familial and intimacy practices among enslaved peoples had taken various forms, such as unofficial marriages, polygamy, and other "illicit" sexual behaviors. The Freedmen's Bureau often forced marriage on African Americans and prosecuted African American men for not complying with proper marriage laws.[23] While marriage rights offered an opportunity for African Americans to claim humanity and some sense of belonging and respect within U.S. structures, immersion into heterosexual marriage norms of citizenship allowed for another avenue through which white supremacy could police African American behaviors.

More recently, marriage has been one of the primary mechanisms for demanding and cultivating proper citizenships for impoverished people of color. The 1996 Personal Responsibility and Work Opportunity Reconciliation Act describes marriage as the "foundation of a successful society" and figured it as the way to police and control single mothers in particular (who often are rhetorically and visually represented as African American women).[24] Since that time, the U.S. federal government has poured millions of dollars into "experimental marriage and fatherhood programs" aimed at producing proper monogamous heteronormative households. Rather than economic redistribution, the answer to America's poverty is located in proper intimacy and familial practices. As Jacqui Alexander points out, the state's demarcation of good citizen bodies (those that are married, heterosexual, reproductive, and white) is drawn in direct opposition to noncitizen bodies (nonheterosexual, nonreproductive, engaging in sex for pleasure, and nonwhite).[25]

By promoting and naturalizing heterosexual marriage as the primary institution of American domestic life, the state not only produces heterosexuality as the norm but also inextricably links heteronormativity to a properly gendered, settled, racialized, and sexualized citizenry. The same-sex marriage debate within the United States has consistently called up this gendered, racialized, and colonial past and present, particularly through the reoccurring appeal to "civilization."[26] The "clarity" that George W. Bush offered not only promoted and supported the Federal Marriage Amendment but also marked heterosexual coupledom and marriage as critical elements that would keep the nation from plunging into the abyss of barbarity.[27] This is not just a conservative impulse, as same-sex marriage proponents have also deployed the discourse of civility in marriage. For proponents and opponents of same-sex marriage rights, marriage is fundamental to modernity, progress, and civilization, and the rights of same-sex marriage will either keep the nation from or immerse it into savagery, barbarity, and degeneration. As Mark Rifkin observes, "The invocation of 'civilization' appears less as a residue of an outmoded nineteenth-century language of Euro-conquest than a trace of the ongoing enmeshment of discourses of sexuality in the project of fortifying the United States against the incursions by uncivilized formations that jeopardize the 'common sense' of national life."[28]

This brief history lesson demonstrates that marriage laws have been a highly productive form of biopolitical governmentality. It also demonstrates the baggage that comes with claims for same-sex marriage rights. Looking at this history, what on first glance might appear to be a private matter, quickly becomes, in practice, a key method of settler colonialism, white supremacy, and heteromasculine sex/gender ordering. The question, of course, is whether same-sex marriage can unsettle any of these operations, or if its success has actually reinforced them. And in a post–September 11, 2001 milieu, it gets even more complicated. The "war on terror" has relied upon discourses of barbarity, civility, and Western enlightenment, whereby a benevolent empire offers to spread American ways of life (such as "citizenship" and "democracy"). These are, as Indigenous studies scholars point out, eerily similar to what the U.S. settler government has continued to "offer" Native nations. This brief history, then, forces us to consider the operations whereby the terrorist, Indigenous, and gay subjects are inextricably locked within the enmeshment of perversity, settler colonialism, the war on terror, and the civilizing functions of marriage.

## Intersectionalities Found

While the marriage movements that have dominated the early twenty-first century U.S. political sphere are what most people think of in terms of political organizing around same-sex marriage, there was an earlier and more radically progressive round of same-sex marriage advocacy in the 1970s. The radical potential of this same-sex marriage advocacy hinged on the ability to expose, at least momentarily, the constructedness of sex, gender, and sexuality, as well as the "gender trouble" that these exposures offered. By "gender trouble" I am referring to Judith Butler's critical understanding of the ways in which sex, gender, and heterosexuality function. For example, Butler's book *Gender Trouble* argues that gender is an obligatory performance that must be repeated over and over in order to maintain the effect of the "naturalness" of sex, gender, and heterosexuality. While not named as such, Butler considers sex, gender, and sexuality intersectional categories; that is, they are a causal sequence, whereby the naturalness, coherence, and normativity of each category relies upon and reproduces the others. For Butler, the "trouble" comes when that causal sequence is paused, exposed, or delinked—even if only momentarily, such as in the case of drag performances. The 1970s marriage rights advocacy actually caused a bit of "gender trouble," even though this trouble was quickly quashed via the (re)deployment of marriage-as-civilizing discourses within the early twenty-first century.

In the early 1970s, feminists successfully implemented many state versions of the Equal Rights Amendment and "sex" was included in equal protection laws throughout the states.[29] This allowed for an opening and an opportunity, whereby same-sex couples came forward to challenge the sex bias of marriage law. For example, in the 1971 Minnesota case *Baker v. Nelson*, two men argued that they should be granted a marriage license because no statute explicitly denied them access to marriage. Moreover, they argued, denial of their "fundamental right" to marriage was tantamount to "sex" discrimination. The court deployed all-too-common tropes of "common understanding" and history to reject their claims. "A sensible reading," the court held, suggested that Minnesota legislators had used marriage in the common sense of the term, meaning a bond between a man and a woman.[30] The existing statutes used words such as husband and wife and bride and groom, which were, according to the court, "words of heterosexual import." Turning to history, the court continued:

> The institution of marriage as a union of man and woman, uniquely involving the procreation and rearing of children within a family, is as old as the book of Genesis. . . . This historic institution manifestly is more deeply founded than the asserted contemporary concept of marriage and societal interests for which petitioners contend. The due process clause of the Fourteenth Amendment is not a charter for restructuring [marriage] by judicial legislation.[31]

According to the court, marriage is irrevocably heterosexual because it is rooted in history, captured in its timeless formation through Christianity. Thus semantics and history precluded rights claims, particularly to such a "contemporary" formation as two male partners.

In the 1973 Kentucky case *Jones v. Hallahan* two female petitioners argued that the denial of same-sex marriage violated their freedom to associate and their freedom of religion.[32] Unfortunately, the court did not directly address these unique arguments but instead fixated on common language. Since the Kentucky statute did not specifically define marriage, the court turned to a variety of dictionaries in order to claim that marriage generally implies a union between one man and one woman. Strangely, the court then argues that the female petitioners have doomed themselves because they do not fit these dictionary definitions. According to the court, "It appears to us that appellants are prevented from marrying, not by the statutes of Kentucky or the refusal of the County Court Clerk of Jefferson County to issue them a license, but rather by their own incapability of entering into a marriage as that term is defined."[33]

In the 1974 Washington case *Singer v. Hara* the petitioners offered a more sophisticated and thorough case for same-sex marriage. They claimed that denial of their application for a marriage license violated the state's Equal Rights Amendment (approved by the voters in 1972), as well as various parts of the U.S. Constitution. Moreover, they contended that the trial court's conclusion was based on "the erroneous and fallacious conclusion that same-sex marriages are destructive to society."[34] To prove their point, they dedicated over forty pages of their brief to the social science literature attesting to the benefits of same-sex marriage and homosexuality. The court responded that while this academic literature was informative, it did not provide a legal argument. This would suggest that appeals to nonlegal sources, such as history or dictionaries or the book of Genesis, are acceptable because they are aligned with the common knowledge as determined by the courts.[35] In regard to the legal issue—that is, the potential violation of the state ERA—the court found that there was no violation as long as men and women were equally denied access to same-sex marriage. And, even more importantly, the court reprimanded the male petitioners for trying to subvert the purposes of the ERA—that is, for taking advantage of and, supposedly, *misusing* the feminist achievement of acknowledging sex discrimination.

These are important moments in which same-sex marriage claims began to expose the intersectionality (that is, the indivisibility and codependency) of sex, gender, and sexuality. Throughout these earlier cases, courts struggled to find ways to clarify and contain the operations of sex, gender, and sexuality in order to reject same-sex marriage arguments. However, following these cases, many state legislatures worked to provide "clarity" by passing laws defining marriage. Maryland led the way in articulating what conservatives had previously considered obvious—"A marriage must be between a man and a woman in order to be valid"—and seventeen states followed suit between 1973 and 1993.[36] These offensive maneuvers demonstrate that there was clearly some gender and heteronormative trouble before the notorious 1993 Hawai'i case *Baehr v. Lewin*, but it was this case particularly that agitated the U.S. Congress.[37] It is certainly worth interrogating why the *Baehr* case ended up causing so much anxiety about the security of heterosexual marriage and resulted in a "backlash" of laws (including federal and state-level Defense of Marriage Acts, discussed later). While most political pundits and scholars focus on how this case was the first high court ruling supporting same-sex marriage, I would argue that there was something else much more radical and frightening afoot in the *Baehr* decision.

Three couples applied for marriage licenses, but were denied by the State of Hawai'i Department of Health. While the district court dismissed their case, the Hawai'i Supreme Court remanded the case back to the district court, requiring that it apply a "strict scrutiny" level of analysis as to whether the refusal to grant them marriage licenses relied on any form of "sex" discrimination—that is, a violation of equal protection based on "sex" as guaranteed by the state constitution.[38] In a footnote, the court observes that these couples are not being denied marriage licenses because of their sexuality or sexual identity. Rather, they are being denied due to what the court refers to as their "sex." As the court states, "'Homosexual' and 'same-sex' marriages are not synonymous; by the same token, a 'heterosexual' same-sex marriage is, in theory, not oxymoronic. . . . Parties to a union between a man and a woman may or may not be homosexuals."[39] In fact, in the original complaint, the plaintiffs did not "proclaim" their homosexuality (an omission that the opposition was quick to point out). But as the court noted, it was the state of Hawai'i that made homosexuality an issue in this case, not the plaintiffs.

By considering same-sex marriage a matter of sex discrimination, the *Baehr* case demonstrates the ways in which sex, gender, and sexuality are intermeshed constructs. Reminiscent of the two men accused of misusing the ERA in *Singer v. Hara*, the Hawai'i Supreme Court was accused of purposefully and willfully misconstruing the meaning of "sex" in this case. Members of the Hawaiian legislature were particularly bereft and criticized the court for deliberately confusing sex-as-in-gender with sex-as-in-sexual orientation.[40] Of course, the point here is that the distinctions among sex, gender, and sexuality are confusing and that courts and legislatures are foolish if they think they can pinpoint discrimination within one category of identity alone. Here, referring to same-sex marriage as a matter of sex, as opposed to sexuality, allowed for and produced *a necessary and appropriate* confusion about the relationship between sex, gender, and sexuality, as well as anxiety that these are, in fact, social constructs.

Soon after the *Baehr* decision, the Hawaiian legislature made two moves that became the quintessential liberal compromise on same-sex marriage. State lawmakers approved a "reciprocal beneficiaries" plan that granted same-sex couples some of the benefits associated with marriage, while also proposing a constitutional referendum "preserving" marriage for "opposite-sex couples" (a referendum that passed with 69 percent of the vote in 1998).[41] And as we now know, the Hawaiian case and other same-sex marriage activisms set off a legislative firestorm of DOMA and mini-DOMAs throughout the United States.[42] The 1996 Defense of Marriage Act (DOMA)[43] had two provisions: first, it defined marriage for federal purposes as "only a legal union between one man and one woman as husband and wife, and the word 'spouse' refers only to a person of the opposite sex who is a husband or a wife"; and second, it permitted states to refuse to recognize same-sex marriages performed in or legitimized by other states.[44] Throughout the DOMA debates, senators and representatives claimed that heterosexual marriage needed to be defended. The "homosexual lobby," according to Senator Jesse Helms, had "chipped away at the moral stamina of some of America's courts and some legislators, in order to create the shaky ground that exists today that prompts this legislation."[45] Helms and the bill's other sponsors argued that while marriage had always been unequivocally, irrevocably heterosexual, recent case law had challenged this presumption. What troubled Helms and other conservatives was that, according to the law, marriage and heterosexuality were no longer synonymous.

If anti–same-sex-marriage law depends on the presumption that "man" and "woman" are discrete, natural, or even identifiable categories, then surely transgender rights advocacy has sounded and will continue to sound an alarm over the supposed natural and distinct differences among sex, gender, and sexuality.[46] Paisley Currah argues that "while the . . . freedom-to-marry challenge engineered by mainstream lesbian and gay rights advocates is apparently articulated in terms of essentialist notions of sex and gender, it is important to recognize that legal advocates of transsexuals [have] already been defending 'same-sex' marriages for some time."[47] While many "same-sex" marriages involving transgender spouses have slipped under legal radars, some marriages appeared on the radar because they involved contestations over property, assets, and financial resources.[48] For example, in the 1999 Texas case *Littleton v. Prange*, a woman who had sued for malpractice following her husband's wrongful death appealed the trial court's judgment favoring the physician, who had countered that she was ineligible for insurance benefits because Texas law defined marriage as a union between a woman and a man, and the appellant, according to the physician, was in fact not a woman.[49] Christie Lee Littleton, a transwoman, had changed her sex designation as well as her name on her birth certificate by court order before the marriage ceremony. Yet her status still plagued the appellate court:

> This case involves the most basic of questions. When is a man a man, and when is a woman a woman? Every schoolchild, even of tender years, is confident he or

she can tell the difference, especially if the person is wearing no clothes. These are observations that each of us makes early in life and . . . [are among] the more pleasant mysteries. The deeper philosophical (and now legal) question is: can a physician change the gender of a person with a scalpel, drugs and counseling, or is a person's gender immutably fixed by our Creator at birth? The answer to that question has definite legal implications that present themselves in this case.[50]

Reminiscent of the drive to declare the nature of marriage obvious and known by all, the court's desire to declare gender unquestionable even as the court admitted gender's questionability, demonstrates the court's (as well as society's) general refusal to acknowledge the social construction and intersectionalities of sex and gender.

Interestingly, the question is not, what is a man or woman? Rather, it is a temporal question: "*when* is a man a man, and *when* is a woman a woman?" (emphasis added). The reference to time suggests that gender may be, after all, historically contextual and constructed. While the court recognized that "there are many fine metaphysical arguments lurking about here involving desire and being, the essence of life and the power of mind over physics," it concluded that Littleton was not entitled to sue because the original birth certificate designated her "real" sex.[51] In the end, the legal-juridical document trumped both science and nature: "Christie was created and born a male. Her original birth certificate, an official document of Texas, clearly so states."[52] While the court acknowledged that Littleton had changed the sex on her birth certificate, this change was a "ministerial one." As the court stated: "The facts contained in the original birth certificate were true and accurate. . . . There are some things we cannot will into being. They just are." Therefore, "we hold, as a matter of law, that Christie Littleton is a male. As a male, Christie cannot be married to another male."[53] The U.S. Supreme Court affirmed this decision by denying certiorari on October 2, 2000.[54]

The same year that the Texas court was pondering when is a man a man, the Vermont Supreme Court brought us civil unions. In the 1999 case, *Baker v. State of Vermont*, the court found that same-sex couples should receive the same benefits as opposite-sex couples and ordered the state legislature to ensure that they did.[55] In making this conclusion, the court applied the "common benefits clause" of the Vermont state constitution, which states that "government is or ought to be instituted for the common benefit, protection and security of the people, nation, or community, and not for the particular advantage of any single person, family, or set of persons." While the *Baker* decision was seen as a breakthrough for gays and lesbians, the court avoided the question of whether homosexuals were a suspect class under the Fourteenth Amendment, thereby limiting the impact of the case to the state of Vermont, and designated marriage as a benefit, not a right.[56] The court delicately suggested that the state legislature should adopt some form of benefit for same-sex partners in the form of either marriage or civil union. In April 2000, the legislature passed a compromise bill, which gave same-sex partners access to civil union while defining marriage as a union "between a man and a woman."[57]

While some gays and lesbians immediately packed their bags for Vermont, it was unlikely that civil unions performed in Vermont would be recognized by other states. Just in case, a few months after *Baker*, Nebraska and Nevada passed anti–civil-union laws, and many states followed suit. Importantly, civil unions serve as an interesting compromise, giving gays and lesbians the right to benefits associated with marriage without the acceptance and legitimacy of marriage itself. In this way, marriage is reinstitutionalized as the foundation of intimate, familial life, while civil unions are designated as a formation that is merely practical, economic, and contractual. Heterosexual couples, however, have rarely been granted the legal right to civil unions, which reminds us that there is as much investment in policing those within the category—that is, the heterosexual couple—as demarcating those outside the categories and keeping them at bay.

## Intersectionalities Lost

Same-sex marriage law expanded exponentially in the first and second decades of the twenty-first century. The transformation in same-sex marriage law began with the landmark 2003 Massachusetts case, *Goodridge v. Department of Public Health*.[58] While this case was the most successful in terms of gay rights advocacy, it was also the most conservative. *Goodridge* embodies and brings to fruition various queer theoretical critiques of same-sex marriage advocacy. A decade later, courts and same-sex marriage advocates continued to apply the conservative logics of *Goodridge* to other same-sex marriage cases. Throughout these two decades, same-sex marriage rights moved toward anti-intersectional arguments and worked to disappear the linkages of (homo)sexuality to race, class, and sexual deviance, while reifying the violence of normative citizenships and expanding the civilizing governmentality of marriage.

The court's final conclusion in *Goodridge* is that the denial of marriage rights to same-sex couples denies equal protection and due process under the Massachusetts Constitution. On the way to this conclusion, however, the court makes three maneuvers that I am particularly concerned with: first, they declare that including same-sex couples within marriage will bolster the exclusivity of marriage; second, they assert that including same-sex couples will allow the state to extend its purview into same-sex relationships, producing and maintaining them as "good citizens"; and last, this decision deploys temporality in such a way to maintain and reproduce the erroneous and dangerously seductive logics that citizenship and marriage are naturally evolving, progressively inclusive institutions.

The court decision begins by describing the seven couples, all vital members of the community, for they are "business executives, lawyers, an investment banker, educators, therapists, and a computer engineer" and "are active in church, community, and school groups."[59] Even more importantly, these are good family members that are in long-term monogamous relationships, most with children and some even responsible for their elderly parents. This is, of course, a useful and productive approach. The state's argument that marriage must be opposite sex only rested upon a "protect the children rationale"—that is, the notion that opposite-sex marriage promotes procreation and child-rearing. But the state's arguments backfire as the court basically accuses the state of not having family values:

> No one disputes that the plaintiff couples are families, that many are parents, and that the children they are raising, like all children, need and should have the fullest opportunity to grow up in a secure, protected family unit. . . . It cannot be rational under our laws, and indeed it is not permitted, to penalize children by depriving them of State benefits because the State disapproves of their parents' sexual orientation.[60]

Rather than protect children, the exclusivity of marriage law harms them. Thus the court cleverly deploys the state's logic against itself and, along the way, suggests that discrimination against gays and lesbians actually targets families, parents, and children.

But then it gets tricky. The court attempts to tackle the conservative argument that U.S. laws should preserve the sanctity of marriage and replies that extending marriage to same-sex couples will do just that. The court suggests that although many are concerned that same-sex marriage "will trivialize or destroy the institution of marriage," it must be understood that this decision in fact strengthens the institution. It is important to trace the trajectory of the court's argument:

> Here, the plaintiffs seek only to be married, not to undermine the institution of civil marriage. They do not want marriage abolished. They do not attack the

binary nature of marriage, the consanguinity provisions, or any of the other gate-keeping provisions of the marriage licensing law. Recognizing the right of an individual to marry a person of the same sex will not diminish the validity or dignity of opposite-sex marriage, any more than recognizing the right of an individual to marry a person of a different race devalues the marriage of a person who marries someone of her own race. If anything, extending civil marriage to same-sex couples reinforces the importance of marriage to individuals and communities. That same-sex couples are willing to embrace marriage's solemn obligations of exclusivity, mutual support, and commitment to one another is a testament to the enduring place of marriage in our laws and in the human spirit.[61]

The argument contains many of the elements that queer theorists have critiqued, particularly the suggestion that same-sex marriage rights will not change or transform the institution of marriage, but will fortify its "gate-keeping provisions." For example, the court references here the ways in which same-sex marriage advocacy has not attacked the "binary nature[s]" of marriage. While same-sex marriage advocates have critiqued the male/female and heterosexual/homosexual binaries latent within marriage law, they have not attempted to undermine the sanctity of the domestic couple. Clearly, there are a variety of intimacies and familial practices that fall out of this narrow construction.

I also want to spend some time interrogating the strategic analogy to race. Most of the case law and popular debate slips into the question as to how similar same-sex marriage rights are to interracial marriage rights. Is the nation at the same crossroads it was back in 1967, when the U.S. Supreme Court struck down Virginia's antimiscegenation law in *Loving v. Virginia*? Proponents of same-sex marriage have often argued that sex orientation *now* is like race *then*. As the logic goes, the majority of the U.S. population used to think that marrying someone of a different race was wrong, just like the majority might think it is wrong for same-sex folks to marry today. But opponents counter that discrimination based on race "back then" was wrong because it was based on prejudice, whereas discrimination based on sexual orientation "today" concerns a legitimate difference that matters. In this framing, conservatives mark racism as a historic wrong while designating homosexuality as a contemporary formation and a conduct that should be regulated by the state.

Either way, my concern is that this narrative holds that "we" all know that racial discrimination is wrong, and "we" will either learn a similar lesson in regard to sexuality or not. Without denying that the *Loving* decision has had an impact on race and marriage rights, or that racial discrimination has changed over time, I am wary of the ways in which a legal decision can be mobilized to suggest that racial discrimination in marriage, employment, education, and so on, is a thing of the past—that is, properly belonging to the past as opposed to the present. As other scholars have also noted, the deployment of the interracial marriage analogy produces painfully inaccurate teleological narratives that racial justice has been accomplished.[62] The analogy is loaded and works to obscure the fact that racialized discrimination remains very much a part of citizenship in the United States. Moreover, understanding the histories of marriage law and citizenship highlights the fact that marriage law has been a primary site for the production and maintenance of a whitenormative citizenry. The deployment of the racial analogy recalls this whitenormative history only to deny its contemporary importance. The analogy works, then, to negate and disavow the intersectionalities of race, sexuality, and gender, marking them, as David Eng eloquently observes, as "parallel issues that never cross."[63]

Ultimately, the court's decision rests on the premise that marriage law is one of the best mechanisms for maintaining and tracking conformity of citizens. The court is refreshingly blunt about this relationship:

> Without question, civil marriage enhances the "welfare of the community." It is a "social institution of the highest importance." . . . Civil marriage anchors an ordered society by encouraging stable relationships over transient ones. It is central to the way the Commonwealth identifies individuals, provides for the orderly distribution of property, ensures that children and adults are cared for and supported whenever possible from private rather than public funds, and tracks important demo-graphic data.[64]

The court suggests that extending same-sex-marriage rights is a way to incorporate and assimilate gays and lesbians into the norms of the national polity. Such rights will provide order, stability, and a means of identifying and recognizing individuals. That is, they will make gays and lesbians intelligible and acceptable to the state as citizens. Moreover, marriage rights privatize responsibilities, in accordance with neoliberalist and conservative rhetoric that promotes marriage among single welfare recipients as a solution to social ills and economic disparities. The court goes on to assert the legitimacy of the state's intrusion into the marital bed, stating "in a real sense, there are three partners to every civil marriage: two willing spouses and an approving State."[65] In this way, same-sex-marriage rights are a means of expanding the number of beds that can be "approved" by the state and raises the question: With whom are gays and lesbians in bed?

Let me clarify, however, that this is not merely a matter of whether particular gay and lesbian couples are making some type of "personal" decision to get in bed with the state. As described earlier, marriage—like citizenship in general—

is a form of governmentality; that is, marriage is a technology of governance, an extension of normative practices and behaviors that are condoned, taught, and disciplined far beyond the state. Foucault pointed out, for example, that while the family was a model of critical importance to disciplinary societies, the family became "the privileged instrument for the government of the population" (i.e., biopolitical governmentality) in the middle of the eighteenth century within Western state formations.[66] Marriage is not a privatized experience—rather, it functions and receives its social value through the work of social recognition and participation. The requirement that state-recognized and non–state-recognized marriages are "witnessed" works to facilitate the governmentality of marriage, dragging all participants and even nonparticipants into the surveillance of romantic relationships, kinship practices, and family formations. Put differently, marriage transforms communities into accomplices in the surveillance apparatus, whereby they are subsumed into the practice of witnessing, congratulating, maintaining, tracking, or rewarding the normative married citizen.

As I mentioned, one of the most dangerous elements of *Goodridge* is the way in which it deploys particularly developmental notions of history, marriage, and citizenship as progressing toward complete and total inclusion. It is not a coincidence that the first successful same-sex marriage case is also the most conservative in tone and the most aligned with the progress narrative of U.S. citizenship. The court refers to history throughout this case, often to state that it agrees that this history shows that marriage "has been" between a man and woman, but is now about to change. In the introduction to the decision the court directly addresses its (presumed) reticent audience by stating, "We are mindful that our decision marks a change in the history of marriage law."[67] But, importantly, the "change" in this supposedly static history of marriage law is being forced by the evolutionary nature and progressive function of citizenship. Here, in the words of the court: "The history of constitutional law is the story of the extension of constitutional rights and protections to people once ignored or excluded."[68] The progress narrative of citizenship, then, works its magic to assist the court in deeming the decision *inevitable* while simultaneously eliding the exclusionary natures of citizenship.

But in order to secure the narrative of evolutionary and inclusionary citizenship and disavow the contemporary violence of racialized citizenship, the court faithfully returns to the racial analogy of antimiscegenation law. Quoting the court:

> As *Loving* made clear, the right to marry means little if it does not include the right to marry the person of one's choice, subject to appropriate government

restrictions in the interest of public health, safety and welfare. In this case, as in *Loving*, a statute deprives individuals of access to an institution of fundamental legal, personal and social significance—the institution of marriage—because of a single trait: skin color in *Loving*, sexual orientation here. As it did in *Loving*, history must yield to a more fully developed understanding of the invidious quality of the discrimination.[69]

By equating "sexual orientation" to "skin color," the court fixes racial discrimination in the past, while simultaneously cementing the progress narrative of citizenship as an inevitable future. Racial discrimination is marked as anachronistic, out of time, compared to the steam train of progressive citizenship—a steam train that is powered by nothing less than the histories of discriminatory citizenship.

In the evolution of same-sex marriage law, *Goodridge* turned out to be the tip of the iceberg. While conservatives continued to agitate for same-sex marriage bans throughout the states, and were quite successful, those bans were in jeopardy the more that the courts and U.S. popular opinion embraced the arguments found in the *Goodridge* decision.[70] Same-sex marriage law transformed rapidly; while in June of 2013, only thirteen states recognized same-sex marriage, by January 2015, there were over thirty-six states. The accelerated speed of same-sex marriage recognition stemmed from the U.S. Supreme Court cases, *United States v. Windsor*, and *Hollingsworth v. Perry*, which marked the most significant transformations in same-sex marriage case law since *Goodridge*.[71]

In *United States v. Windsor*, the majority decision (penned by Justice Kennedy) invalidated the Defense of Marriage Act (DOMA) definitional provision, Section 3, which specified "the word 'marriage' means only a legal union between one man and one woman as husband and wife, and the word 'spouse' refers only to a person of the opposite sex who is a husband or a wife" throughout federal law.[72] The case revolved around the question as to whether Edith Windsor could qualify for the federal marital tax exemption when she inherited the estate of her wife (whom she married in Canada in 2007), Thea Spyer, who passed away in 2009. Without the tax exemption, Windsor paid $363,053 in taxes and was, therefore, challenging DOMA as a means to get a refund. In a five-to-four decision, the Supreme Court held that Section 3 violates the equal liberty of persons as protected under the Fifth Amendment.[73]

Many of the logics within the *Windsor* decision followed in step with *Goodridge*. Predictably, perhaps, this case was very much a question of neoliberal citizenship, whereby marriage law continues to be one of the primary means to channel property and capital among the financially privileged. Moreover,

Windsor and Spyer were a long-term couple, together for over 44 years. Echoing elements of *Goodridge*, Kennedy's opinion emphasizes that refusing to recognize their marriage perpetuates social stigma on same-sex couples and makes them feel unworthy and humiliates children of same-sex couples. DOMA creates "two contradictory marriage regimes" by marking some marriages more worthy than others, thereby "writing inequality into the entire United States code."[74] But as much as same-sex marriage advocates celebrated the decision, a careful reading would reveal that Kennedy's decision is much more invested in recognizing states' rights (over federalism) than in recognizing same-sex relationships. The Kennedy decision marks the State of New York as the injured party, rather than same-sex couples. As Justice Scalia notes in his dissent, "the opinion does not argue that same-sex marriage is 'deeply rooted in this Nation's history or tradition,'" because Kennedy is actually only invested in recounting the history of states' rights to regulate marriage laws.[75] According to the majority opinion, history and tradition tell us that the "regulation of domestic relations" is "an area that has long been regarded as a virtually exclusive province of the States."[76]

The other landmark U.S. Supreme Court decision on same-sex marriage, *Hollingsworth v. Perry*, was even more limited in scope as the Court focused the decision on the narrow question of "standing," that is, whether the parties in the case are qualified to bring suit. In another five-to-four decision, the Court held that the proponents of California's Proposition 8 did not have standing before the Court. *Hollingsworth v. Perry*'s trajectory to the Supreme Court is a convoluted one, but it began when two same-sex couples challenged California's Proposition 8, a state constitutional amendment voted in by California voters that restricted marriage to "a man and a woman."[77] In its first incarnation, the district court case of *Perry v. Schwarzenegger*, Judge Walker offered an impressive and extensive decision overturning Proposition 8 for violating Due Process and Equal Protection clauses of the Fourteenth Amendment.[78] Notably, the State of California did not appeal the decision, and in their stead the activists behind Proposition 8 stepped up to challenge Judge Walker's decision. The Ninth Court of Appeals did recognize their standing but followed the district court's lead in finding Proposition 8 unconstitutional (though on narrower grounds).[79] Hence, when it came to the Supreme Court's decision, they averted the constitutional questions around Proposition 8 and same-sex marriage altogether by reversing the finding that the advocates of Proposition 8 had standing.[80]

The *Perry* cases offer important lessons as to what Dean Spade calls "the mystique of marriage."[81] Because California had a substantial domestic partnership law that offered an extensive array of benefits for same-sex couples, both the district court and the circuit court were forced to wrestle with the question as to what makes "marriage" special, unique, and so worthy of fighting over. The ninth circuit opinion goes out of its way to, in the words of Judge Reinhardt, "emphasize the extraordinary significance of the official designation of 'marriage.'"[82] As the court explains, "That designation is important because 'marriage' is the name that society gives to the relationship that matters most between two adults. A rose by any other name may smell as sweet, but to the couple desiring to enter into a committed lifelong relationship, a marriage by the name of 'registered domestic partnership' does not."[83] Trying to capture the sentimentality of marriage and national cathexis, the court explains that, "we are excited to see someone ask, 'Will you marry me?' whether on bended knee in a restaurant or in text splashed across a stadium Jumbotron. Certainly it would not have the same effect to see, 'will you enter into a registered domestic partnership with me?'"[84]

But an intersectional analysis would offer a slightly different reading as to why marriage matters. The value of marriage stems from the fact that it is a religious-, social-, and state-enforced institution that creates a hierarchical relationship of value between those relationships that are within what Gayle Rubin named "the charmed circle," and those castigated to "the outer limits" of social acceptability.[85] In her famous essay, "Thinking Sex," Rubin attempted to articulate the ways in which normative belief systems perpetuate discrimination against sexual minorities. At the time, Rubin was also invested in exposing how some feminist scholars and activists (especially antipornography scholars and activists) participated in reifying systems of differentiation between "perverts" and those deemed sexually acceptable. But since the emergence of same-sex marriage advocacy, queer theorists have offered a similar alarm: marriage matters because it offers a shorthanded means to locate acceptable sexual practices and forms of intimacy, and LGBT organizations are relying upon and reproducing these very same hierarchies.

Many scholars have argued that same-sex marriage invites dangerous state-based regulations of intimacy and relationships,[86] and most importantly, that same-sex marriage exacerbates the vulnerability of nonnormative folks,[87] which is especially dangerous within the contexts of the "war on terror" and widespread expansion of U.S. empire.[88] Intersectional queer scholars have pointed out, for example, the ways in which same-sex marriage advocacy is particularly dangerous when understood through the contexts of the "global lockdown" and mass incarceration of people of color (especially African American men) and undocumented migrants through the prison industrial complex. As Anna Agathangelou, M. Daniel Bassichis, and Tamara L. Spira eloquently observe, "the privatization of the freedom of the queer subject enshrines a culture of loss of rights for non–U.S. citizens while naturalizing the backdrop of (specifically black) (non) subjects within the United States whose civically dead or dying status has rarely been assigned rights to lose."[89]

Queer Indigenous studies scholars have pointed out that same-sex marriage advocacy participates in the reification of settler colonialism in a variety of ways. As described earlier, part of the problem is the ways in which "civility" is deployed throughout same-sex marriage debates, whereby marriage-as-the-mark-of-civilization reproduces the logics of elimination that have been used (and continue to be used) to dismantle Native sovereignty, self determination, and kinship practices. But another aspect of the settler colonial violence of same-sex marriage advocacy stems from the ways in which it has selectively fixated on presumptions of Native sexual and gender alterity in order to argue that Native traditions have long-recognized same-sex marriages and, therefore, the U.S. nation should follow suit. Same-sex marriage advocates have presumed an alliance with Natives merely through claiming a shared history of nonnormative sexualities and genders. But as Joanne Barker points out, this presumption rests on the "incredible proliferation of stereotypes and misrepresentations of Native traditions about marriage and sexuality" that were forged in colonialist anthropology and historiography, as well as other discourses.[90] This is not to suggest that there are not diverse and varied conceptions of gender and sexuality within Native systems; rather, this is to call out the ways in which same-sex marriage advocacy appropriates colonialist representations of Native genders and sexualities for white settler belonging.[91] As Scott Morgensen argues, when same-sex marriage advocates selectively appropriate Native histories and traditions, they not only attempt to obscure their own roles as settlers, but they also absorb Native history and traditions as their own in order to "legitimate their place on stolen land."[92]

Same-sex marriage advocates' promotion of "marriage tourism" is another site whereby they reenact and solidify U.S. settler colonialism. As states recognized same-sex marriage rights, advocates rewarded them by promoting the state as a tourist spot for the celebrating couples. In the process of binding marriage rights to consumer gay practices, marriage advocates reproduced gay tourism rhetoric in which the mobility of the modern, mobile, and cosmopolitan gay subject relies upon and reproduces the immobility of "premodern," "exotic," racialized "others."[93] For example, soon after Governor Abercrombie signed same-sex marriage legislation in Hawai'i, the Human Rights Commission sent out an email blast with the title, "Say ALOHA to Marriage Equality." The email celebrates the Hawaiian State Senate's approval of a bill that allows "all loving and committed couples to marry," and although this law does not, in fact, allow "all" couples to marry, that is the least of my concerns with HRC's notice. Rather, I am troubled by the suggestion that the best means to "celebrate" same-sex marriage in Hawai'i is to, "Vote with your wallet" and "Consider taking your next vacation to the Aloha state or others—as well as our nation's capital—where marriage equality is the law of the land." The HRC's promotion of marriage tourism moves beyond a mere homonormative logic of voting with dollars, particularly when it suggests that same-sex couples can consume Native Hawaiian difference.

As described in more detail in the next chapter, settler colonial rhetorics consistently distort the Hawaiian concept of "aloha" in order to create a permanent invitation for settlers to visit, consume, and exploit the islands—an invitation that is made to appear to be from Kanaka Maoli themselves. It is in and against this seemingly endless invitation that activists such as Haunani-Kay Trask implore all potential tourists to reconsider visiting. Many Kanaka Maoli activists have been quite vocal in their opposition to the tourism industry in Hawai'i, and the ways in which this industry has wreaked havoc on Indigenous lifeways, land claims, and sovereignty movements. "If you are thinking of visiting my homeland," Trask implores, "please do not. We do not want or need any more tourists, and we certainly do not like them. If you want to help our cause, pass this message onto your friends."[94] The tourism promoted by HRC is just one more way in which same-sex marriage advocacy naturalizes and reproduces settler colonialism.

The considerable gains made in the recognition of same-sex marriage have come at a substantial cost, as the intersectionalities of sexuality with class, race, sexual deviance, and settler colonialism continue to get buried under the increasing absorption of many gay and lesbian subjects into normative citizenships. Same-sex marriage has reinforced and resolidified the nonnormativities and abjections of racialization, working-class lifestyles, sexual perversities, and Native sovereignties, and it has continued the work of severing the potential for intersectional political alliances. In the aftermath of same-sex marriage law, the raging success of practical, anti-intersectional political strategies, and the reification of normative citizenship, it is critical to ask, in Amber Hollibaugh's eloquent phrasing from the epigraph that began this chapter, "What if we said that no one, not a single one of us, would get traded for socioeconomic access or the achievement of short-term legal goals?"[95]

## The Monstrosities of Alliance

The movement to legalize same-sex marriage marks a critical opportunity to reflect on the potential of queer political organizing and the possibilities of contesting normative citizenship. Many scholars and activists argue that there has been a severe loss of queer political goals. For example, some argue that the loss of queer political values stems directly from how neatly same-sex marriage rights reproduce conservative "family values." As Urvashi Vaid observes, "the LGBT marriage movement echoes traditional arguments in seeking marriage, arguing for the value of monogamy, for the idea that marriage promotes stability and social integration, and for the position that its extension to same-sex couples would not change the institution in meaningful ways."[96] In fact, Vaid argues that same-sex marriage advocates have been willing to "sacrifice large segments of the LGBT communities (single parents, uncoupled people, those not interested in marriage) in order to secure the support of right-wing allies."[97]

Scholars and activists have not only raised questions as to how and in what ways same-sex marriage advocacy has appealed to conservatives, but they have also questioned why conservatives have increasingly come on board the same-sex marriage train. However, when we return to the issue of how, as marked by the *Goodridge* court, marriage is one of the primary means to produce and regulate normative citizens, we glean important lessons as to why conservatives might increasingly support same-sex marriage. Consider the following prescient warning raised by legal scholar Katherine Franke in 2004:

> I am inclined to end with a prediction: Within a relatively short period, opposition to gay marriage will dissipate, but not because those who now disfavor it will come around to the righteousness of the cause. Rather, it will subside because the decriminalization of sodomy and of gay and lesbian sexual relationships will have created a social terrain in which a vast number of sexual relationships will appear to stand outside the legal order altogether. This, I believe, will prove to be an unbearable state of affairs for those who have always favored the governance, surveillance, and supervision of sexuality. Bringing same-sex couples within the regulatory reach of marriage will in the not too distant future emerge as a better choice than leaving these sexual subjects in the underregulated space that lies between criminalization and legitimization through marriage.[98]

In other words, Franke argues that especially after the *Lawrence v. Texas* (2003) decision that forced states to abandon sodomy laws, conservatives would increasingly need to turn to other mechanisms to regulate queerness. And as noted in *Goodridge*, marriage is such a mechanism.

These scholars and activists also explain that the turn toward regulation, in the form of marriage rights, marks a direct rejection of queer political values. As Vaid explains, "values like standing up for all LGBT people, including those who are immigrant, in unions, women, in need of reproductive health services, or low-income . . . are sidelined in the rush to gain the support of right-wing funders who oppose the rights of these parts of our communities."[99]

Other scholars and activists articulate the loss of queer political values as a turn away from the "origins" of queer politics. For example, Willse and Spade argue that "the winning decision in *Lawrence* and its aggrandizement in LGBT legal circles represents a frightening reduction in the demands of what was, at its inception, a movement against violent and coercive systems of gender and sexual regulation." Importantly, these scholars do not mark the "inception" of the queer political movement in any whitewashed historical narrative of the 1969 Stonewall uprising, as promoted through gay pride parades. Rather, they locate the origins of queer politics within an intersectional historical narrative that emphasizes how mostly "low income gender and sexual outsiders," especially queer and transgender people of color, rioted against state surveillance, regulation, and harassment. Therefore, as they lament, "in the decades since that time, we have seen the consolidation of legitimacy and power in organizations whose leadership, priorities and strategies sharply depart from these origins."[100]

While I find these analyses of the "loss" of queer political values very insightful, I would describe the process slightly differently. Upon reflecting on the success of same-sex marriage advocacy, especially in the process of watching LGBT communities explode with marriage fervor after the Supreme Court decisions, it has gradually become clear to me that the loss of radical queer politics has less to do with the "origins," and more to do with monstrosity. Throughout the past, the radical potential for queer politics has, in part, hinged on the fear and anxiety that has been evoked by what I call "monstrous queerness." While scholars have found a long historical association between homosexuality and monstrosity, especially within gothic literature and science fiction,[101] what I am attempting to name here is slightly different. Through queer activism, they capitalized on, rather than alleviated, the correlation of queerness with the lawlessness, criminality, and sexual contagion that were forged throughout heteronormative systems of knowledge, especially as manifest within science, psychology, criminal justice, and legal discourses.

Queer political actions took advantage of queer's association with sexualized, racialized, and gendered perversities, and inhabited monstrous queerness as a way to exploit heterosexist fears of angry queers gone amok. In so doing, these actions capitalized on the ominous threat associated with queerness, including notions that queers are sexual outlaws, and that they are the sick and perverse sexual beings that required (and excused) numerous "sex panics" throughout U.S. history. Same-sex marriage has severely wounded, if not eliminated, the monstrous queer and its radical potential to use fear and anxiety (along with campy fun, frolic, and a lot of sex) as a means to disrupt normative systems of knowledge and power. Importantly, however, the ultimate fear and anxiety produced by queer monstrosity was less about sexual alterity and more about the ways in which queer activists inhabited a politics of perversity that could directly ally with the racialized monsters of U.S. colonialism, U.S. imperialism, white supremacy, and the carceral state.

Queer activism has prolific examples of activists adopting and utilizing heteronormative anxieties and fears of monstrous queerness.[102] Rather than advocating for inclusion via rights claims, queer activists utilized "in your face" subversive tactics, from theatrical demonstrations to infiltrations of presumably heterosexual spaces. As Lauren Berlant and Elizabeth Freeman explain, these queer activists used "alternating strategies of menace and merriment" in order to exploit heterosexist fears.[103] The names of the organizations themselves are telling: Sex Panic!, ACT UP (AIDS Coalition to Unleash Power), Queer Nation, and Lesbian Avengers, to name a few. Each of these names invokes images of enraged queers acting up to avenge the violence that the norms of citizenship enact and to, perhaps, forge a new queer nation in which heterosexuals will become the abjected others.

By staging "kiss-ins" in shopping malls, infiltrating straight bars, and making passes at heterosexuals, queer activists exploited the fear of liminal queerness, the contamination of uncontainable homosexuality, and the spread of utter debauchery. As Berlant and Freeman suggest, queer activist infiltrations of heterosexual spaces derailed key tenets of heteronormative culture, including the notion that what appeared to be a "bounded gay subcultural activity" is, in fact, "restless and improvisatory, taking its pleasures in a theater near you." Queer activists took advantage of the fear of militant queers creating "an army of lovers," that offered, at the very least, a "psychic counterthreat" to heteronormativity.[104] For example, groups like the Pink Panthers and the San Francisco Street Patrol (originally named DORIS SQUASH, an acronym for Defend Our Rights In the Streets/Super Queers United Against Savage Heterosexism) not only guarded the streets against homophobic gay bashing, but also promised to "Bash Back!"[105] The Lesbian Avengers also provoked these fears by having a cartoon image of a bomb with a lit fuse as their signature, splattered throughout their pamphlets and protest materials.[106]

In declaring their "gay rage," Anonymous Queers distributed the infamous "Queers Read This! I Hate Straights!" leaflet at the Chicago and New York City gay pride parades in 1990, which unabashedly proclaimed an active disdain for U.S. national, heteronormative institutions such as the government, police, education, and military.[107] Calling out to comrade queers, the pamphlet declared that straights would never give up privilege voluntarily. Rather, "straights must be frightened into it. Terrorized into it. Fear is the most powerful motivation. No one will give us what we deserve. Rights are not given they are taken, by force if necessary. It is easier to fight when you know who your enemy is. Straight people are your enemy."[108] Throughout this diverse array of tactics, queer political power capitalized on the monstrosity of queerness and the ways in which queerness evoked both panic and awe.

Of course, the queer actions described above were not without their faults, and I do not mean to idealize them here. Scholars and activists have noted that some of these actions lacked intersectional alliance, especially when they mobilized discourses of racism and settler colonialism or refused to be accountable to white- and malenormativities within the organizations. For example, as Christina Hanhardt's work shows, while some incarnations of queer street patrols focused on structural critiques of state and police violence, others actually participated in furthering racialized discourses of criminality in ways that fixed manifestations of "homophobia" onto racialized masculinities.[109] But my aim is to emphasize that the radical potential of monstrosity is most profoundly located within practices of intersectional alliance that work to build relationships across queered practices, behaviors, bodies, and identities.

I also mean to extend and build on the analysis offered by Jasbir Puar and Amit Rai on the monstrosities that have been vital to the "war on terror." Through their readings of terrorism studies and media portrayals of the Taliban, Osama bin Laden, and other so-called "militant Islamists," Puar and Rai argued that the United States was in the midst of an "uncanny return of [the] monster" in the early twenty-first century.[110] They read this return in not only the more blatant name-calling of Islamic militants as "monsters," but also within the discipline of terrorism studies that claims to offer "insights" into the terrorist psyche. Throughout this scholarship, the terrorist mind is characterized as exceptionally self-destructive, irrational, violent, and, most notably, a product of failed heterosexuality. Therefore, Puar and Rai demonstrate that post–September 11 U.S. nationalist rhetoric has constructed the terrorist into an amalgamated "monster-terrorist-fag." Puar and Rai show how monstrosity has been a productive method to queerly racialize Islamists and create "docile patriots" in the United States who inadvertently and consciously reproduce the normative and violent disciplining of U.S. heteronormative patriotism and imperialism.

Yes, monstrosity has been one of the mechanisms by which hegemonic discourses have justified profound social violence, but monstrosity is not just a weapon wielded against the gendered, racialized, and colonized Other—it is also a powerful resource for the oppressed. The power for monsters lies in recovering the anxieties that the hegemonic mark of monstrosity is attempting to foreclose. As Puar and Rai argue, the "monster-terrorist-fag is both a product of the anxieties of heteronormative civilization and a marker of the noncivilized—in fact, the anxiety and the monster are born of the same modernity."[111] If monstrosity is a product of anxiety that signals the settler colonial, imperial, and racial project of heteronormativity, how might we exploit these anxieties through a monstrous coalition?

The historical strands of marriage law and U.S. citizenship that I rehearsed earlier in this chapter are teaming with monsters. The settler colonial project marked Natives as outside of civilization through discourses of savagery, working to construct Natives as "monstrously raced and sexed."[112] The antimiscegenation laws, not to mention the widespread practice of lynching, were implemented through the white supremacist mission of marking African American men as sexually monstrous, male beasts that could not be controlled around white women. White women who thwarted expectations of heteropatriarchal reproductive sex within marriage, especially those who had sex for money, were abjected from the norms of U.S. citizenship through discourses of monstrosity. And there are many contemporary monsters among us: the incarcerated, the undocumented, Islamic fundamentalists, people living with HIV and AIDS, people seeking abortions, and Natives refusing the "gifts" of U.S. citizenship and federal recognition. These are just a few of the many types of bodies that are marked through discourses of monstrous difference in the age of U.S. terrorism, global lockdown, settler colonialism, and empire. Each of these forms of monstrosities serves as limit cases—that is, they are the *specters that haunt* normative citizenship.

If same-sex marriage advocacy relies upon notions of acceptability, normality, inclusion, civility, and sameness to heterosexual marriage; if same-sex marriage has increasingly made queers palatable to the mainstream and even conservative public; if same-sex marriage actively requests state-based regulation of intimacy and kinship; and if same-sex marriage has worked to negate the intersectionalities of sexuality with race, class, and Indigeneity, then perhaps the best way to understand marriage advocacy is to see it as an active attempt to eradicate the monstrosities that have been integral to sexual deviancy, Indigeneity, and racialized, gendered difference. Perhaps, beneath all of these longings for acceptance and inclusion lies an active desire to slay that monstrous queer within. And as Jasbir Puar's work on homonationalism demonstrates, one might even see the increasing decoupling of queerness from monstrosity through same-sex marriage advocacy as partly responsible for the increased reliance upon the colonial racialized monstrosity in the United States post–September 11.[113]

I cannot help but hope for an intersectional, queer backlash to the aspirations of same-sex marriage: a counterattack that is resolved to reinhabit and reignite queer monstrosity and its potential alliances to the gendered, racialized, and Indigenous monsters as a means to thwart normative citizenship. Monstrosity is that performative ethic than can link the queerly racialized, gendered, sexualized, colonized Other. This is a call, then, for an accountable coalition of monstrosity that works to link the vulnerable, the displaced, the dejected, and the abjected, not in order to value the devalued, but to forge a protective alliance that nurtures the anxieties of a normative public. As Anonymous Queers point out, "fear is the most powerful motivation,"[114] and nothing is as frightening, and as monstrous, as an intersectional alliance against citizenship.

# CHAPTER 3

# Legal Detours of U.S. Empire

## Locating Race and Indigeneity in Law, History, and Hawai'i

In the summer of 2014, the U.S. Department of Interior (DOI) announced an "Advance Notice of Proposed Rule Making" in which they held a series of public meetings in Hawai'i and across Indian Country. The public meetings were to determine whether they should initiate a process for "reestablishing an official government-to-government relationship with the Native Hawaiian community and if so, what that procedure should be."[1] As DOI representatives continued to clarify throughout these public meetings, the DOI was merely seeking information as to whether they should "open a door" to the process of federally recognizing a Native Hawaiian government, and were offering to "help" the Native Hawaiian community begin such a process. But federal recognition is a particularly vexed operation of U.S. settler colonialism, as the United States offers to "recognize" a limited and contorted level of sovereignty for Native nations as "domestic dependent nations." Federal recognition comes with benefits, including the creation of a political relationship between a tribal nation and the United States, as well as responsibilities across this relationship. But recognition also comes with significant burdens, not the least of which includes the (further) subjection of Indigenous peoples to processes of U.S. racialization. As Joanne Barker observes, "The rub, as it were, for Native peoples is that they are only recognized as Native within the legal terms and social conditions of racialized discourses that serve the national interest of the United States in maintaining colonial and imperial relations with Native peoples."[2]

Across the DOI hearings in Hawai'i, the majority of Kanaka Maoli constituents not only refused to "open the door" for recognition, but slammed it shut on the DOI representatives. Testifier after testifier declined the "offer" of recognition and scolded the DOI and the U.S. government for presuming they had any authority over Hawai'i. Self-identified Kanaka Maoli vehemently declared "'a'ole" or "no" to recognition, and told the DOI to "pack up and go home." Moreover, many testifiers refused the racialization that this recognition entails. Kanaka Maoli argued that they are "not Indians," and that the offer to recognize a "government to government" relationship on the U.S. nation-state's terms was a process of transforming Kanaka Maoli into "tribes" and "Indians."[3] Some of these rejections of "Indianness" were marked in solidarity, that is, with an understanding that Native Americans have been racialized and made into "Indians" through U.S. settler-colonial processes. For instance, as one testifier accurately observed, "even the Indians [are] not Indians."[4] But others deployed rhetoric that not only obscured the potential alliances among Kanaka Maoli and American Indians, but also resolidified the colonial normativity of the U.S. continent. For example, in refusing the DOI's offer, one testifier argued, "This is my ancestral homeland. Not yours. So, the best thing you could do is get up and get out. And take Pocahontas with you."[5] And another conflated tribal identity with the lack of sovereignty by stating, "I say no because we are not Indians. We are not a tribe. We are a nation."[6]

As Jodi Byrd points out, this type of distancing makes sense. It is strategic and accurate to refuse the offer to Indianize Kanaka Maoli, especially when "Indianness" is used to facilitate the spread of U.S. empire. In her foundational text, *Transit of Empire*, Byrd argues that Indianness "becomes a site through which U.S. empire orients and replicates itself by transforming those to be colonized into 'Indians' through continual reiterations of pioneer logics, whether in the Pacific, the Caribbean, or the Middle East." But are there ways to do this work of refusal without, in the process, "reflecting and reinscribing the very colonialist discourses used to possess and contain American Indian nations"?[7] As scholars and activists have shown, alliances are indeed possible, but they require work and an attention to the ways in which U.S. citizenship and U.S. empire rely on anti-intersectionalities, not only across state-produced differences such as race, Indigeneity, gender, and sexuality, but *within* these categories as well. When anticolonial gestures in Hawai'i replicate and reproduce the colonialism of American Indians, it shows the force and power of anti-intersectional logics within categories of identity.

Since this book argues that a politics of alliance requires activisms against U.S. citizenship, this chapter works to flesh out how decolonization and Native self-determination are central to an intersectional alliance against citizenship. While Native and Indigenous Studies scholars and activists have described different models for decolonization, many argue that decolonization requires, at a minimum, the repatriation of land, the reinstatement of Native governance in all of its distinct varieties, and the unsettling of white settler colonialism and its constitutive logics.[8] Decolonization also requires, as Byrd so eloquently describes, the ability to dismantle and deconstruct the "cacophonies" of U.S. multicultural colonialism, whereby the cacophonies are the competing interests, investments, and "interactions of divergently targeted peoples along the transit of empire."[9] This chapter joins Byrd in working to acknowledge the differential placements of settlers, arrivants, and Indigenous peoples within U.S. empire, while also working to configure an intersectional and coalitional decolonial politics against U.S. citizenship.

In this chapter, I follow the lead of Kanaka Maoli scholars and activists that expose the ways in which the U.S. settler state colonizes/occupies Hawai'i through a distinct process of racializing Kanaka Maoli within and through U.S. laws and U.S. settler historiography.[10] Law and historiography, together and separately, have been powerful mechanisms in constructing Kanaka Maoli and their lands as always-already benevolent, hospitable people and spaces. Reading across Hawaiian Studies, I argue that these scholars are, collectively, demonstrating the ways in which the distinct—as in a specific type of Indigenous—racialization of Kanaka Maoli was produced through a comparative racialization project; Kanaka Maoli were and are marked as a biopolitical community in and against their similarities and differences to Native Americans, Asian Americans, and white settlers. In this chapter, I work to unravel only a small part of the story as to how the U.S. colonization/occupation of Hawai'i relies upon and reproduces several discourses of racialization, including U.S. orientalism, Indianness, and whiteness. Along the way, I examine how U.S. law works to disguise and obscure the collective mechanisms of racialization and colonization in Hawai'i through deployments of history that mark them as occurring in separate times and spaces. I argue that in order to dismantle and denaturalize U.S. settler colonialism in Hawai'i, scholars and activists must work against the anti-intersectional histories of racialization and colonization as manifested in law.

One of the most prescient examples of how U.S. law works to historically segregate and refuse the coordinating processes of racialization and colonization is within the U.S. Supreme Court decision, *Rice v. Cayetano* (2000). This case took up the question as to whether the State of Hawai'i could restrict voting for representatives to the Office of Hawaiian Affairs to those defined by the State as "Native Hawaiian." Throughout the case, history is mobilized to confirm the colonialist enterprise of the U.S. nation-state by reproducing citizenship as a progressively inclusive and evolutionary paradigm. Moreover, history is deployed to segregate the processes of racism and colonialism. Importantly, as my analysis demonstrates, in the process of working to dismantle U.S. colonization, some decolonial and antiracist activists, scholars, and their allies have unintentionally replicated this bifurcation of racism and colonialism, thereby inadvertently reproducing anti-intersectional strategies that obscure the co-ordinating operations of racism, U.S. orientalism, and U.S settler colonialism.

Of course, as Noelani Goodyear-Ka'ōpua points out, Kanaka Maoli activists are struggling, like many Indigenous nations, for strategies that can "unsettle settler state authorities, without replicating the violences and exclusions we aim to stop."[11] While the decolonization/deoccupation movement includes an extremely diverse array of perspectives and strategies, collectively they aim to expose and depose the U.S. nation-state as an unlawful occupier and colonizer of Hawai'i.[12] Some Kanaka Maoli activists and organizations, including many leaders within the Office of Hawaiian Affairs, call for federal recognition of a government-to-government status, similar to federally recognized American Indian tribes/nations. Other activists and organizations appeal to intergovernmental organizations (such as the United Nations) and governing bodies (such as the U.S. Department of State) to accept Hawai'i as a completely sovereign nation-state that has been illegally occupied by the United States.[13] Included within and across these different strands of Kanaka Maoli activisms are: legal claims for monetary and land reparations, "illegal" or antistate strategies for reoccupation of land and antieviction activisms, and cultural justice organizing that center Hawaiian epistemologies within education, culture, historiography, and law. And, as seen throughout the DOI hearings that I describe above, a majority of Kanaka Maoli activists showcase a remarkably brave, inspiring, and avowedly nonpractical politics that refuses the offer of federal recognition on the U.S. nation-state's terms. In demonstrating the active, collective, and visionary work of Indigenous self-determination, Kanaka Maoli demand that they, as a diverse and contested community, will decide the terms of governance and futurity beyond U.S. settler colonialism.

It is not a coincidence nor an accident that the Supreme Court case that directly set up civil rights against Indigenous rights involved Hawai'i. As many Kanaka Maoli scholars and activists have pointed out, colonialist discourse on Hawai'i deploys multiculturalism on behalf of settler colonialism, and vice versa. This collusion functions through two framing devices: first, a willful distortion of the Hawaiian concept of "aloha" in order to excuse and explain U.S.

settler colonialism; and second, the mythic representations of Hawai'i as an immigrant and multicultural paradise. The Hawaiian term *aloha* has been violently co-opted throughout the colonization of Hawai'i in order to be twisted into a permanent invitation for settlers and arrivants to come explore and exploit the islands. This co-option has been perpetuated by the State of Hawai'i, the tourist industry, and most of the early scholarship on Hawai'i that reproduces the notion that Hawai'i is the postcolonial playground for U.S. empire. Moreover, as Rona Halualani and Lisa Kahaleole Hall argue, aloha is a central part of the "Hawaiianness at heart" discourse that twists Kanaka Maoli's supposed natural inclinations of generosity and benevolence into an invitation for haoles (white settlers) and migrants to become "Native Hawaiian."[14] Put differently, through the colonialist reframing of aloha, Indigeneity is imagined as one of those many cultural traits that "Native Hawaiians" are more than willing to share.[15] To compound the issue, sociologists, ethnic studies scholars, and tourist discourses offer up Hawai'i as "The Rainbow State" which promises a "true ethnic mosaic" and mixture of peoples and cultures from around the world.[16] These discourses not only buttress U.S. exceptionalism and the continuing erasure of whitenormative U.S. citizenship, but they also transform Hawai'i into the paradigmatic success story of multicultural settler colonization—a land of and for immigrants.

These are the contexts for *Rice v. Cayetano*, one of the most important Supreme Court decisions that served to entrench the colorblindness doctrine against Indigenous people (in this case, Kanaka Maoli) in order to renaturalize colonialnormativity and whitenormativity.[17] In short, *Rice* was the culmination of the efforts of the Campaign for a Color-Blind America Legal Defense and Educational Foundation, which teamed up with a "Caucasian rancher" named Harold "Freddy" Rice to bring a suit against the State of Hawai'i.[18] Their claim alleged that the election protocol for the trustees for the Office of Hawaiian Affairs (OHA) violated the Fourteenth and Fifteenth Amendments of the U.S. Constitution by limiting the eligibility of voters to Native Hawaiians and Hawaiians.[19] The Office of Hawaiian Affairs was formed by a 1978 state constitutional amendment and is responsible for utilizing monetary proceeds from the "ceded" land trusts in order to administer programs for the benefit of Hawaiians and Native Hawaiians, as defined by state statute.[20] Harold Rice argued that the voting schema for OHA trustees was based on racial classifications and, therefore, unconstitutional. The State of Hawai'i and the OHA countered that the voting schema was not racial, but political, and therefore did not violate the Fourteenth or Fifteenth Amendments. The Supreme Court ruled on behalf of Rice. This ruling furthered the Rehnquist Court's use of the "colorblindness doctrine" to equate affirmative action and "entitlement" programs with "racism," and, along the way, disaggregated the collective and mutually constituting mechanisms of colonialism and racism.[21]

Critical race scholars use the *Rice* case to demonstrate the ways in which the discourse of colorblindness in the United States in general, and in U.S. law in particular, serves to encapsulate the U.S. nation-state's regression from civil rights. Hawaiian sovereignty scholars use the case to discuss the possibilities of Hawaiian sovereignty claims, and mark it as a recent incarnation of the U.S. nation-states' racialization and perversion of Kanaka Maoli identity and belonging. And lastly, Native Studies scholars use the case to talk about the precarity of Indigeneity as a political status in U.S. law and are concerned about whether *Rice* marks a turn toward the dismantling of the albeit limited "entitlements" that are linked to Indigenous political statuses.

My goal here is to place these fields of study and their corresponding interventions in conversation, with a focus on how we might achieve an intersectional, antiracist, and decolonial analysis of the *Rice* case. But I also want to offer an intervention into the usefulness (and dangers) of calling for a more historically accurate analysis within U.S. legal mechanisms. Unfortunately, the *Rice* case provides valuable lessons on how historical narratives and legal structures work to replicate the whitenormative, colonialnormative, and anti-intersectional operations of U.S. citizenship. This conundrum raises serious challenges for activists and scholars invested in alliance politics. Therefore, this chapter uses the *Rice* case as an entry point into debates and struggles over race, Indigeneity, and coalitional politics and tactics. Here, I work to understand what types of "queer mergers" might expose the historical and contemporaneous residues of the racialization and U.S. settler colonization/occupation of Hawai'i.

## Dismembering Settler Historiographies and Legalized Colonialisms

In the late twentieth and early twenty-first centuries, Hawaiian Studies has expanded exponentially, and a great deal of the scholarship offers profound revisions to the historiography of Hawai'i and the legal record.[22] In many ways, this scholarship is rooted in and inspired by Kanaka Maoli activisms against U.S. empire. And the cycle continues, as deoccupation and decolonization activists rely upon and utilize this scholarship to build complex, Kanaka-centered histories and theories against U.S. empire.[23] While the following is far from a complete literature overview, my aim here is to explain how this scholarship has greatly informed this chapter and my analysis of the *Rice* case.

Hawaiian Studies scholarship joins American Indian Studies scholarship by exposing the ways in which U.S. legal mechanisms are used in the project of settler colonialism. In *Dismembering Lāhui*, Jonathan Kamakawiwoʻole Osorio details the encroachment of Western law and politics as processes that dismembered social relations, land tenure, economic structures, and governance, which thereby created a space in which white foreigners increasingly and *legally* (according to U.S. law) colonized Hawaiʻi.[24] Sally Engle Merry's work is aligned and demonstrates how U.S. colonial law, especially through legal reformulations of family, sexuality, and community, marked Native Hawaiians and the Nation of Hawaiʻi, as in need of "moral reform" and, hence, U.S. colonization.[25] And while Osorio, Merry, and others focus on how U.S. law was central to nineteenth-century colonial incursions, scholars such as J. Kēhaulani Kauanui have offered meticulous evidence of the ways in which U.S. law has continuously reinforced U.S colonization of Hawaiʻi through the racialization of Kanaka Maoli Indigeneity in various federal and state-level "entitlement" programs, such as the Hawaiian Homes Commission Act of 1921, as well as within U.S. Congressional debates around the statehood of Hawaiʻi.[26] Critically, these scholars also describe the ways in which Kanaka Maoli have reappropriated U.S. legal mechanisms within strategies of resistance.

Kanaka Maoli scholar and activist Haunani-Kay Trask also implicates history—as a discourse and an academic discipline—in the colonization of Hawaiʻi. As she describes throughout her text, settler historians, along with settler anthropologists, produced a static, unified, and simplistic narrative of Hawaiian history, culture, and people that excused the imperialist and colonialist intrusions onto Hawaiian soil (that were also alibied by U.S. law). Not known for mincing words, Trask observes, "historians, I realized, were very much like missionaries. They were part of the colonizing horde. One group colonized the spirit; the other the mind."[27] And Trask is not alone. Other scholars, activists, and writers have also indicted history and historians for participating in the Othering of Kanaka Maoli and the colonization of Hawaiʻi. Elizabeth Buck describes how settler historiography has served as a tourist spectacle based on "Western assumptions as to what constitutes social progress and morality."[28] Merry, foreshadowing the historiography used in the *Rice* decision perfectly, describes the historical narratives on the colonization of Hawaiʻi as a story "of gradualism and invitation. . . . There was no apparent violence, confrontation, or resistance, only easy accommodation."[29] It has been as critical, then, that Hawaiian Studies has diffused what Noenoe K. Silva describes as the "cultural bomb" of colonial historiography, particularly by relying on the very rich archive of Ōlelo Hawaiʻi (Hawaiian language) documents, media, chants, and Kanaka Maoli–centered moʻolelo.[30] Silva's brilliant archival work, for example, rediscovered the extensive Kanaka Maoli opposition to U.S. annexation in which over 95 percent of the Native population in Hawai'i signed antiannexation petitions in an organized (and women-led) movement against U.S. empire.[31] And as Goodyear-Ka'ōpua points out, the rediscovery of these petitions served as another spark that has reignited the decolonization/deoccupation movements in Hawai'i.[32]

The history of Hawai'i is a hotly contested one, and the political stakes are high. While there are certainly similarities, the various strands of the decolonization/deoccupation movement rely upon and utilize "substantially disparate histories" in order to serve their own needs.[33] These are purposeful and willful negotiations with history and law, negotiations that are as risky as they are strategic and hopeful. Native theologian, lawyer, and scholar Vine Deloria Jr. once warned about the dangers of the ways in which history and law, when combined, were formidable mechanisms for perpetuating U.S colonialism. As he explained, "It is no mistake . . . that the most distressing [legal] cases in Indian affairs today are those cases in which history has become a determining factor."[34] The reason, he pointed out, is that these cases place the history of U.S. colonization "on trial," and force the United States settler populace to come face to face with their past and ongoing violence and privilege. It is clear that Kanaka Maoli scholars and activists are more than aware of this struggle. "Something is remarkably optimistic," Osorio observes, "about the ways in which small, patriotic Native groups vulnerable to many things, including hopelessness, grasp the mechanics of law and the potions of history and contend with one another for shaping the national spirit. We have certainly changed in many ways, but in our rapt absorption with, and our refusal to concede, either law or history to anyone, we demonstrate how very like our nineteenth-century ancestors we are."[35] These are the challenges that are brought to bear, and collide into view, in the *Rice v. Cayetano* decision.

## The Violence of History: Historical Emplotments in *Rice vs. Cayetano*

History is evoked in the *Rice v. Cayetano* case at multiple levels. The Supreme Court's majority and dissenting opinions, as well as the briefs for both sides of the case, begin by telling different histories of Hawai'i, each claiming that their versions provide the proper historical context for the case. Justice Kennedy, writing for the majority, reminds us that while history is central to understanding the case, his role is limited to simple recantation. "Historians and other scholars who write on Hawai'i," he writes, "will have a different purpose and more latitude than we do. . . . Our limited role, in the posture of this particular case, is to recount events as understood by the lawmakers, thus ensuring that we accord proper appreciation to their purposes in adopting the policies and laws at issue."[36] But the dissenting opinion, penned by Justice Stevens, directly admonishes Justice Kennedy for telling the *wrong* history, which results in the wrong conclusions. In Justice Stevens's view, "The Court's holding today rests largely on the repetition of glittering generalities that have little, if any, application to the compelling history of the State of Hawaii."[37] And while I focus primarily on the legal briefs and court decisions, most of the scholarship on this case follows similar trajectories in offering history lessons on Hawai'i, history lessons that are then used to explain their conclusions regarding the case. This reoccurring theme—that is, the need to (re)tell the "proper" history of Hawai'i—is informative of the uses of history in law, and, in particular, the uses of history to displace coloniality from structures of racism, and vice versa.

While there are numerous historical accounts available to legal actors and scholars, there are really only three historical narratives, or what Hayden White calls "historical emplotments," circulating in and around the *Rice* case.[38] These narratives reflect what I would loosely refer to as the conservative, liberal, and counter-hegemonic analyses of the U.S. nation-state's relationship to Hawai'i. My goal in this first half of the chapter is to provide an overview of these historical narratives, with an emphasis on their discursive structure—that is, which moments and events count as "history" and the language used to describe these moments.[39] Methodologically speaking, I use what I call a "ventriloquist" writing method here in order to showcase how competing and conflicting historical narratives work—differently—to stitch settler colonialist versions of Hawai'i into whitenormative narratives of U.S. citizenship. To be clear, the following narratives are not being read for their correctness, completeness, or historical accuracy. Perhaps, after reviewing the three different, though related, accounts, one can glimpse a part of the nuanced landscape that is Hawaiian history, but I also hope interested readers will look into the increasingly expansive decolonial historiography and mo'olelo on Hawai'i.[40]

As I demonstrate, the court opinions and legal briefs tell competing narratives of the history of Hawai'i that serve to either acknowledge or deny the story of U.S. colonialism. Importantly, these historical narratives take place separately from discussions on the "legal" issue of the case, which is the question as to the appropriateness of racial categories in law. The critical point here is that this "legal" matter also requires competing narratives of the historical trajectory of "race" in law. In the process, colonialism and racism are given different histories and, thus, recognized as distinct processes in time and place, and, therefore, as anti-intersectional issues.

## COLORBLIND COLONIALISM

I want to spend a bit more time recounting the historical narrative (re)pro-
duced in Justice Kennedy's majority opinion, not only because it reflects the
reoccurring colonialist script on Hawai'i, but also because, according to legal
registers, this account holds weight as the story that mattered most.[41] As described above, Kennedy sees himself as a transcriber rather than a producer of
history, and even suggests that his account comes from history texts that the
"litigants seem to agree" upon, namely Lawrence Fuchs's *Hawaii Pono: An Ethnic
and Political History*, published in 1961, and Ralph Kuykendall's *Hawaiian Kingdom*,
a three-part volume that was published, respectively, in 1938, 1953, and 1967.
Two quick points need to be made in regard to Kennedy's sources. First, due to
his inconsistent citational method, it is not clear whether he is relying on former
legal documents or the text of Fuchs and Kuykendall for his historical account.
Second, Fuchs and Kuykendall have been widely criticized for their colonialist
historiographies of Hawai'i. This is, perhaps, another reminder that history is
contested and that how we traverse history and historiography are political acts.

The majority opinion's historical narrative is a very familiar narrative indeed; it relies heavily on key colonialist tropes such as empty lands, naive and
uncivilized Indigenous folks, brave Western explorers, and benevolent missionaries. According to Kennedy, historical progress—which is distinguished
by markers of capitalism, Christianity, and liberal democracy—swept over the
unsuspecting, and at times, grateful, Native Hawaiian population. Importantly,
according to this narrative, capitalism, democracy, and even the Christianizing
mission occur without processes of racial differentiation, racism, or even ill will.
This narrative functions, then, to reframe colonialism; rather than a project that
is predicated upon producing, locating, and classifying racialized differences
(as well as gender and sexual differences that are mapped onto these racial
categories), colonialism is reframed as a colorblind endeavor. In this narrative
of colorblind colonialism, colonialism is merely the natural route of Western
progress and evolution, and is thereby divorced from its racist motivational past
as well as its present.

The tale begins with the story of vacant lands and inevitable arrival, as the
"first" Hawaiian people are "Polynesian explorers" who settled on the islands.[42]
These migratory explorers then become immobile and static Native Hawaiians
until Captain Cook's arrival in 1778. While most stories detail the horror that
goes hand-in-hand with Cook's arrival, such as myriad devastating diseases and
degradations, Kennedy describes the process in much more egalitarian terms,
such as "reciprocity" and "amalgamation." There are no power differentials in
his narrative, just equal exchanges among easily definable groups. For example,

as Kennedy explains, Hawai'i is "a story of increasing involvement of westerners in the economic and political affairs of the kingdom,"[43] whereby "involvement" suggests welcome or needed "contributions" from well-intentioned Westerners. Moreover, in a revealing use of passive voice, Kennedy notes that "Their [Westerners'] intermarriage with the inhabitants of Hawaii was not infrequent."[44]

Again, Kennedy's narrative relies upon the progressive and natural evolution and eventuality of capitalism and American empire. In this story, colonialism occurs without intention (similar to his own historical narrative). Although Kennedy explicitly acknowledges that land and property are inherently volatile topics in Hawai'i, he reminds the reader that he is merely a neutral transcriber: "The status of Hawaiian lands has presented issues of complexity and controversy from at least the rule of Kamehameha I to the present day. We do not attempt to interpret that history, lest our comments be thought to bear upon the issues not before us."[45] But then Kennedy proceeds to describe a series of events in which the so-called "feudal" land system was transformed into private property and foreigners were granted the legal right to own land. While many historians have argued that the privatization of land in Hawai'i stemmed from a far more complex negotiation among the monarch, ali'i, and Western advisers, Kennedy's narrative locates the agency (and, therefore, responsibility) of these life- and nation-altering transformations on the shoulders of Hawaiian monarchs alone.

Once Kennedy arrives in the 1890s, we start to hear a few rumblings about power, military occupations, and control, but the terms Kennedy employs are telling. For example, Kennedy describes this period as a time when Queen Lili'uokalani was in power, the Hawaiian government was "uncontrolled," and the situation was "tense" between "an anti-Western pro-native bloc in the government on the one hand and Western business interests and property owners on the other."[46] According to this narrative, Queen Lili'uokalani is an impotent leader, and her lack of political savvy sets the stage for the U.S. takeover. While Harold Rice's legal brief argues that the "monarch abdicated and was replaced by a provisional government," Kennedy describes a "power struggle" in which the victors just happen to be American businessmen (the self-proclaimed "Committee of Safety"), who have some assistance from a U.S. minister and "a small force of Marines."[47] Again, Kennedy's deployment of value-free terminology is noteworthy. According to Kennedy, "tensions intensified" and later "peaked" in 1893, when the Committee of Safety acted "in response to an attempt by the then Hawaiian monarch, Queen Lili'uokalani, to promulgate a new constitution restoring monarchical control over the House of Nobles and limiting the franchise to Hawaiian subjects."[48] In "response" to this supposedly ineffective Hawaiian monarch's attempt to enforce control over her kingdom, the Committee of Safety, the U.S. Minister to Hawai'i John Stevens, and the U.S. armed forces "replaced the monarchy with a provisional government" and then "sought annexation by the United States."[49]

Despite President Cleveland's public "denounce[ment of] the role of American forces," the United States moves into the formal position as colonial occupier without much ado. In Kennedy's words, "The Queen could not resume her former place, however, and in 1894 the provisional government established the Republic of Hawaii."[50] The Republic is annexed a few years later in the 1898 Newlands Resolution, signed by President McKinley. In the annexation process, lands were "ceded" to the United States and a provision was passed that revenues from public lands were to "be used solely for the benefit of the inhabitants of the Hawaiian Islands for educational and other public purposes."[51] Annexation, like Westernization and U.S. expansion, is simply part of the evolutionary process that just so happens to take place on the body of Hawai'i.

While this marks the end of the first part of Kennedy's historical narrative, his next section is dedicated to providing the context for the Office of Hawaiian Affairs (OHA). Kennedy's history lesson skips from annexation to the Hawaiian Homes Commission Act (1921) twenty-three years later. Skipping over the formal settler colonization of Hawai'i, we find that the U.S Congress is "concerned with the condition of the native Hawaiian people" and enacts the HHCA to "rehabilitate the Native Hawaiian population."[52] The 1921 Act set aside 200,000 acres of the "ceded" public lands and instituted a home loan and lease program. Importantly, in the process it also codified racial definitions of Hawaiians, in which the U.S. colonial empire defined a "Native Hawaiian" as "any descendant of not less than one-half part of the blood of the races inhabiting the Hawaiian Islands previous to 1778." Critically, the U.S. nation-state demonstrates its "concern" by simultaneously racializing and infantilizing Native Hawaiians. The next event is statehood via the Admissions Act (1959), which is only notable because the federal government transfers 200,000 acres of "ceded" lands, as well as an additional 1.2 million acres of land, to the State of Hawai'i. According to the Admissions Act, these lands are to be held as a "public trust," that can be used for only five purposes, including the "betterment of the conditions of Native Hawaiians."[53]

We have finally arrived at the moment in which the Office of Hawaiian Affairs (OHA) was established through a 1978 state constitutional amendment. As Kennedy quotes from the proceedings, convention members hoped that the OHA would "provide Hawaiians the right to determine the priorities which will effectuate the betterment of their condition and welfare and promote the protection and preservation of the Hawaiian race, and that it will unite Hawaiians as a people."[54] The OHA is figured as a goodwill restorative gesture initiated by the State of Hawai'i to "protect" and "preserve" Hawaiians, who are already being reimagined as an antiquated "race" that are, as settler colonialism requires, increasingly extinct in a modernized world. Structurally, the OHA is overseen by nine trustees, members of which "shall be Hawaiians" and "shall be elected by qualified voters who are Hawaiians, as provided by law."

In order to distinguish who are the benefactors and administrators of the OHA, the U.S. legal regime returns to the issue of how to define (as in produce) Hawaiians as a racial group. Again, this process (taken up in 1978) links the identity of beneficiaries with dependency and expresses the goodwill of the state through the power to define race:

> "Hawaiian" means any descendent of the aboriginal peoples inhabiting the Hawaiian Islands which exercised sovereignty and subsisted in the Hawaiian Islands in 1778, and which peoples thereafter have continued to reside in Hawaii.
> "Native Hawaiian" means any descendent of not less than one-half part of the races inhabiting the Hawaiian Islands previous to 1778, as defined by the Hawaiian Homes Commission Act, 1920, as amended; provided that the term identically refers to the descendants of such blood quantum of such aboriginal peoples which exercised sovereignty and subsisted in the Hawaiian Islands in 1778 and which peoples thereafter continued to reside in Hawaii.[55]

Directly after reproducing these definitions in the text, Kennedy jumps into the details of the case. He does not offer any analysis of the racial definitions, and I leave the implications of these definitions for later in the chapter. For now, I want to emphasize the way in which he ends his history lesson on Hawai'i with regurgitations of U.S. settler laws and their racial definitions. We have finally ended up where, according to Kennedy, Freddy Rice enters the story and Hawaiian "history" ends. The end of history is marked by Hawaiians' full immersion as a racial group defined by and for the state. And yet, the demarcation of Hawaiians as an undeveloped yet definable and classifiable racial group under a paternalist state obscures how the *Rice* case hinges upon these very same racial definitions.

In Kennedy's historical narrative, Westernization and U.S. settler colonialism simply come to pass through benign and neutral events. History happens, Westerners move westward, and Hawaiians get caught underfoot in the march of progress. According to this narrative, the colonialist usurpation of Hawai'i happens through a series of legal maneuvers that work to give U.S. colonialism the cover of law. There are no power differentials here, just a battle between two opposing ways of life, one of which would naturally and inevitably be deemed the victor. Consider the majority opinion's final commentary on the case:

When the culture and way of life of a people are all but engulfed by a history beyond their control, their sense of loss may extend down through generations; and their dismay may be shared by many members of the larger community. As the State of Hawaii attempts to address these realities, it must, as always, seek the political consensus that begins with a sense of shared purpose. One of the necessary beginning points is this principle: The Constitution of the United States, too, has become the heritage of all the citizens of Hawaii.[56]

As far as the Supreme Court majority is concerned, U.S. settler colonialism is not purposeful, willful, nor violent. It is a colonialism without intention and without discrimination; in other words, it is a colorblind colonialism. This colorblind colonialism is a central element of manifest destiny and the divine sanctioning of naturalized and nonviolent expansion of U.S. empire.[57] And when law is constricted to the history of colorblind colonialism, Harold Rice's claim is the only claim that makes any sense at all.

## APOLOGETIC LIBERALISM (AKA U.S. SETTLER MULTICULTURALISM)

The most prevalent historical narrative found throughout the discussions of the *Rice* case is one I refer to as apologetic liberalism, which allows for some sort of willful colonialism, but a colonialism that is circumscribed to the past and assuaged in the multicultural present and future. This narrative is echoed in Justice Stevens's dissenting opinion, the State of Hawai'i defense, numerous amicus briefs, the Apology Resolution of 1993, and the majority of the legal scholarship on the case.[58] Throughout this narrative, the United States is more directly identified as colonialist, but at the same time this colonialism is reconfigured as a "mistake" that is written in history, at a time when the United States did not know any better. Within this discourse, Native Hawaiians are given somewhat more agency; unlike Kennedy's narrative, history does not just happen to roll over Native Hawaiians. However, the liberal narrative is invested in imagining Native Hawaiians as well-meaning and good-natured Natives that were taken advantage of by a *few* not-so-well-intentioned Westerners. This narrative provides a few functions, not the least of which is to figure white settler guilt and responsibility as residual artifacts of the past and to turn to the potential of law and multicultural liberal democracy as a means for redemption. I weave together various sources—the Apology Resolution, Justice Stevens's dissent, and the State of Hawai'i's brief—in order to show how apologetic liberalism functions. As shown here, apologetic liberalism claims that the settler colonialism of Hawai'i was established through individualized and skillful trickery. In order to resolve these egregious mistakes, the U.S. nation-state must offer a few nonbinding apologies, as well as make good on its promise of multicultural recognition of "Native Hawaiians."

In 1993, President Clinton signed a joint resolution that is most commonly called the U.S. Apology Resolution. The title of the law is telling, as is the stated objective, which is, "To acknowledge the 100th anniversary of the January 17, 1893 overthrow of the Kingdom of Hawaii, and to offer an apology to Native Hawaiians on behalf of the United States for the overthrow of the Kingdom of Hawaii."[59] The resolution consists of a series of "declarations" that reflect and produce a history of Hawai'i. The Apology Resolution enshrines history, not only by being imprinted into law, but also due to the style of the document with over forty decrees. The resolution begins, for example, with the following pronouncement:

> *Whereas*, prior to the arrival of the first Europeans in 1778, the Native Hawaiian people lived in a highly organized, self-sufficient, subsistent social system based on communal land tenure with a sophisticated language, culture, and religion.[60]

I will return to this narrative in a moment, but for now I want to point out a few more issues relating to the resolution. First, the Apology Resolution has become a central part of apologetic liberalism—that is, the U.S. Apology Resolution is a moment in which the colonialist history of Hawai'i is at least acknowledged as an "illegal overthrow."[61] It is important to note that the majority decision as penned by Justice Kennedy, as well as other conservative historical narratives, completely neglect to mention the resolution altogether. Moreover, this resolution has become a key tool in Kanaka Maoli decolonization efforts against both the State of Hawai'i and the U.S. nation-state as a whole.[62] My goal in deconstructing the Apology Resolution is not to contest any of these decolonization efforts, but, rather, to describe how the structure, language, and emphasis of the document itself coincides with other liberal historical narratives that reproduce multicultural liberal teology of Hawai'i.

As mentioned above, the apologetic liberalist historical narrative of Hawai'i begins with an acknowledgment and recognition of Hawaiian systems and organizations—a recognition that works to relate Hawaiian systems to a Western litmus test of a "civilization." Moreover, this narrative argues that while the islands were divided into different kingdoms, "they had a uniform culture, language and religion."[63] It is here that we see the liberal multicultural impulse to "respect"—and *typify*—groups and communities as unified monocultures. King Kamehameha I plays a significant role in this historical narrative, since he was the King who "unified the islands"[64] around 1810 "with the assistance of western advisors and weaponry."[65] The description of Hawai'i as a unified kingdom sets the stage for the next historical "fact" of recognition, which is that the U.S. nation-state recognized Hawai'i as an independent nation. The point here is that the apologetic liberalist narrative routinely deploys the framework of "recognition" not only because of liberal claims to recognize and respect "difference," but also to showcase the recognizable components of liberal nationhood.

In turning to the turbulent series of events in the 1890s, the liberal narrative is much more willing to use negative evaluative terms, especially regarding U.S. actions. It names, for example, the 1893 event as an "illegal overthrow" of the Hawaiian monarchy. Moreover, this narrative fleshes out some of the central characters in this overthrow, such as U.S. Minister John Stevens who conspired with American businessmen and the Committee of Safety in order to mislead the U.S. government. In this narrative, a few mischievous men fool Hawaiian and American leaders alike. Importantly, these nations and their leaders join together—momentarily—to deal with the situation; in response to Queen Lili'uokalani's request, President Cleveland sent Congressman James Blount to Hawai'i to investigate the events. According to the Blount Report, the Hawaiian nation experienced nothing less than a military coup. Therefore, President Cleveland demands that the monarchy be restored while simultaneously declaring that Stevens and the Committee of Safety committed an unsanctioned "act of war."[66]

While this historical narrative acknowledges these events as "illegal" acts of aggression, the story places accountability on a few men rather than the U.S. nation-state as a whole. Here, a democratic political system and U.S. legal mechanisms are not flawed in and of themselves, even though individual acts of corruption can lead to tyranny if left unchecked. In fact, the Apology Resolution offers detailed information as to how President Cleveland, the Blount Report, and various congressional hearings all acknowledged that the Republic of Hawaii (i.e., the U.S.-led government put in power through the military coup) was an illegal occupier. And yet, according to this story, history required the legal sanctioning of the illegal occupier's actions. As the resolution states, "as a consequence of the Spanish-American War" President McKinley signed the Newlands Resolution which sanctioned the formal colonial annexation of Hawai'i. Therefore, even the various good-willed intentions and mechanisms of U.S. governance cannot stop the evolution of U.S. empire.

As the State of Hawai'i's legal brief points out, the Apology Resolution is actually the second formal liberal apology to Native Hawaiians. According to the brief, "President Cleveland refused to recognize the new Republic, and denounced—as did Congress a century later—the role of United States agents in overthrowing the monarchy, which the President likened to an 'act of war, committed without authority of Congress,' and called [the overthrow] a 'substantial wrong.'"[67] The point that must be emphasized here is that the Apology Resolution marks the 100-year anniversary of the coup and President Cleveland's apology, rather than the series of events that transformed this "illegal act" into the legally sanctioned colonization/occupation of Hawai'i.[68]

Apologies from well-intentioned white men are followed by more good intentions as the narrative maneuvers quickly from the Hawaiian Homes Commission Act (HHCA) of 1921 to the formation of the Office of Hawaiian Affairs (OHA) in 1978. What makes the HHCA significant is that it initiates and illustrates a multicultural and benevolent Congressional investment in "rehabilitating the native people and culture," an investment that explains the OHA.[69] These good intentions also provide cover for the expedient processes of settler colonialism in which statehood (the 1959 Admissions Act) is merely a legal transfer of land trusts rather than an especially violent operation of denigrating Hawaiian sovereignty. The good intentions also explain the connections between the HHCA and the OHA, as the OHA can continue the settler project as the administrator and arm of the state to ensure "the betterment of the conditions of native Hawaiians."[70]

The rhetoric of rehabilitation, betterment, and benevolence are actually opportunities to establish a guardian-ward, or trust relationship, between the U.S. and Native Hawaiians. One of the central objectives of the apologetic liberal historical narrative is to prove that there is such a trust relationship, a trust that was transferred to the State of Hawai'i and, eventually, the OHA as well. The historical account stops here in order to emphasize this point: the liberal nation-state is responsible for carrying through this trust relationship, a relationship that mirrors the so-called trust relationship between Native Americans and the U.S. government. Justice Stevens is, in fact, dismayed that Kennedy's majority decision neglects this relationship:

> While splendidly acknowledging this history—specifically including the series of agreements and enactments the history reveals—the majority fails to recognize its import. The descendants of the native Hawaiians share with the descendants of the Native Americans on the mainland or in the Aleutian Islands not only a history of subjugation at the hands of colonial forces, but also a purposefully created and specialized "guardian-ward" relationship with the Government of the United States.[71]

And yet, it is here that we can also see the ways in which the discourses of "trust" and "guardian-ward" relationships between the United States and Indigenous people in the early twentieth century actually forecast the rhetoric and operations of U.S. multiculturalism. Trust relationships operate through hierarchical designations of parental settler-states and childlike Indigenous peoples. Within trust relationships and multiculturalisms, settler states grant themselves the power to name, locate, and set the terms of "difference," as well as mark what types of Indigenous authenticity they really have to "respect."[72]

While Stevens's dissent acknowledges and references colonial power (what he calls "subjugation"), he makes sure to describe these operations in the past tense. Stevens argues that there is "compelling similarity . . . between the *once subjugated* indigenous peoples of the continental United States and the peoples of the Hawaiian Islands whose *historical sufferings* and status parallel those of continental Native Americans" (emphasis added).[73] This narrative evokes a sense of culpability, but only for past wrongs as opposed to present-day infringements on sovereignty, rights, and status. More importantly, this narrative has proceeded to tell a history of the colonization of Hawai'i as a process that is led by greedy individualism and unchecked illiberal governance, rather than liberal nation-state investments in strategic geopolitical positioning and resource extraction.

Apologetic liberalism offers reparations in the form of formal and nonbinding apologies, as well as promises to make good on the so-called trust relationships between Indigenous Hawaiians and the United States government. According to this narrative, citizenship and law can and must live up to these promises in order to rectify not just the wrong done to Native Hawaiians, but to salve the blemishes on the face of the U.S. liberal state. But it is important to notice one of the most important similarities between colorblind colonialism and apologetic liberalism, which is the refusal to acknowledge how racism and racialization of Native Hawaiians have been central to the myriad projects of settler colonialism, including, if not especially, the pre-multiculturalist discourse of rehabilitating impoverished Natives. Put differently, according to apologetic liberalism, the settler colonial project of racializing Native Hawaiians is done in their best interests and provides an alibi and futurity for the settler state to continue to strive toward fulfilling its promise of managing the vestiges of Indigeneity.

## COUNTER-NARRATIVES AND THE LIMITS OF STRUCTURE

Resistance is not futile, but it is challenging, particularly within the contexts of U.S. law and colonial historiography. As described above, Native activists and scholars debate about the usefulness of turning to U.S. legal mechanisms, and the various contortions that are required in order to "make sense" within colonial structures. But these contortions are even more painful when it comes to the legal deployments of history. As Diane Kirby and Catharine Coleborne describe, "'law' and 'history' are culturally specific ways of knowing and ordering experience, inherently implicated in relations of power."[74] While the primary texts of the *Rice* case reflect the more expected narratives of U.S. settler history and law, there were a series of amicus briefs that demonstrated a contested and alternative framing of Hawaiian history, and began to expose the relationships among racialization, political recognition, and Indigeneity.[75] While these counter-histories also claim to be offering the "proper" historical contexts for the case, these histories are quite distinct from the apologetic and colorblind narratives described earlier. These counter-histories describe at least *some* of the history of Native Hawaiian resistance, and work to lay the foundations for decolonization platforms.

These counter-histories also reflect the constraints of the case and state-focused activisms. As a reminder, the respondent here is not Kanaka Maoli activisms writ large; rather, it is the State of Hawai'i. Therefore, legal experts and organizations that filed amicus briefs on behalf of the state were either invested in or required to support the State of Hawai'i's institutionalization of Hawaiian "entitlement" programs.[76] There are numerous branches of Kanaka Maoli activisms that are not interested in furthering U.S. state-level colonization/occupation of Hawaiian lands and the various programs that oversee these processes. The counter-history that is offered in regards to *Rice*, then, is a very limited story of Kanaka Maoli activisms, Indigenous solidarities, and the politics of recognition in Hawai'i. But these narratives do critical work by marking the politics of language and translation, the histories of U.S. colonization, and a few of the many examples of Kanaka Maoli resistance.

In terms of language and translation, the brief from the State Council of Hawaiian Homestead Association outwardly critiques the use of colonial tropes by placing common colonizing terms within the appropriate quotation marks in order to emphasize the politics of representation. Note, for example, the brief's description of the colonial event:

> Captain James Cook's 1778 "encounter" with Hawai'i and with Hawaiians produced social consequences no less profound than Christopher Colombus's trans-Atlantic crossing did for the native peoples of North America. . . . As with the "Indians" of North America, death rates for Hawaiians rose precipitously after contact due to their vulnerability to common European diseases and other maladies of "civilization."[77]

Moreover, these counter-narratives are invested in producing as well as representing Kanaka Maoli knowledge, belief systems, and cultural representations. For example, many of the briefs deploy Hawaiian terminology throughout, working to encourage readers to understand that the history of Hawai'i is not wholly transparent. Collectively, these briefs are inconsistent as to when they offer possible English translations of the Hawaiian terms and when they do not, thereby reminding readers that comprehension and translation are, at best, partial and inconsistent.

These narratives also refuse colonial "precontact" tropes in which Indigenous structures are depicted as simple political, social, and spiritual systems, especially as compared to always-already complex Western systems. The Kamehameha Schools Bishop Estate brief, in particular, stands out by offering detailed descriptions of Kanaka Maoli agricultural and fishing practices, skilled artisans, complex religious traditions, and diverse political interests. In an example of the empire writing back, the brief points out, "Hawai'i was not Utopia. There were wars between the island chiefs and among other ali'i. Natural disasters, such as tidal waves and volcanic eruptions, often killed or displaced whole villages. But Hawai'i's social, economic, and political system was highly developed and evolving, and its population, conservatively estimated to be at least 300,000, was relatively stable before the arrival of the first westerners."[78]

These kind of counter-histories are exceptional for their detailed explications of historical transformations and events, particularly those that are notably absent from both the colorblind and apologist narratives. For example, they vigilantly describe the transformation of the communal land systems in Hawai'i. As they explain, "the land tenure system was communal and subsistence-based," until the Māhele land reform in 1848, which "effectively ended Hawai'i's ancient communal land tenure system, and gave Westerners a way to acquire fee simple ownership of Hawaiian lands."[79] Moreover, these counter-histories connect land dispossession of Kanaka Maoli to the land dispossessions of other Indigenous communities. As they state, "the Mahele opened the way to the same massive loss of native land that occurred among Indians in North America. There was also a devastating loss of population as Hawaiians, like other aboriginal peoples, succumbed in great numbers to small pox and childhood diseases."[80]

These accounts emphasize another gaping omission in the other narratives: the Bayonet Constitution of 1887. The name suggests the political importance of this moment, as well as a reminder that "legal" transformations often occur through force, violence, and other *illegal* means. The Bayonet Constitution dramatically transformed the kingdom's government structure and decreased the monarchy's power, but more notably it extended the franchise to non-Hawaiians and enforced a property requirement for voting rights. The result was that the vote was given to American and European landowners at the expense of the majority of non-landowning Kanaka Maoli. As these counter-histories emphasize, the Bayonet Constitution provided the backdrop for the sequence of events leading up to the illegal overthrow of the Hawaiian government in the 1890s.

While some of these counter-narratives offer detailed information about the slow creep of U.S. colonialism in Hawai'i, the Kamehameha Schools brief offers critical information as to how U.S. government agencies sanctioned the imperialism and colonization of Hawai'i. This is not, then, a story of a few bad apples, but, rather, a coordinated effort between "Americans living in Hawai'i" and the United States government. The Kamehameha Schools brief describes the series of governmental actions that sanctioned the colonial occupation of Hawai'i, including the Tyler Doctrine (1840s extension of the Monroe Doctrine to Hawai'i), the Reciprocity Treaty of 1875 (limiting trade to the United States), the U.S. Marine suppression of Native resistance after the Bayonet Constitution, and the various ways leading officials in the U.S. government (such as the Secretary of the Navy, as well as the U.S. Minister to Hawai'i) coordinated with American annexationists in the provisional government. Moreover, this brief describes the ways in which Presidents Harrison and McKinley both participated in the colonization/occupation of Hawai'i.[81]

As a whole, these briefs offer many more specifics about the process of annexation, and emphasize how it was a critical part of the settler colonial project. One of the many important interventions they make is to contextualize the annexation of Hawai'i within geopolitical contexts of U.S. empire. For example, as the Kamehameha Schools brief notes, even though proannexation leaders in the U.S. Congress could not obtain the necessary two-thirds Senate majority, "The balance was tipped at this moment by the United States' entry into the Spanish-American War. American troops were fighting in the Pacific, particularly the Philippines, and the United States needed to be sure of a Pacific base."[82] There is, of course, another side to the story of annexation, specifically Kanaka Maoli opposition. As the State Council of Hawaiian Homestead Association's brief states, "There was never any plebiscite of the Hawaiian people on the question of annexation, and contemporary observers were convinced that if there had been a popular vote, it would have been overwhelmingly against annexation."[83] Unfortunately, when the briefs include details about the massive activisms against annexation, these details are relegated to a footnote.

The choice as to what to put in the body of the text and what to relegate to a footnote is difficult, particularly due to the limitations of U.S. legal structures. Unfortunately, some of the most powerful instances of Kanaka Maoli resistance are hidden in the footnotes of the briefs. In another example, the State Council of Hawaiian Homestead Associations' brief consigns one of the most important Hawaiian songs of resistance to a footnote:

> After the overthrow, the Queen's Royal Hawaiian Band was ordered by the new government to sign a loyalty oath. Band members were "threatened with dismissal, and told that they would soon be eating rocks (since they would have no money to buy food)." The Band members refused to sign the oath, and told their story to a local songwriter who then composed a famous protest song entitled *Kaulana Nā Pua* (Famous are the Children), also known as *Mele ʻAi Pōhaku* (the Stone-Eating Song). The lyrics repeated the Band members' resolve that they would rather eat stones than give up their land. *Ua lawa mākou i ka pōhaku, I ka ʻai kamahaʻo o ka ʻāina.* The song's sweet melody belies the bitterness of its lyrics. This song is still sung today, in remembrance of the love that Hawaiians have for their land.[84]

The footnote showcases one of the many powerful examples of Kanaka Maoli resistance. In fact, embodied sovereignty is one of the central features of Hawaiʻi. Therefore, the Mele ʻAi Pōhaku does not belong in a footnote; rather, it should be one of the main arguments of the brief itself.

The various trajectories of annexation provide the setting for the Hawaiian Homes Commission Act in 1921 and the land trust program by the U.S. federal government, earmarked for Native Hawaiian homesteading. However, while many of the counter-narratives critique the colonial "rehabilitation" tale, some of the briefs actually reproduce colonial epistemic violence by describing Kanaka Maoli as childlike, uneducated, and crippled with inferiority complexes. For example, the Kamehameha Schools brief describes Kanaka Maoli as "not extremely sophisticated in governmental matters," as having "a debilitating sense of inferiority," and that they "were bitter about the loss of their lands to foreigners."[85] These moments, juxtaposed against the marginalization of resistance, work to undermine the histories of Indigenous agency and endurance, and open painful wounds within the counter-histories.

There are, importantly, a few moments in which they expose the combined processes of racialization and colonization, but they are rare. For example, the OHA et al. amicus brief is the only legal brief to discuss congressional negotiations over the racial category "Native Hawaiian." According to the brief, the original HHCA did not include any racialized restrictions (i.e., "blood quantum") until (haole) plantation owners pushed for narrower restrictions on who could qualify for land allotments. With a smaller number of "qualified" Native Hawaiians, the State of Hawaiʻi could lease more land to the plantations. The brief points out, then, that the racialization of Native Hawaiians was in the service of the haole plantation elite. However, they also somehow end up describing the final law as a "compromise bill" in that the racial definition of "Native Hawaiian" was not as narrow as the plantation elite requested.[86]

Thus far, I have tried to describe how some of the amicus briefs offered counter-histories that highlight Kanaka Maoli agency and resistance, as well as expose the U.S. nation-state and government as liable for the colonization/occupation of Hawai'i. There is, however, an additional discursive narrative throughout these briefs that attempts to position Kanaka Maoli as like-Indians enough to protect Hawaiian entitlements. These narratives aim to make Native Hawaiians intelligible to law via demarcating their similarity to Native Americans, who are themselves marked and made intelligible to U.S. legal systems through subjectification as "Indians" and as "tribes."[87] While many of the parallels between Native Americans and Native Hawaiians are quite profound given the colonialist and imperialist endeavors of European and American governments, there is a much more strategic maneuver at work here. At one level, these briefs demonstrate possibilities for Indigenous alliance. But at another level, they analogize Kanaka Maoli to Native Americans in ways that evacuate their specificities.

The National Congress of American Indians (NCAI) brief is the most explicit example of alliance politics, and they choose their terms carefully. They never describe Kanaka Maoli as Native Americans; rather, they describe them as part of many peoples that have been mistakenly referred to (thanks to Christopher Columbus) as "los Indios."[88] Moreover, they offer numerous examples in which U.S. law has recognized different types of land tenure and different forms of governance (i.e., not just "tribal"). Therefore, the NCAI offers a delicate negotiation that connects Kanaka Maoli to other Indigenous groups, but in such a way as to create possibilities for connections rather than consolidation.

The Hawai'i Congressional Delegation has a complicated narrative, as it recognizes Indigenous sovereignty but also subsumes Kanaka Maoli and all other Indigenous groups under the sign of Native American. For example, they argue that U.S. Congress understands that the sovereignties of "America's indigenous peoples" have existed long before the formation of the United States.[89] They also suggest that these Indigenous peoples have different histories, but somehow end up with the same conclusion:

> Although the differences in their languages, their cultures, their belief systems, their customs and traditions, and their geographical origins may have kept them apart and prevented them from developing a shared identity as the native people

of this land - with the arrival of western "discoverers" in the United States, their histories are sadly similar.[90]

The end of history for Indigenous nations, notably, comes hand in hand with their designation as "Native American." Here, the Hawai'i Congressional Delegation works to explain that while there might be different terms (that is, whether they were called "'aborigines' or 'Indians' or 'natives'") the result, like the end of history, is the same.[91]

Because Native Americans have been recognized as a "political" group having a "political" relationship with the United States, it is productive—within law—to figure Kanaka Maoli as a "political" rather than a "racial" group.[92] But the problem is that the U.S. legal structure reroutes these narratives through a colorblind, multicultural, liberal ideological gauntlet that forces the disaggregation of race from colonialism. These counter-narratives are responding to the need to assert not only intelligible claims, but legally viable ones as well. But intelligibility requires coherence—and when law and history work to disjoin racism and colonialism, *counter-narratives are required to follow suit.*

## At the Dead End of Analogies

While reflecting on the various debates around the *Rice* case and Native Hawaiian recognition, R. Hōkūlei Lindsey observes, "Despite their right to self-determination, the legal reality for Native Hawaiians has become a *race* between those who would protect Native Hawaiian rights and those who would destroy a peoples and their culture" (emphasis added).[93] This quotation highlights the diverse ways in which "race" is used throughout law in general and in this case in particular. While Lindsey is not using the term "race" to designate a sociopolitical category, the apt word choice reflects a larger dynamic within legal discourses, whereby this case showcases the battle over the proper meanings and uses of "race" in law. Scholarship on this case devotes almost as much energy on the proper meanings and importance of race in law as it does on the history of Hawai'i. Yet history rears its head once again, here as a means to tell the story as to the supposed "proper" meanings and contextualizations of race in the United States. Importantly, these historical tales of race in law end up transposing and projecting specific U.S. contexts onto Hawai'i, thereby offering and requiring analogies that continue to erase the specificities of Kanaka Maoli racialization and Indigeneity.

When Harold Rice based his claim on protections against racial discrimination as found in the Fourteenth and Fifteenth Amendments, the case required a series of competing historical narratives about these amendments. As described throughout this chapter, historical narratives are anything but neutral, but Kennedy's narrative on the history of race in law is a perfect example of how dangerous and selective historical narratives can be. In the *Rice* decision, the history of race in law begins elsewhere, that is, not in Hawai'i but in the U.S. South. The specter of the U.S. South serves as a history lesson about Black/white racial segregation and white supremacy, rather than a story about the concurrent processes of settler colonialism, African enslavement, and apartheid policies in the U.S. South. The result is, once again, the disaggregation of colonialism and racialization, Indigeneity and race.

But it is hardly a surprise that Kennedy neglects settler colonialism in the U.S. South, as he only begrudgingly acknowledges slavery and white supremacy. Note, for example, his rhetorical choices: Kennedy claims the primary aim of the Fifteenth Amendment was to protect newly emancipated slaves and "to *reaffirm* the equality of races" (emphasis added).[94] With this careful and selective phrasing, Kennedy renarrates the Reconstruction Era amendments and postemancipation U.S. racial dynamics as if there was some state of equality that merely needed endorsement. Later, Kennedy reproduces a direct quote from a 1915 case that claimed, erroneously, "By the inherent power of the [Fifteenth] Amendment the word white disappeared."[95] Here, white privilege is rewritten as something that was named and identified directly in law, rather than acknowledging the fact that whiteness and white privilege were rarely named or identified directly in U.S. legal history (hence their endurance). Moreover, white privilege is described as part of the past, that is, *already over* by 1915.

Kennedy simultaneously acknowledges and disavows the historical contexts and outcomes of nineteenth-century voting rights and racial antidiscrimination laws. After offering the renarrativized context for the Fifteenth Amendment, Kennedy offers a brief overview of various disenfranchisement cases (cases challenging grandfather clauses, literacy tests, and so forth) from 1876 well into the 1960s. He lists, then, almost a century of cases (often referred to as the "white primary cases") that provide evidence that the Fifteenth Amendment did *not* extinguish white privilege and white supremacy. But, apparently, while "[p]rogress was slow . . . important precedents did emerge which give instruction in the case before us."[96] In Kennedy's reading, the numerous cases challenging Black disenfranchisement in the U.S. South provide the instruction that "racial exclusion" can occur without naming specific racial categories. This (re)contextualization is used as a perfect setup for the *Rice* case, where a case involving the vote for Native Hawaiian representation becomes analogous to the white primary cases throughout the U.S. South. By way of Kennedy's analysis, this case turns out to be even more atrocious since, "Unlike the cited cases, the voting structure now before us is neither subtle nor indirect. It is specific in granting the vote to persons of defined ancestry and to no others."[97]

I highlight this transition—from white supremacy in the U.S. South to Native Hawaiian representation in Hawai'i—because it is just one more example of how court decisions reframe the history of race in order to enforce notions of equalized citizenship, colorblind constitutionalism, and colonialnormativity. Via Kennedy's historical detour, the OHA voting schema is maneuvered into a particular historical narrative where the problem is not racism, and certainly not colonialism, but mere racial categorization itself. This explains, then, the peculiar claim that "the word white disappeared." The issue is not the existence of systemic racism and white privilege; the issue is any transparent use of racial categories. The difference between white supremacy in the nineteenth-century voting schemes and the Native Hawaiian vote gets rewritten as a difference in directness and transparency, not in the cause, effect, or intent. Within this logic, race is inherently problematic because it was a horrific category of analysis that was used to demean a particular group, but that particularity is *no longer relevant*. Because "this" (Hawaiian representation) is like "that" (white supremacy, systemic racism, and racial segregation) Kennedy's tour through the historical trajectory of the 15th Amendment has ended up at the dead end of analogy.[98] As Kennedy explains, "Hawaii may not assume, based on race, that petitioner or any other of its citizens will not cast a principled vote. To accept that position advanced by the State would give rise to the *same* indignities, and the *same* resulting tensions and animosities the Amendment was designed to eliminate" (emphasis added).[99]

But as described above, various briefs and Justice Stevens's dissent offer an analogy of their own. According to Stevens, there is a critical difference between voting schemes aimed at excluding a racial group versus the OHA's program for empowering a historically disenfranchised group. And beyond any remedial intentions, Stevens argues that the federal government as well as the State of Hawai'i has a special duty to Native Hawaiians, a duty parallel to the relationship between the federal government and Native American groups. The proper analogy, then, is not that Native Hawaiians in Hawai'i are like white supremacists in the Jim Crow South; the proper analogy is that Native Hawaiians are like Native Americans. The result of this analogy is to argue that the federal government has a responsibility to "compensate for past wrongs to the ancestors of these peoples."[100]

But these analogies—to be like white supremacists in the United States South or to be like Native Americans—serve as shorthand for the complex racialization of Kanaka Maoli. These analogies also mirror the ways in which race and Indigeneity are warped into "parallel issues that never cross."[101] As legal scholar Chris Iijima rightfully points out, this framing creates a "false dilemma." In his words, "The Supreme Court's decision in *Rice* was driven, in essence, by a framework that squeezed complex identities into a simple binary universe—whether Native Hawaiians were either a 'political entity' or a 'racial group.'"[102] Throughout U.S. legal mechanisms, racial identities and political identities have been contorted into polarized positions, rather than as codependent elements that are both products and outcomes of U.S. colonialism, slavery, and empire.[103] The danger, however, is in the ways in which the avenues for racial reparations and Indigenous political rights are blocked through these anti-intersectional logics. As illuminated in the *Rice* case, the expansion of the colorblindness doctrine has put reparative racial justice projects in serious jeopardy. Therefore, in response, Indigenous rights advocates need to distance themselves from race and racialization in order to protect Indigenous rights claims from being dismantled. But the *Rice* case is also an example of the precarity of U.S. courts' recognition of and respect for the distinction between racial statuses and political statuses. Indigenous political status is easily denied by U.S. courts invested in selectively acknowledging the racialization of Indigeneity in order to dismantle Native sovereignty. The false dilemma between racial and political statuses is, in fact, a destructive anti-intersectional mechanism that upholds racial violence and Native dispossession while impeding coalitional antiracist, decolonial actions against the U.S. nation-state.

## The Racial Politics of Decolonization in Hawai'i

This "false dilemma," in which racial categorization is configured as oppositional to political organization, reverberates throughout Native American studies and has a long legal history. As described in the introduction to this chapter, Native Studies scholars, such as Joanne Barker, Jodi Byrd, Kēhaulani Kauanui, Mark Rifkin, and Audra Simpson, have described the ways in which Indigenous peoples have been racialized through U.S. legal systems in such a way as to undermine their sovereignty, epistemologies, kinship structures, and relationships to land.[104] As Joanne Barker observes, the construct of "Indians" in U.S. law "depends on an especially racialized notion of Native authenticity, one that is recognizable by national narrations as valuably unique to the national polity."[105] Mark Rifkin adds to this point by arguing that "if native peoples are understood as *Indians*, a category defined by the procreative transmission of a certain kind of 'blood' . . . they can be characterized as (primarily) a racial population, which also means . . . that they are not first and foremost *political* entities whose status is irreducible to U.S. jurisdictional formulations."[106] These arguments demonstrate how racialization has become a critical problem for Indigenous peoples in the United States, a problem that was produced through U.S. legal terminologies and U.S. empire.

This takes us back to Jodi Byrd's insightful analysis about the cacophonies that drown out or subsume analyses. As Byrd points out, there has been a problematic tendency in which colonization has been conflated with racialization, and "when these two historical processes are so enmeshed that racialization in the United States now often evokes colonization as a metonym, such discursive elisions obfuscate the distinctions between the two systems of dominance and the coerced complicities amid both."[107] Echoing Byrd on the violence of privileging racialization when thinking through Indigeneity, Audra Simpson argues that these race-based analyses "obfuscat[e] the profound difference of difference—the 'difference' of indigenous moral and philosophical orders, their matrix of connectedness, and their complexity, all of which lay before and now lie within, settler societies."[108] These scholars argue that it is critical to work against the conflation of racialization with Indigeneity and work toward analyzing the distinct and specific racializations of Indigeneity in ways that can support and bolster Native epistemologies and sovereignty.

Hawaiian Studies scholars have worked to piece together the very complicated histories of the racialization and colonization of Hawai'i. These scholars demonstrate how Kanaka Maoli have been configured, throughout the U.S. colonial enterprise, as benevolent and lazy Natives, emasculated warriors and spectacled hula girls, and much more, through historiographies, travel narratives, U.S. policies and laws, and museums. For example, J. Kēhaulani Kauanui's book, *Hawaiian Blood*, provides a genealogy of how Native Hawaiians have been increasingly constructed into a racial group through legal measures that worked to create and circumscribe the legal identity of "Native Hawaiians" into calculable blood quantums.[109] She locates the consolidation of this formation in the congressional debates on the Hawaiian Homes Commission Act (HHCA) of 1921, which offered to "rehabilitate" the Native Hawaiian and save her from herself and her own self-destructive nature. Kauanui's research also helps us see how the HHCA's successful legalization relied on two racializations: first, that Native Hawaiians are not only hospitable, but more importantly, assimilable types; and, second, the racialization of Native Hawaiians' Indigeneity as naturally assimilable and, therefore, worthy of "saving" was directly organized in and against Asian immigrants, who were positioned as the inherently alien and unassimilable alternative.[110] Sally Engle Merry's research places this comparative racialization—of Native Hawaiian against

Asian immigrant—within a longer historical trajectory of anti-Chinese and anti-Japanese rhetoric in Hawai'i, beginning as early as the 1850s.[111] These scholars illuminate how Native Hawaiians were cemented into particular amounts of racialized Indigenous types through the comparative racialization projects of U.S. orientalism and U.S. settler colonialism.[112]

But to talk about U.S. orientalism as intertwined with settler colonial racializations is not to suggest that the racialization of Asian Americans, especially through U.S. orientalisms, is primary, more important, or the same process as the racialization of Kanaka Maoli Indigeneity in Hawai'i. And I need to clarify this point because of those very loud cacophonies that Jodi Byrd talked about. Scholars that are working to piece together the various strains of race and Indigeneity in Hawai'i have had to work against the numerous discourses that have fetishized Hawaiian racial politics in the service of U.S. multiculturalism. These scholars and activists work against the ways in which Hawai'i, already figured as the multicultural success story, is now, quoting the official State of Hawai'i's tourism Web site, "Barack Obama's Hawai'i." Therefore, my goal here is to argue that U.S. orientalisms are a *part*, but not the whole, of the genealogical conditions of contemporary discourses of U.S. settler multiculturalism within Hawai'i.

Scholars in Asian Settler Colonial studies and Hawaiian Studies have been working against the cacophonies, especially the tendency to narrate the historical as well as contemporaneous migration to Hawai'i in ways that obscure and perpetuate settler colonialism. This includes, then, the delicate and controversial work of trying to articulate the responsibilities between and across Asian migrants and Kanaka Maoli. Asian settler studies, for example, demonstrates how Asian migrants can be interpellated into settler subjects, as well as participate in practices that solidify U.S. colonialism/occupation in Hawai'i. They argue that Asian migrants/settlers resolidify U.S. settler colonialism by appealing to the U.S. nation-state via civil rights projects, by claiming the identity "local," and by outright support of U.S colonial projects such as statehood.[113] This work is inspired by the ever-so-direct Haunani-Kay Trask, who, in the keynote address at the Multi-Ethnic Literature of the United States (MELUS) Conference in 1997, called out "Asians in Hawai'i as settlers who benefit from the colonial subjugation of Hawaiians."[114]

Trask followed up her keynote with a more extensive essay, where she argued that some Asian migrants have positioned themselves as Indigenous Hawaiians through the deployment and embrace of the identity "local." She contends, "Our Native people and territories have been overrun by non-Natives, including Asians. Calling themselves 'local,' the children from Asian settlers greatly outnumber us. They claim Hawai'i as their own, denying indigenous history, their long collaboration in our continued dispossession and the benefits there from."[115] In response, some Asian American scholars criticized Trask for re-deploying anti–Asian-immigration rhetoric (such as the reference to being "overrun" by Asian immigrants), as well as for utilizing racialized discourses of Asians as model minorities within the U.S.[116] And yet, scholars within Asian settler studies such as Candace Fujikane and Dean Saranillio honor, as well as extend, Trask's calling out of Asian migrant complicities in the dispossession of Kanaka Maoli. For example, in response to Asian American critiques of Trask's bold assertions, Fujikane argues that "the construction of Asian Americans as 'victims' of Native 'racism' tells us much about the way in which Asian Americans, like the plaintiffs in the court cases threatening Native rights, see themselves as oppressed citizens of a democratic nation-state: they do not want to see the United States as a colonial nation-state, and they refuse to see themselves as beneficiaries of that colonial system."[117]

The tension offered here within the context of Hawai'i echoes conversations throughout multicultural settler nation-states, as white antiracists, allied de-colonialists, people of color, and Indigenous activists explore ideas, terms, and practices in order to dismantle the anti-intersectionalities of settler multicul-turalisms.[118] Within these various spaces, these allies work through the various contexts that inform and forge the cacophonies around them. In the specific context of Hawai'i, part of the goal is to tease apart the ways in which U.S. orientalism, U.S. settler colonialism, and U.S. racializations work together to thwart coalitions and produce distractions. And the challenges are profound, as scholars and activists negotiate a myriad of challenges. How might scholars and activists explore a sustained analysis of how Asian migrants get interpellated into settler colonial projects, while also being wary and mindful of how these very same subjects are also subjugated and displaced via ongoing operations of U.S. orientalist rhetoric? And how might scholars and activists articulate the pain and violence of ongoing dispossession of Kanaka Maoli sovereignty and land through, among other processes, the ascendancy of a distinct Asian American power bloc within Hawaiian State politics, without falling back on the racist shorthand of the "model minority" myth? These are just some of the legacies of U.S. orientalism, U.S. racialization, and U.S. colonialism/occupation that hover across antiracist, anticolonial alliances.

The struggle to articulate coalitions and accountability within multicul-tural settler states is also mirrored within arguments as to whether civil rights are incompatible with sovereignty organizing. As Trask argues, civil rights frameworks are inappropriate for Indigenous peoples and do not value "Native relationships to land, to language, to culture, to family, to self-government, indeed, to anything Natives value."[119] Kauanui extends Trask's analysis, and it is worth quoting at length:

> Despite the expansive and changing notion of civil rights, as a political project it is insufficient for Indigenous and other colonized peoples and the ongoing and often pressing questions of sovereignty and nationhood. This is not to say that Indigenous and other colonized peoples are not or should not be concerned with education, health, housing, and employment and the right to live free from the structures of white supremacy, racial oppression, male domination, and homophobia, all of which are integral to the civil rights project. Of course, many are concerned with all these elements of livelihood and citizenship. However, because of its very origins, the concept of U.S. civil rights is, by definition, inadequate. It cannot address the nation-to-nation governance and land issues as they affect American Indians and Alaska Native villages, as well as those from the U.S. territories in the Pacific Islands and the Caribbean.[120]

Indigenous scholars such as Deloria, Kauanui, and Trask are particularly critical of the ways in which the rhetorics of U.S. citizenship and civil rights serve to deny colonialism and Native claims.[121] Civil rights is a negotiation of who can be included within the American polity and how to have a "right" to U.S. citizenship. Worse yet, civil rights and citizenship discourses rarely, if ever, account for the ways in which they take place on Native land. Therefore, as Kanaka Maoli and Indigenous scholars and activists point out, while civil rights can be a strategy to contest (white-, male-, hetero-)normative citizenship, it is also a mechanism by which minoritized subjects reify settler colonial citizenship.

While it is critical that activists and scholars address the ways in which racism and civil rights, as understood within dominant discourses, work to obscure Indigenous claims, this conversation might reproduce the disaggregation of racism and colonialism in ways that confound abilities to dismantle the enduring racializations of settler colonialism. Moreover, their arguments can be read as presuming or presupposing a success or an inclusion of racialized people of color within U.S. citizenship. In other words, there are ways in which some sovereignty-based critiques of "civil rights" can be read as replicating the progress narrative of U.S. multicultural citizenship. This can obscure the very long tradition of critical race and antiracist assessments as to how liberal nation-states appropriate and contort civil rights (for example, Martin Luther King argued that civil rights was an inadequate framework for racial justice).[122] There is, then, a much larger array of misrecognitions and anti-intersectionalities at work here. Civil rights rhetoric fails to recognize sovereignty claims in part because it is immersed in U.S. citizenship discourses, but more profoundly, *civil rights rhetoric fails people of color and Indigenous peoples because U.S. citizenship is whitenormative and colonialist in nature.*

But is it a matter of abandoning the language of civil rights in favor of sovereignty claims or vice versa? While the critiques of their limitations are extremely important, the *Rice* case showcases how this "tug of war" between antiracism and anticolonialism merges neatly into settler colonialism, which serves to deny both the structures of racism within, as well as the colonial occupation of, Hawai'i. The challenge is to expose not only the ways in which citizenship discourses and civil rights doctrines work to undermine sovereignty claims, but also the ways in which these very same discourses serve to reproduce a whitenormative, colonialnormative citizenship. Put differently, the challenge here is to depose the anti-intersectional, either/or setup that has overdetermined the failure of both antiracist and anticolonialist claims. If colonialism and racism have worked hand in hand, if one is essential for the successful operations of the other, then it is critical to expose their codependence and constitutive natures through an intersectional "coalition through incommensurability."[123]

This either/or setup is (re)produced within the structure of law and history, especially through segregating the history of racism from the history of colonialism. An intersectional approach to the *Rice* case exposes the complex interactions of racism and colonialism within the histories of Hawai'i, from the occupation of Hawaiian national and cultural formations to anti–Asian-immigration policies and beyond. An intersectional approach describes the formation, production, and maintenance of multiple identity categories, born out of U.S empire and manifested in law. Rather than leaving race and colonialism to their own time, to their own proper historical context or proper legal rationale, I suggest that we focus our energies toward *queering*—as in, denaturalizing—the disaggregation of race and colonialism. This queering does not rely upon a single, coherent narrative, but deploys a series of disjointed, discontinuous narratives that tell the stories, over and over, of their complex, contradictory, intersectionalities. I am suggesting that we make a series of queer detours through the histories and legal narratives of Hawai'i in order to mark the presentness of racism and colonialism within modern-day U.S. empire.

## Stranger Mergers: Toward Queering U.S. Empire

Before I wrap up this chapter, I want to tell you about a fascinating moment in the chronicles of the *Rice* case. Long before *Rice* made its way to the Supreme Court, Harold Rice's complaint was first heard at the federal district court level.

But at this time, he was not focused on voting for representatives of the Office of Hawaiian Affairs; rather, he was concerned with being excluded from the 1996 sovereignty vote that was held by the State of Hawai'i. The Hawaiian sovereignty vote was initiated by state law, and the Hawaiian Sovereignty Elections Council (HSEC) distributed a ballot to an estimated 85,000 voters worldwide, who were registered as "Native Hawaiians," with this question: "Shall the Hawaiian people elect delegates to propose a Native Hawaiian government?" It was, then, the rumbling of sovereignty that got Harold Rice's and the Campaign for a Color-Blind America's attention.

What makes this earlier incarnation of the *Rice* case important is that Harold Rice's claim was consolidated with a complaint by folks referenced as the "Kakalia plaintiffs" by Judge Ezra of the District Court of Hawai'i.[124] The Kakalia plaintiffs were comprised of a group of sovereignty activists, including members of the organization, Ka Lāhui Hawai'i, an OHA trustee, and a "non-Hawaiian" sovereignty ally, who were also trying to stop the vote.[125] For some reason, this strange merger went unnoticed. Even the district court's decision did not acknowledge or even infer that there might be some critical tensions between the plaintiffs. In searching for commentary on the consolidation, I found only one newspaper article that called the consolidation "ironic," and claimed that it came about at the behest of sovereignty activist, lawyer, and (former) leader in Ka Lāhui Hawai'i, Mililani Trask.[126]

But how queer—as in, odd, unnatural, strange—that Harold Rice would have something in common with sovereignty activists. We can only speculate as to what would have happened—that is, what types of historical narratives would have been possible or necessary—had this consolidated version gone all the way to the Supreme Court. While I have already familiarized you with Harold Rice's claim, the Kakalia plaintiffs described the illegality of the vote from a different perspective; the Kakalia plaintiffs contested the vote not for being *excluded* from it, but for being *forcefully included* in it.

By the time this merged case arrived at the district court, ballots had already been received and tabulated by the HSEC, so the district court quickly placed a restraining order to hold off on disclosing the results. The Kakalia plaintiffs claimed the vote violated the Supremacy Clause of Article VI of the U.S. Constitution, the First and Fourteenth Amendments, the Admission Act of 1959, and various Hawai'i State laws. Harold Rice, who was ineligible to vote, argued that his rights were violated via the Fourteenth and Fifteenth Amendments, the Voting Rights Act, the Civil Rights Act, and parts of the Hawai'i State Constitution.

While Kakalia and Rice wanted the court to apply a "strict scrutiny" analysis, as is generally applied in cases involving racial categories, the court sided with the State of Hawai'i's argument that the classification in question, "Native Hawaiian," was a political rather than a racial category.[127] As a political category, the State of Hawai'i needed to provide only a "rational basis" for the vote's restriction to "Native Hawaiians" only. The court found that there was a very rational basis because money, land, and the rising tide of sovereignty activism are at stake. The court suggests that, in many ways, due to the importance of the sovereignty question, the State has *a right to know* where Kanaka Maoli stand on sovereignty, and it is this very same demand for the right to knowledge that Kakalia plaintiffs suggest is the problem.

Without strict scrutiny, Rice's complaint is pretty much resolved—according to the court, Rice might be concerned and even directly impacted by the vote, but he does not get to be included with it. Therefore, the majority of the decision is dedicated to considering the Kakalia plaintiff's arguments. The Kakalia plaintiffs are challenging the ways in which the State of Hawai'i positioned itself in relationship to sovereignty; the Kakalia plaintiffs are attempting to name the colonialist gesture of the vote itself. One concern, for example, is that the vote would solve and/or resolve the question of sovereignty in simplistic (that is, *state-determined*) language, and it is here that they suggest that there has been a violation of free speech. The speech wanted and needed, according to the Kakalia plaintiffs, is the ability to determine the ways in which sovereignty, as an issue, gets articulated. Language is far from transparent, and it makes a difference as to how the question of sovereignty gets raised, by whom, and when. The court fails to understand this concern, however, arguing that there cannot be any harm in raising the question in this way, at this time, because this is merely a vote and nothing more. The court can only see this vote within neoliberal terms, as one idea among many; in the court's words, "At this point, all that Act 359 accomplishes is the release of yet another idea into the already vast marketplace of ideas."[128]

The Kakalia complaint also alleges that this vote violates the Supremacy Clause, which restricts states from infringing upon the power of the federal government to enter into agreements with foreign entities. Importantly, this discussion circulates around the question of whether Native Hawaiians are a foreign power or can be understood as such. The court offers two answers to this question, the first of which is that the Kakalia plaintiffs have jumped the gun. Again, misunderstanding the sovereignty activists' claim, the court thinks that they are only worried the vote will constrict the form a Native Hawaiian government could take. Since the vote is only the first step in what would be an elaborate process, the court argues, "Plaintiff's claims are based on a scenario that may never occur."[129] But this argument makes more sense after the court's second point on the topic, in which the court invokes the language of universal citizenship. As the court explains, the State of Hawai'i is "not attempting to deal with a foreign entity" because "[f]or the most part, the Native Hawaiian voters are full citizens of the State of Hawai'i and the United States of America."[130]

So, admittedly, this early incarnation of the *Rice* case ends on a disappointing note. The court concludes that the sovereignty vote is valid and the results should be disclosed because "the public interest in announcement of the results is quite high" and, apparently, the plaintiffs' arguments are unconvincing. But the qualification made by the district court, that is, the suggestion that Native Hawaiians are "for the most part . . . full citizens," directs our attention toward the ways in which discourses of universal citizenship work to foreclose critiques of U.S. colonialism. In the court's logic, because Native Hawaiians are almost full citizens, they cannot be sovereign or independent. Sadly, this is exactly what the Kakalia plaintiffs were trying to explain—that is, the ways in which *the inclusionary gesture of universal citizenship works to recolonize the Indigenous.*

Frankly, the court refuses to understand the Kakalia plaintiffs' claims, while being quite empathetic to Harold Rice and his folk. For example, the court infers that the only people who should be "anxious" about the sovereignty vote would be "non-Native Hawaiians" like Harold Rice. But despite Rice's discomfort, the State should have access to the body of Native sovereignty. As the court summarizes:

> Recognizing that there was much discourse about Native Hawaiian sovereignty in academic, social and political circles, the legislature established the HSEC as a barometer to gauge the momentum and direction of popular support for any such movement. While there is undoubtedly some interest and anxiety generated by this issue among non-Native Hawaiian citizens of the State, the fact of the matter is that the State as guardian of the Hawaiian home lands should be able to periodically check the Native Hawaiian pulse.[131]

In the court's imaginary, the State of Hawai'i is reconfigured into some type of kindly doctor merely checking on a patient, rather than one of the victimizers that put this patient in the hospital in the first place. And while the court might see the vote as merely a matter of "access," as far as the Kakalia plaintiffs are concerned, this is a matter of control, regulation, and subjection. It is critical to acknowledge, then, how the State of Hawai'i has maneuvered to access and, importantly, *contain* knowledge about sovereignty, a process that has been perpetuated by the 2011 Hawai'i Act 195, the "First Nation Government Bill," which created the Native Hawaiian Roll Commission and furthered the process of state-defined federal recognition.[132]

Regardless of the outcome, the tale about the strange merger between Harold Rice and sovereignty activists is worth exploring. It is worth speculating what kinds of historical narratives—about citizenship, settler colonialism, and racism—would be possible had this merger continued forward, onto the Supreme Court perhaps or even just within scholarly and political debates surrounding the *Rice* case. We have seen how, without the Kakalia plaintiffs, Harold Rice's complaint aligns neatly with the rhetoric of universal, white-normative, and colonialnormative citizenship. But together, this queer merger between Harold Rice and sovereignty activists provides a space to imagine an alternative: an intersectional space where colonialism is marked as complicit with notions of racial difference and vice versa. What kinds of historical narratives would have been necessary to explain, excuse, or even just situate both Harold Rice's argument for racial exclusion, on the one hand, and the Kakalia's arguments about colonialist inclusion, on the other? Is it possible to tell the competing histories of Harold Rice and the Kakalia plaintiffs' without acknowledging the ways in which Rice's history invades and occupies Kanaka Maoli history? Might this merger finally expose the painful irony that Harold Rice is challenging a racial classification system that was formulated by the U.S Congress in order to benefit white plantation owners and U.S. businessmen from whom he is descended? In the trajectory of trying to trace what Harold Rice and the Kakalia Plaintiffs have in common, we are smack-dab in the middle of the production of legalized racial categories that lie at the heart of the U.S. colonialist project in Hawai'i.

Discussion of this merger contextualizes the fierce debates about deoccupation and decolonization that resonated throughout the 2014 DOI hearings and will, no doubt, continue to reverberate throughout Hawai'i. Understanding that some sovereignty activists opposed the state-held Native Hawaiian sovereignty vote, while others worked within the OHA and the Hawaiian Sovereignty Elections Council on defending and promoting the vote, illustrates the fact that critiques of U.S. settler colonialism are complex, strategic, multiple, and not necessarily aligned. It allows—*forces*—a refusal of any easy characterizations as to what Kanaka Maoli want, think, or do on behalf of sovereignty. Kanaka Maoli activists are located on all different sides of this question of how, where, and when there might be a direct opposition and exposure of the U.S. colonial empire in Hawai'i. These different positions do not point to a lack of solidarity—rather, they point to the complex ways U.S. colonialism has been legalized and maintained through a variety of forces, from the national level with momentary recognitions of Native Hawaiians as a "tribe" and/or a "political group," to the state level with its sometimes remedial, oftentimes paternalistic gestures on behalf of Native Hawaiians through rehabilitation programs involving land, language, education, employment, and so forth.

The project of unraveling this web of racial difference and coloniality that is the heart of U.S. legal systems can start by actively working against their normalization and naturalization via anti-intersectionality. The lack of alignment—here between Harold Rice and the Kakalia plaintiffs—provides a small window for us to see how we can work to denaturalize and disrupt the series of maneuvers whereby colonialism is made intelligible in and through its segregation from racism, and vice versa. This is the challenge of intersectionality: to queer the normativities that are all around us and refuse to rest until we can finally, once and for all, make antiracist and anticolonialist gestures in the same step.

# CONCLUSION

# In and Out of Time

Despite the productivity of various borders, gatekeeping apparatuses, and boundary mechanisms that are used to promote, retain, and maintain the exclusivities of citizenship, citizenship is not merely a spatial formulation. Citizenship is also temporal. Citizenship's meaning and value is forged through pledges to restore its idyllic past and through promises of an "improved tomorrow."[1] While some citizenship studies scholars have recently observed a tempo to citizenship, these authors have tended to see this relationship as newly invoked via the increasing velocities of globalization, technology, and neoliberalism.[2] But citizenship has always been a temporal formation, and this temporality has been used to produce difference. As Elizabeth Povinelli observes, "the temporality of social belonging that emerged with democracy, colonialism and capitalism emerged not merely as a dialectic but also as a division."[3] Within liberal governance, citizenship is part of larger processes that position subjects within differential temporalities, or, in Povinelli's words, "tense[s] of social belonging."[4] Therefore, citizenship is an anti-intersectional temporal structure that situates normative and nonnormative subjects within time.

Without the promise and premise of futurity, and the potential for eventual inclusion, citizenship would not be able to retain the tight hold it has on the political imagination, particularly for the excluded. Similarly, without the idyllic past, normatively privileged citizen-subjects would be left without the sentimental material to bemoan their supposed loss and to forge their cultural defenses of normative citizenship (as described in the Introduction). In these ways, and more, the temporalities of citizenship constrict political visions and create a dissociated existence—"a present that is not fully present."[5] Instead of being constrained by citizenship, I want to imagine a politics that is against citizenship—one that refuses both futurity-as-inclusion as well as retroactive and restorative political visions of the past, in order to enact a coalitional, intersectional, and decolonial politics in and of the present.

The anti-intersectional tenses of citizenship were particularly evident in the Supreme Court decisions of June 2013—*United States v. Windsor, Hollingsworth v. Perry, Fisher v. The University of Texas, Shelby County v. Holder,* and *Adoptive Couple v. Baby Girl.* As described in Chapter Two, the Supreme Court issued some of the most powerful decisions for and against the rights of gays and lesbians, people of color, and Indigenous nations, all in one week. While I outlined the two decisions involving same-sex marriage in the earlier chapter (*United States v. Windsor* and *Hollingsworth v. Perry*), here I want to flesh out the logics and implications of the other cases. Combined and juxtaposed against each other, these cases highlight and expose the anti-intersectional and temporal schemas of white settler citizenship.

In *Fisher v. The University of Texas,* the Supreme Court continued its dismantling of affirmative action programs.[6] The case involved a "Caucasian" petitioner, Abigail Fisher, who sued the University of Texas (UT) after being denied admission, claiming that UT admission programs utilize "race" in such a way as to violate the Equal Protection clause of the Fourteenth Amendment. In the end, the Supreme Court decision did not make a huge splash because it only remanded the case back to the Court of Appeals, telling them to apply a "strict scrutiny" burden—that is, to apply the strictest of standards for using a "racial" category. But it would be a mistake to think of *Fisher* as a benign decision, because along the way the Supreme Court actually reinsured the futurity of and property interest in whiteness within university and college admissions programs.[7] In *Fisher,* the majority decision, penned by Justice Kennedy and joined by six other Justices, tightens the noose around affirmative action programs by demanding that any uses of "race" in admissions must meet two tests, both of which must pass strict scrutiny: first, that "diversity" is essential to the educational mission, and second, that the university has proven there are no workable race-neutral alternative admissions programs that would produce this diversity.[8] Of course, the first test makes the second test redundant; that is, the demand to fulfill the multicultural state's interest in "diversity" already requires admission programs to ignore the historical and contemporary structures of racialized rights. That is, the turn toward "diversity" denies the violence of racialized exclusions as well as the assets of white privilege that have accumulated over time.

While the majority decision is seemingly short and not terribly detailed, it says enough to offer troubling premonitions of future decisions where affirmative action programs and/or remedial programs will be reframed into unconstitutional assertions of race-based law, thereby ensuring a futurity for white privilege. But this decision also returned us to the specter of the Jim Crow South, whereby it serves as a temporal-spatial metaphor to mark racialized remedies as out of time. As Justice Thomas laments in his concurrence, "there is no principled distinction between the University's assertion that diversity yields educational benefits and the segregationists' assertion that segregation yielded those same benefits."[9] Sounding disconcertingly familiar to Justice Kennedy in the *Rice* decision, the specter of the Jim Crow South is deployed to mark justice-based programs as out of time and out of place. And for Justice Thomas, the problem is that there is no end in sight, no future in which justice will or can be complete. According to Thomas, previous Supreme Court decisions have rejected remedial programs because "the interest in remedying societal discrimination . . . had no logical stopping point."[10] Here, the capitalist logic of scarce resources becomes transposed onto temporality, whereby there is not enough time in the world to remedy societal discrimination, so why bother trying. In the process, conservative justices' apathetic imaginations reestablish the future as the proper inheritance of whiteness and white privilege.

*Shelby County v. Holder* is a more complicated story.[11] In this case, Shelby County of Alabama argued that Congress exceeded its power by renewing the Voting Rights Act in 2006 and reauthorizing various sections of the law that are, according to Shelby County, no longer relevant. The Voting Rights Act of 1965 was part of a series of civil rights legislation, and it targeted the continued disenfranchisement of African Americans, especially in (but not limited to) the South. The Voting Rights Act is a complex and nuanced law that sets into motion various monitoring programs. For example, section 5 requires certain counties and states to obtain federal "preclearance" before they can make any changes to their voting laws. And section 4(b) has an elaborate formula to configure which counties and states should be required to obtain this "preclearance." This formula is based on "the past"; that is, the formula focuses on those areas that have marred histories of discrimination. Therefore, history became, once again, a battleground, here to stage the fight over the Voting Rights Act.

The majority decision, penned by Chief Justice Roberts, argued that the Voting Rights Act coverage formula was out of time, that is, nearly 50 years old, and, therefore, fixes "decades-old data to decades-old problems, rather than current data reflecting current needs."[12] Roberts was concerned with how Congress reauthorized the Voting Rights Act in 2006 without offering substantial changes to the coverage formula. According to Roberts, things have changed over time, and "during that time, largely because of the Voting Rights Act, voting tests were abolished, disparities in voter registration and turnout due to race were erased, and African-Americans attained political office in record numbers."[13] Justice Ginsberg, in her passionate dissent, argued that Roberts is ignoring the vast record compiled by Congress in the process of reauthorizing the law. Congress accumulated over 15,000 pages of data and held 21 hearings that detail both change over time—in the form of "second-generation barriers"—as well as current, present-day effects of discrimination. Therefore, according to Ginsberg, the coverage formula continues to capture and locate municipalities that disenfranchise people of color, but through more complex mechanisms such as racialized gerrymandering. As she states, "True, conditions in the South have impressively improved since passage of the Voting Rights Act. . . . But Congress also found that voting discrimination had evolved into subtler second-generation barriers, and that eliminating preclearance would risk loss of the gains that had been made."[14]

Eerily similar to the debates on hate crime legislation that I described in Chapter One, the past is used to define and delimit voting discrimination into horrific, extraordinary acts of violence, thereby negating subtle forms of disenfranchisement. Even when Roberts looks at that vast record compiled by Congress, he sees only that the present is not as bad as it once was, hence the renewal is inappropriate. In Roberts's words, "Regardless of how to look at the record, however, no one can fairly say that it shows anything approaching the 'pervasive,' 'flagrant,' 'widespread,' and 'rampant' discrimination that faced Congress in 1965."[15] For Roberts, voting disenfranchisement is a photograph in time, captured in 1965 via the "extraordinary problems" of white supremacy in the Jim Crow South. Anything that diverges from this picture is, again, not worth our collective time. The spatial-temporal specter of the South here works to dislodge and dismember reparative justice, and mark African Americans as worthy of protection only when they experience extreme forms of bodily violence at the hands of vigilante white citizens. Racialized remedies had their time, and were appropriate (and woefully inadequate, we might add) back then, but in this moment, the here and now, those remedies are out of time.

*Adoptive Couple v. Baby Girl* works to suture the settler colonial project of eliminating Indigenous peoples to the anachronistic projects of reparative racialized justice, as marked by *Shelby* and *Fisher*.[16] In this case, a white adoptive couple argued that the biological father, who is Cherokee, cannot invoke the protections of the Indian Child Welfare Act (ICWA). The ICWA was enacted in 1978 as a remedial and reparative effort to foreclose or at least significantly reduce the long history of the white settler state removing Native children from their families and nations. The ICWA sets minimum standards for the majority of custody hearings involving Native children, supersedes state laws on custody, and recognizes tribal jurisdiction over the hearings (either concurrent with state jurisdiction or exclusive jurisdiction if the child lives on tribal land).

In the decision, Justice Alito fixates on terms used in the ICWA in order to yank them out of context and renarrate the purpose of the law. By providing textual readings that would trouble many literature majors, Alito pulls out his diction-ary in order to investigate the meanings of the terms "family," "continuous," and "breakup." According to Alito, the biological father was never part of a "family," did not have "continuous" custody of the child, and that there could not have been a "breakup" of the family because, again, there was no "family" to begin with. So even though the ICWA is clearly aimed at setting into motion a series of hurdles in order to keep Native children with Native nations, communities, and especially relatives/ancestors, Alito uses the dictionary in order to bypass those hurdles. In the end, he argues that the ICWA does not apply to noncustodial parents, and, therefore, that the biological father could not block the adoption.

This case exemplifies what Patrick Wolfe described as the settler colonial deployment of Native "mixed-bloodedness" as "the postfrontier version of the vanishing Indian."[17] Justice Alito consistently and unnecessarily goes out of his way to mark a Cherokee child as a victim of remote ancestry. Alito racializes Indigeneity right out of the gate, as his first comment on the case inappropri-ately classifies the child. As he states, "This case is about a little girl (Baby Girl) who is classified as an Indian because she is 1.2% (3/256) Cherokee."[18] This characterization is offensive in at least three ways: it deploys settler colonial racialization rhetoric of blood quantum; it employs racialized discourses of vanishing, diluted, and therefore "inauthentic" Indigeneity; and it completely mischaracterizes Cherokee citizenship practices. As the Cherokee Nation de-clares, "Cherokee Nation citizenship does not require a specific blood quantum. It does require that you have at least one direct Cherokee ancestor listed on the Dawes Final Rolls."[19] But Alito continues to return to the settler colonial racialization schema of blood quantum in order to invalidate Cherokee citizen-ship practices and to claim they are race-based and, therefore, subject to the colorblindness doctrine. And, to make the conflation complete and mark this Indigenous-based program as the same as a race-based program, Alito claims that "a biological Indian father could abandon his child . . . and then could play his ICWA trump card at the eleventh hour to override the mother's decision and the child's best interests."[20] This "ICWA trump card" is a not-so-subtle play on conservative white America's favorite idiom, the "race card," which is used to denigrate any attempt to call out white supremacist and racist discourses.

By marking Baby Girl within the terms of settler colonial racialization, Alito creates a doubled violence through situating both reparative race-based programs and remedial Indigenous-based programs as anachronistic efforts that are out of time.[21] But we must also consider the ways in which Indigenous peoples and people of color are located within different (though connected) temporal logics within multicultural settler states. If the Jim Crow South fixes people of color's experience of white supremacy and the violence of citizenship as only, and especially, heinous and in the past, the temporal logics of settler colonialism fixes Indigenous peoples as *embodiments* of the archaic past. As critical Indigenous studies scholars have shown, one of the ways in which settler colonial claims to Native land and resources are continuously and repeatedly performed is through temporal constructions that situate Natives as temporally bounded to and imprisoned within premodernity.[22] This temporal framing positions enduring Indigenous presence in the present as bare traces and distant relatives of colonial violence, configuring Natives into what Jodi Byrd so eloquently and painfully describes as "signposts and grave markers along the roads of empire."[23] Therefore, Alito's investment in referencing Baby Girl's so-called "distant" relationship to her Cherokee citizenship efficiently reproduces the settler colonial temporal schema that positions Indigenous-based rights and remedial efforts as too removed, and far too late.

Even though the Supreme Court did not consider whether the ICWA invokes the "strict scrutiny" measures of race-based programs (as seen in *Fisher* above), Alito offers a very ominous concluding remark. Directly after his comment on the "ICWA trump card," Alito points out that *if* the ICWA was interpreted in such a way—as in, a "trump card" that could be played to override other interests—it would "raise equal protection concerns."[24] The reference to "equal protection concerns" is, as Justice Sotomayor points out in her dissent, a veiled threat to dismantle ICWA by marking Indigeneity as a racial-not-political identity. Moreover, Alito's final remarks explain his fixation on racializing Baby Girl; as Sotomayor astutely notes, "The majority's repeated, analytically unnecessary references to the fact that Baby Girl is 3/256 Cherokee by ancestry" alongside the last-minute intimation of the Equal Protection Clause, offer troubling threats to "second-guess the membership requirements of federally recognized Indian tribes."[25]

This threat is especially ominous if we understand the Supreme Court's decision in the *Rice* case, as shown in Chapter Three, as a "cautionary tale" as to what can happen when the Court chooses to designate Indigenous rights as racially based rather than political.[26] These are reminders that the Court's willingness or interest in recognizing Indigenous peoples as political communities is tentative at best, and that the U.S. judicial system will use the colorblindness doctrine to racialize (in order to deem inappropriate) Indigenous nations especially when it perpetuates the settler colonial project of reducing Indigenous membership and their claims to land.[27]

Thinking through these cases individually exposes some of the violent temporalities of U.S. settler colonization and racialized citizenship. However, juxtaposing them against the same-sex marriage cases that were decided in the same Supreme Court term exposes the ways in which temporality is manipulated to suture homonormativity to white settler multiculturalism. As described in Chapter Two, in *United States v. Windsor* and *Hollingsworth v. Perry*, the Supreme Court ended up supporting same-sex marriage rights. While the Court decision in *Hollingsworth v. Perry* was limited, the decision in the *United States v. Windsor* undermined federal efforts, in the form of the 1996 Defense of Marriage Act (DOMA), to constrict the federal definition of marriage to opposite sex only. As a reminder, the Court decision, penned by Justice Kennedy, argued that DOMA produced "two contradictory marriage regimes," and "writes inequality into the entire United States code."[28] And as I described in the earlier chapter, this case announces the legalized absorption of sexual difference, here gay and lesbian coupledom, into heteronormative, class-based, racialized citizenship.

When we compare these decisions across the Supreme Court term, from *Fisher* to *Windsor*, the problem is not just that *Windsor* happened to grant rights to gay and lesbians while the other cases took rights away from people of color and Indigenous peoples. Rather, the problem is the means by which the rights of gays and lesbians were secured through the past tensing of racialized discrimination and settler colonialism and the alignment of gay and lesbian relationships with heteronormative reproductive futurity. Kennedy continuously deploys the language and terminology of mid-twentieth-century racial de/segregation cases, particularly by repeatedly describing the ways in which DOMA created a two-tiered, dual regime that results in a state-imposed segregation of marriages within states. As the decision observes, "DOMA's principal effect is to identify a subset of state-sanctioned marriages and make them unequal." Moreover, the effect of segregated marriages fits with DOMA's principal purpose, which is to "impose disadvantage, a separate status, and so a stigma upon all who enter into same-sex marriages."[29] These are uncannily akin to the findings in *Brown v. Board of Education* (1954), when Chief Justice Warren declared for a unanimous Court that the "separate but equal" segregation of African American school-children produced an inescapable "sense of inferiority," a wound that was only deepened via the sanction of law.[30] Desegregation discourse labored to describe how segregation created separate statuses and stigmas on African American communities, and this discourse is now being used—exclusively—for gays and lesbians.[31] How confusing, as in concerning, that the stigma of racialization is projected onto sexuality at the same time that other decisions delimit the pain and agony of current-day racializations of Indigenous folks and people of color, as seen in *Fisher, Shelby*, and *Adoptive Couple*.

As described in Chapter Two, it is not just that gays and lesbians are described as the new rightful owners of racialized remedies and rights. They are also deemed the proper beneficiaries of rights and benefits of citizenship through their new roles in the scripted "conventions of family, inheritance, and child rearing."[32] In this script, gay and lesbian parents now possess the rights to reproductive futurity, a temporality premised around the investment in the child, nuclear familial units, and proper, privatized routes of inheritance. As Lee Edelman describes, "reproductive futurity" is a contortion of politics, whereby the (ideal) Child is the "perpetual horizon" and "fantasmatic beneficiary of every political intervention."[33] *Windsor*, like *Goodridge*, marked same-sex marriage rights as a means to protect the future/child, but *Windsor* was much more direct about how marriage rights are primary mechanisms for the transmittal of property and capital accumulation. In these processes, a particular type of familial, class-based gay rights inherit the right to futurity, and the futurity of rights.

According to the Supreme Court decisions in June of 2013, racialized discrimination of people of color must be extraordinary in order to be deemed valid (*Shelby*), reparative racialization policies are always-already analogous to white segregationists (*Fisher*), Indigenous rights are about-to-be reparative racialization policies (*Adoptive Couple*), and gay and lesbian rights is the new site of racialized justice (*Windsor*). These distortions are familiar; they were continuously echoed within debates around hate crime legislation, the same-sex marriage cases, and the *Rice* decision. Within this worldview, racialized rights are out of time, Indigenous rights where never in time, and gay rights' time has come. Through these framings, temporality perpetuates and maintains the anti-intersectionalities of citizenship, thwarts intersectional coalitions, and tears apart communities and subjectivities by forcing them to work at different times, in different tempos, for different futures.

Citizentime produces the temporal imaginary in which the past is deemed particularly aberrant (or idyllic, depending on the standpoint) for its reign of normativities, and with patience and adherence to state and social norms, progress will come in time. The past-as-exclusion is the pedagogical lesson of citizenship; the past provides the evidence of the violent histories of nonnormative citizenships and explains (and, often, rationalizes) the violence in the present.

But within citizentime, the past is a retrospective tutorial that confirms the narrative of progressive citizenship; in time, more and more will be included—if not now, then soon. The past-as-exclusion references the future-as-inclusion as the salvation to pain, violence, and exclusion. And yet, citizenship's vision of the future-as-inclusion is not an intersectional one; rather, the future is plotted as a series of partial, group-based inclusions, one axis of (normativized) difference at a time. In this way, Justice Thomas's premonition in his concurrence in *Fisher* that there is "no logical stopping point" for remedying societal discrimination is, in fact, the point of citizenship discourse itself. Citizenship is a self-referential system that continuously deploys anti-intersectional epistemologies in order to ensure its own futurity.[34]

These temporalities of citizenship are a means to restore normative citizen-subjects as the rightful heirs to the past-as-future. As Stephen Dillon so incisively describes, one of the essential qualities of privileged, normative existence is the ability to wait and presume "the passage of time washes away the violence of the then and now so that the future is free from the horrors of the past." But the violence of citizenship, like time, does not pass, it *accumulates*; the variable distributions of the brutalities and precarities of social life build, intensify, and modify. "Power does not get better, friendlier, or less brutal," Dillon observes, "it just changes name and shape. The wreckage of the past keeps piling up, so that what the liberal imagination hopes it has left behind, is actually what makes the present and the future unlivable."[35] For the "death-bound subject," there is no future, and there is no time to waste.[36] In and against state projects that claim that racialized, heteronormative, colonial abjection is past, and that the complete normativization of difference is in the future, there is no time for intersectional coalitions but now.

This book is merely an explication of what Audre Lorde already diagnosed in the infamous essay, "The Master's Tools Will Never Dismantle the Master's House." In that essay, and her subsequent work on difference, Lorde argued that U.S. state mechanisms (and Western epistemologies) reframe difference and contort it into a system of dehumanization, whereby the differences between and within us all are valued or devalued through the combined operations of white supremacy and capitalism, and we can add to her analysis, settler colonialism, neoliberal globalization, and U.S. orientalism. This form of difference—as a systemized mechanism for human de/valuing—is the distortion, the "master's tool" that keeps people focused on either "ignoring or misnaming difference." It is this form of difference that is the "master's tools" that "will never dismantle the master's house. They may allow us temporarily to beat him at his own game, but they will never enable us to bring about genuine change." And this is why she called for a radical reclaiming of difference, a process that would work to recognize and value differences in order to dismantle that house. As she so powerfully (and famously) described, "Difference must be not merely tolerated, but seen as a fund of necessary polarities between which our creativity can spark like a dialectic. Only then does the necessity for interdependency become unthreatening."[37]

U.S. citizenship is the difference engine of human devaluing. It twists and contorts arguments for social change into narratives of citizenship that consistently return us to the master's tools. Thinking outside of and beyond citizenship requires an active disrespect toward the unifying themes and promises of citizenship, particularly as articulated through appeals to American orthodoxies of white settler heteronormative multiculturalism. Being against citizenship is a coalitional stance against systemized human de/valuing, and calls for the envisioning of difference "as a fund of necessary polarities" that Lorde asked for so many years ago. It is a "coalition of incommensurability," that comes together in order to "spark like a dialectic" to forge an intersectional present.[38]

This is happening right now . . . as I write these words. Against the practical, pragmatic politics of single-issue, liberal politics, activists, scholars, and visionaries are enacting intersectional politics against citizenship. It is in prison abolition movements, divestment organizing against border militarizations, queer economic justice work, decolonial activisms against border patrol violence, migrant activisms in defense of Indigenous sovereignties, Black-led coalitions against police assassinations, queer youth of color reclaiming access to public spaces, and radical feminists of color-led organizing against violence. These are just a few of the many ways in which people refuse the politics of anti-intersectional inclusion. And these coalitions are not easy, they are not perfect, and they are not without their shortcomings, momentary lapses, and painful faults. They negotiate power and their own varied and variable intersectional positionalities, sometimes replicating normative power and its embodiments, oftentimes trying to configure what accountability looks like. And they try to refuse, work against, and sometimes fall prey to the script that political actions should contort to the anti-intersectionalities of citizenship in order to be successful. And then they regroup and try again.

*Against Citizenship* is an argument for and vision of coalition building, political organizing, and justice that abandons the normative frameworks of citizenship, law, and temporality. These normative frameworks continue to limit and thwart intersectional political visions; dismantling the violence of citizenship and normativities requires a radical rerouting of faith, a process in which the devalued and disenfranchised and their allies give up any belief in citizenship, law, and futurity as avenues for salvation and justice. Rather than continuing the faithful return to these frameworks, I ask that we mark the faiths in time, law, and citizenship as *queer*—as in odd, off the mark, unnatural—in order to demand knowledge, envision justice, and claim responsibility, not based on time, law, or citizenship, but in spite of them. Queering the faiths in citizenship, law, and temporality creates a space in which decolonial, queer, feminist and critical race scholars and activists work toward imagining and restructuring accountability in order to see oppression, seek change, and envision justice in the present. *Against Citizenship* not only suggests that we *can* embark on such intersectional present, but insists that we *must*. And it is about time.

# Notes

## Preface

1. Brown and Halley, *Left Legalism/Left Critique*, 28.

2. Ibid., 27, 29.

3. For a related critique of political hierarchies within queer studies, see Wiegman, *Object Lessons*.

4. For more on the It Gets Better Project, see http://www.itgetsbetter.org/ (accessed June 15, 2013).

5. Duggan, "New Homonormativity," 190.

6. Eng, *Feeling of Kinship*, 3, 4.

7. Agathangelou et al., "Intimate Investments," 129.

8. Puar, *Terrorist Assemblages*, xii.

9. Ferguson, *Aberrations in Black*, 82.

10. Ferguson, "Of Our Normative Strivings," 98.

11. Agathangelou et al., "Intimate Investments," 129.

12. Ibid., 123.

13. Wiegman, *Object Lessons*, 339–340.

14. Hanhardt, *Safe Space*, 29.

15. Whitlock, *In a Time of Broken Bones*, 7.

16. For more on the ways in which groups are set up in opposition to each other and positioned as having competing interests, see Cacho, *Social Death*, and Jun, *Race for Citizenship*.

17. Cacho, *Social Death*, 148.

## Introduction

1. Importantly, I refer to Arizona's onslaught of dehumanizing legislation not in order to underwrite the discursive production of Arizona as more racist or xenophobic than other states, but because Arizona has served as a role model for other state legislative actions against nonnormative folks. Therefore, Arizona serves as an example of antinormative logics not because of its spectacularity, but because of its centrality.

2. There were other notoriously conservative laws passed in Arizona that year as well, such as the "Birther Bill" that was focused on the racism and phobia against President Obama. The law was vetoed by Governor Brewer, but continued to resurface in the state legislature.

3. *Arizona et al. v. United States*, 567 U.S. ____ (2012) (11-182). The majority decision struck down three other provisions in the law and worked to reaffirm federal authority on issues of immigration.

4. For more on Section 287g, see http://www.ice.gov/287g/, and for "Secure Communities," see http://www.ice.gov/secure_communities/ (both Web sites accessed April 22, 2013).

5. While scholars of immigration have pointed out how anti-immigration rhetoric resurfaces throughout U.S. history as a means to shore up U.S. national identity, we might also understand these moments as part of the performativity of settler colonialism, whereby the U.S. stakes its claim over Indigenous land over and over again.

6. The law does offer the exemption of teaching about the Holocaust and "any other instance of genocide." Ariz. Rev. Stat. § 15-112 (2010); for full text, see http://www.azleg.gov/FormatDocument.asp?inDoc=/ars/15/00112.htm&Title=15&DocType=ARS (accessed March 15, 2014). For analyses of the anti–ethnic studies law, see Cacho, "But Some of Us Are Wise"; Cha-Jua, "Obama, the Rise of the Hard Right"; Kunnie, "Apartheid in Arizona?"

7. Many states, cities, and counties copied Arizona's "show me your papers" laws, including Alabama, Georgia, Indiana, South Carolina, and Utah.

8. For example, many states (including Arizona and Nebraska) have followed model legislation drafted by the National Right to Life Committee (NRLC), referred to as the "Pain-Capable Unborn Protection Act," that attempts to increasingly curtail access to abortion. Moreover, many states have followed Arizona's lead of proposing "Bathroom Bills" (also dubbed "Toilet Papers Bills") that target transgender communities and their use of restrooms without "proper" identifications of their "sex." And while there have been versions of Religious Freedom laws throughout the states, conservative legislators are attempting to enact stricter versions of these laws that grant businesses rights to turn away customers and refuse to provide medical benefits such as contraceptive coverage as practices of the company's religious freedom.

9. Soto and Joseph, "Neoliberalism and the Battle," 48. For other intersectional analyses of Arizona's legislation against nonnormative peoples, see Chávez, "Exploring the Defeat," and "Border (In)Securities"; Gutiérrez et al., "Nativism, Normativity, and Neoliberalism in Arizona."

10. Brandzel and Desai, "Race, Violence, and Terror," 62. While the notion of a "cultural defense" is most often equated with (especially Asian) immigrant defendants in U.S. courtrooms, we purposefully redeployed the term in order to call attention to the ways in which United States popular culture and legal mechanisms are replete with white, heteromasculine cultural expectations and protections.

11. Berlant, *Queen of America*, 2.

12. Thank you Wendy Kozol for this insight.

13. The one exception is the very explicit language of fear and anxiety regarding "Muslim-looking terrorists," as discussed in more detail in Chapter One.

14. Isin and Turner, "Citizenship Studies," 2; Kymlicka and Norman, "Return of the Citizen," 283; Somers, *Genealogies of Citizenship*, 12.

15. For example, see Miller, "Introducing . . . Cultural Citizenship"; Ong, "Cultural Citizenship as Subject-Making"; Rosaldo, "Cultural Citizenship and Educational Democracy."

16. For example, Kymlicka, *Multicultural Citizenship*.

17. For example, Bruyneel, *Third Space of Sovereignty*; Hoxie, *Final Promise*; Mandell, *Tribe, Race, History*; Rosen, *American Indians and State Law*.

18. Young, "Polity and Group Difference."

19. For example, see Bell and Binnie, *Sexual Citizen*; Cossman, *Sexual Citizens*; Evans, *Sexual Citizenship*; Stychin, *Governing Sexuality*; Weeks, "Sexual Citizen."

20. Plummer, "Square of Intimate Citizenship."

21. Berlant, *Queen of America*.

22. Ong, *Flexible Citizenship*.

23. For example, see Bosniak, *Citizen and the Alien*; Sassen, "Towards a Post-National and Denationalized Citizenship"; Soysal, "Toward a Postnational Model of Membership."

24. For example, see Dower and Williams, *Global Citizenship*; Isin and Nyers, *Routledge Handbook of Global Citizenship Studies*.

25. For example, see Hutchings and Dannreuther, *Cosmopolitan Citizenship*; Linklater, "Cosmopolitan Citizenship."

26. For example, see Cronin, *Advertising and Consumer Citizenship*; Grewal, *Transnational America*; Lipsitz, "Learning from New Orleans."

27. Although I am not as familiar with this scholarship, there is a vast body of business, economics, and management literature on "corporate citizenship."

28. Isin and Turner, "Citizenship Studies"; Kymlicka and Norman, "Return of the Citizen."

29. Kymlicka and Norman, "Return of the Citizen."

30. Young, "Polity and Group Difference."

31. Isin and Turner, "Citizenship Studies," 4.

32. See, for example, Gotanda, "Race, Citizenship, and the Search for Political"; Karst, *Belonging to America*, and "Citizenship, Law, and the American Nation"; Smith, *Civic Ideals*; Spiro, "Citizenship Dilemma"; Yuval-Davis and Werbner, *Women, Citizenship, and Difference*.

33. Lister, *Citizenship*, 4–5.

34. Bell and Binnie, *Sexual Citizen*; Evans, *Sexual Citizenship*; Stychin, *Governing Sexuality*; Weeks, "Sexual Citizen."

35. Bell and Binnie, *Sexual Citizen*, 141, 146.

36. Isin and Nielsen, *Acts of Citizenship*, 2, 4.

37. See, for example, Brown, *RePlacing Citizenship*; Lee, "Undocumented Workers' Subversive Citizenship Acts," and "Suicide Bombing?"; Sparks, "Dissident Citizenship."

38. Newman, "'But We Didn't Mean That,'" 96; Rasmussen and Brown, "Radical Democratic Citizenship," 185.

39. For undocumented migrant actions and contestations of citizenship, see Chávez, *Queer Migration Politics*; De Genova, "Production of Culprits," and "Queer Politics of Migration"; Lee and Pratt, "Spectacular and The Mundane"; McNevin, "Irregular Migrants"; Tyler and Marciniak, "Immigrant Protest"; Walters, "Acts of Demonstration."

40. Bosniak, "Varieties of Citizenship"; Sassen, "Towards a Post-National and Denationalized Citizenship."

41. Scholars have pointed out how Natives are embroiled in multiple citizenships across nations and states. This is why Jessica Cattelino refers to "overlapping" citizenship, Renya Ramirez discusses "multilayered" citizenship, and David Wilkins refers to three layers of citizenship that includes U.S. federal and state-level citizenship as well as Native citizenship. For more on these points, see Cattelino, *High Stakes*; Ramirez, *Native Hubs*; Wilkins, *American Indian Politics and the American Political System*.

42. For more on Native citizenship as resistance, see Simpson, "On Ethnographic Refusal," and *Mohawk Interruptus*.

43. Alfred, *Peace, Power, Righteousness*, and *Wasáise*; Cook-Lynn, *Separate Country*; Lyons, *X-Marks*; Simpson, *Mohawk Interruptus*.

44. Barker, *Native Acts*, 216. See also Denetdale, "Securing Navajo National Boundaries," and "Chairmen, Presidents, and Princesses."

45. Ramirez, *Native Hubs*, 18.

46. Henderson, "Sui Generis and Treaty Citizenship."

47. Deloria, *Playing Indian*.

48. Iverson, *Carlos Montezuma and the Changing World*, 113. See also Bruyneel, *Third Space of Sovereignty*, 105.

49. Bosniak, "Universal Citizenship," 965. See also Bosniak, *Citizen and the Alien*; Cole, *Enemy Aliens*.

50. Baines and Sharma, "Migrant Workers as Non-Citizens."

51. See, for example, Gotanda, "Race, Citizenship, and the Search"; Johnson, "Race, the Immigration Laws, and Domestic Race Relations"; Saito, "Model Minority, Yellow Peril"; Trucios-Haynes, "Legacy of Racially Restrictive Immigration Laws."

52. Johnson, "Race, the Immigration Laws," 1116.

53. Cole, *Enemy Aliens*, 8–9. See also Cole, "Against Citizenship."

54. De Genova, "Production of Culprits," 440.

55. Hindess, "Citizenship in the International Management," 1495.

56. Baines and Sharma, "Migrant Workers as Non-Citizens," 76.

57. Somers, *Genealogies of Citizenship*, 20, 69, 26.

58. Volpp, "'Obnoxious to Their Very Nature,'" 72–73.

59. Shildrick, "Sexual Citizenship, Governance and Disability," 138.

60. The majority of the scholarship in sexual citizenship tends to be anti-intersectional.

61. I am very thankful to Wendy Kozol for this brilliant insight.

62. Ong, *Flexible Citizenship*, 120. Importantly, Foucault pointed out that disciplinary power did not disappear through biopolitical power, but, rather, became intensified. As he states, "discipline was never more important or more valorized than at the moment when it became important to manage a population." Foucault et al., *Foucault Effect*, 102.

63. Foucault et al., *Society Must Be Defended*, 242–243.

64. Ibid., 240. See also Mbembé, "Necropolitics."

65. Hindess, "Citizenship for All." This is also a key premise of postcolonial theory. See, for example, Alexander, *Pedagogies of Crossing*; Chakrabarty, *Provincializing Europe*.

66. Hindess, "Citizenship in the International Management," 1496.

67. Baines and Sharma, "Migrant Workers as Non-Citizens," 85.

68. Foucault, "Subject and Power," 781.

69. Ong, "Cultural Citizenship as Subject-Making," 747. See also Ong, *Buddha Is Hiding*, xviii.

70. Bell and Binnie, *Sexual Citizen*, 141.

71. Deloria and Wilkins, *Legal Universe*, 171. Indian General Allotment Act of 1887 (Dawes Severalty Act), chap. 119, 24 Stat. 388 (1887), amended by 25 U.S.C. § 331. For more on federal citizenship as a mechanism of assimilation, see Bruyneel, *Third Space of Sovereignty*; Hoxie, *Final Promise*.

72. Indian Citizenship Act of 1924 (Snyder Act), chap. 233, 43 U.S. Stats. At Large 253 (1924). For example, the *Citizenship Act of 1901* (24 Stat. 388, vol. 1, 33 (1887), amended by 31 Stat. 1447, vol. 1, 114) "granted" citizenship to the "Five Civilized Tribes." However, as American Indian studies scholars have shown, many Indigenous people were "granted" state-level citizenships throughout the nineteenth century. For state-level "gifts" of citizenship to Native Americans, see Mandell, *Tribe, Race, History*; Rosen, *American Indians and State Law*. And, as Kevin Bruyneel notes, U.S. citizenship was imposed on Pueblo tribes in the Southwest through the Treaty of Guadalupe Hidalgo in 1848. See Bruyneel, *Third Space of Sovereignty*, 249, n. 35.

73. According to Deloria and Wilkins, acts including the 1924 law "were largely ineffectual because the doctrine of compatibility of indigenous legal incompetence remained good law and nullified efforts by Congress to provide Indians with constitutional protections with respect to their lands and tribal benefits." Deloria and Wilkins, *Legal Universe*, 197.

74. Ibid.

75. This practice was initiated in treaties that offered Natives an opportunity to become U.S. citizens on the condition that they abandon their tribal citizenship and tribal property. Wilkins, *American Indian Politics*, 51.

76. In her essay, "Captivating Eunice," Audra Simpson describes the ways in which First Nation women lost their tribal citizenship upon marrying Canadian male citizens as a "citizenship of grief."

77. For more on Indigenous claims of U.S. citizenship, see Lomawaima, "Mutuality of Citizenship and Sovereignty"; Maddox, *Citizen Indians*. For more on the ambiguities of Indigenous claims to U.S. citizenship, see Bruyneel, *Third Space of Sovereignty*; Ramirez, *Native Hubs*. For more on Indigenous resistance to U.S. citizenship, see Kauanui, *Hawaiian Blood*; Mandell, *Tribe, Race, History*; Merry, *Colonizing Hawai'i*; Rosen, *American Indians and State Law*; Silva, *Aloha Betrayed*. For the "refusal" of U.S citizenship, see Henderson, "Sui Generis and Treaty Citizenship"; Simpson, *Mohawk Interruptus*. Of course, refusing settler citizenship can be very difficult, especially for members of Native nations whose land is now claimed as a border zone between settler states. For more on this struggle, see Luna-Firebaugh, "Border Crossed Us"; Ramirez, *Native Hubs*; Simpson, *Mohawk Interruptus*.

78. Bruyneel, *Third Space of Sovereignty*, 110.

79. As quoted in ibid.

80. Ibid.

81. Berlant, "Slow Death," 754, 759. As quoted in Lee and Pratt, "Spectacular and the Mundane," 891. See also Berlant, *Cruel Optimism*.

82. Lee and Pratt, "Spectacular and the Mundane," 891.

83. Cacho, *Social Death*; Gilmore, *Golden Gulag*.

84. De Genova, "Queer Politics of Migration," 113, 119. For an excellent discussion of activists that contest the racialized discourses of valued migrants, see Chávez, *Queer Migration Politics*.

85. Agathangelou et al., "Intimate Investments," 129–130.

86. Gilmore, *Golden Gulag*, 28.

87. Cacho, *Social Death*, 18.

88. McClintock, *Imperial Leather*, 4.

89. Crenshaw, "Demarginalizing the Intersection." See also Crenshaw, "Mapping the Margins."

90. Stewart, "Lecture Delivered at Franklin Hall." For a thought-provoking analysis of the various appropriations of Sojourner Truth and her speech, see Painter, *Sojourner Truth*.

91. Collins, *Black Feminist Thought*.

92. Collective Combahee River, *Combahee River Collective Statement*.

93. For example, Norma Alarcón's complex or multiple-voiced subjectivity, Gloria Anzaldúa's "mestiza consciousness," Audre Lorde's "coalitional subjectivity," and Cherríe Moraga's "theory in the flesh" might all be considered articulations of, or alternatives from, "intersectionality." Alarcón, "Theoretical Subject(s)"; Anzaldúa, *Borderlands*; Lorde, *Sister Outsider*; Moraga and Anzaldúa, *This Bridge Called My Back*.

94. Hong and Ferguson, *Strange Affinities*, 11.

95. Bilge, "Beyond Subordination vs. Resistance," 23.

96. See, for example, Roberts and Jesudason, "Movement Intersectionality."

97. For critiques of intersectionality, see Carastathis, "Invisibility of Privilege"; Erel et al., "On the Depoliticisation of Intersectionality Talk"; Garry, "Intersectionality, Metaphors, and the Multiplicity of Gender"; Nash, "Re-Thinking Intersectionality," and "'Home Truths' on Intersectionality"; Prins, "Narrative Accounts of Origins"; Staunæs, "Where Have All the Subjects Gone?"; Zack, *Inclusive Feminism*. For examples of some of the responses to these critiques, see Berger and Guidroz, *Intersectional Approach*; Davis, "Intersectionality as Buzzword"; Hancock, "Intersectionality as a Normative and Empirical Paradigm"; Lewis, "Celebrating Intersectionality?"; McCall, "Complexity of Intersectionality"; May, *Pursuing Intersectionality*; Tomlinson, "To Tell the Truth," and "Colonizing Intersectionality."

98. For example, see Ehrenreich, "Subordination and Symbiosis"; Hutchinson, "Out Yet Unseen"; Kwan, "Jeffrey Dahmer"; Valdes, "Sex and Race."

99. Crenshaw, "Mapping the Margins," 1244–1245, n. 9.

100. Carbado, Crenshaw, and Mays, "Intersectionality," 305. For an example of scholarship that refuses to soothe this anxiety and argues intersectionality is rightfully and politically for and about women of color only, see Floyd-Alexander, "Disappearing Acts."

101. Prins, "Narrative Accounts of Origins," 279.

102. Tomlinson, "Colonizing Intersectionality," 266.

103. Puar, "'I Would Rather Be a Cyborg'"; Nash, "'Home Truths' on Intersectionality."

104. Berger and Guidroz, *Intersectional Approach*; Cho et al., "Toward a Field of Intersectionality Studies"; Dill and Zambrana, *Emerging Intersections*.

105. Nash, "Re-Thinking Intersectionality," 2.

106. Carastathis, "Reinvigorating Intersectionality," 60. See also Carasthatis, "Invisibility of Privilege."

107. Collins, "Forward," vii–xiv; Erel et al., "On the Depoliticisation of Intersectionality Talk," 277.

108. For more on this point, see Bouchard, *Community of Disagreement*.

109. Bouchard, "Women's Studies' Guilt Complex," and *Community of Disagreement*; Hemmings, *Why Stories Matter*; Wiegman, "Feminism's Apocalyptic Futures," and "Academic Feminism against Itself."

110. Okin, *Is Multiculturalism Bad for Women?*; Zack, *Inclusive Feminism*.

111. Brandzel, "Haunted by Citizenship," 505.

112. Puar, *Terrorist Assemblages*, 215.

113. Puar, "'I Would Rather Be a Cyborg,'" 63.

114. Puar, *Terrorist Assemblages*, 212.

115. Berlant, *Queen of America*; Brown, *States of Injury*; Cott, *Public Vows*; Grewal, *Transnational America*; Luibhéid, *Entry Denied*; Ong, *Flexible Citizenship*; Rand, *Ellis Island Snow*

*Globe*; Somerville, "Notes toward a Queer History," and *Queering the Color Line*; Volpp, "Citizen and the Terrorist," "Impossible Subjects," and "Divesting Citizenship."

116. Desai, *Beyond Bollywood*; Duggan, *Twilight of Equality*; Eng, *Feeling of Kinship*; Ferguson, *Aberrations in Black*; Halberstam, *In a Queer Time and Place*; Puar, *Terrorist Assemblages*; Reddy, *Freedom with Violence*; Spade, *Normal Life*.

117. Eng, with Halberstam and Muñoz, Introduction, 2.

118. Barker, *Native Acts*; Byrd, *Transit of Empire*; Denetdale, "Chairmen, Presidents, and Princesses," and "Securing Navajo National Boundaries"; Kauanui, *Hawaiian Blood*.

119. Byrd, *Transit of Empire*, xxiii–xxiv.

120. Puar and Rai, "Monster, Terrorist, Fag."

121. "Kanaka Maoli" (singular and categorical plural) and "Kānaka Maoli" (countable plural) are Hawaiian language terms for the Indigenous, aboriginal peoples that have genealogical ties to the Islands of the Hawaiian Archipegelo. Other terms include "Kanaka ʻŌiwi," or the more abbreviated "Kanaka," "ʻŌiwi," or "Maoli." I use "Native Hawaiian" (both with and without quotation marks) whenever I am referring to the U.S.-based legal, cultural, and political production of Indigenous Hawaiians. Otherwise, I use the proper term, "Kanaka Maoli." For more on naming and identifications of Kanaka Maoli, see Goodyear-Kaʻōpua et al., *Nation Rising*; Kauanui, *Hawaiian Blood*; Silva, *Aloha Betrayed*.

122. Dillon, "'It's Here, It's That Time.'"

## Chapter 1. The Specters of Citizenship

1. For more on the ubiquity of patriotic consumer practices after September 11, 2001, see Grewal, *Transnational America*.

2. The lack of foreclosure within "These colors don't run" is emphasized through some of the playful variations of the slogan, such as "These colors don't run . . . The World" and "These colors don't bleed, the innocent do." One of the most enjoyable iterations of the phrase is from a queer rights bumper sticker in which a rainbow flag–filled triangle lies next to the phrase "These colors don't run. They skip & jump."

3. By using the term "Muslim-looking peoples" I am not attempting to provide an umbrella term for easy reference. Rather, I am attempting to name and pinpoint what Leti Volpp has referenced as the "consolidation of a new racial identity that groups together persons who appear 'Middle Eastern, Arab, or Muslim.'" As Volpp points out, this new racial identity brings together older racialized and orientalist tropes (such as the Asian despot, the Arab terrorist, the victimized veiled woman) into a purposefully broad category through the "war on terror." See Volpp, "Citizen and the Terrorist," 1575. Ahmad furthers Volpp's argument by suggesting that there has been a recent deployment of the "logic of fungibility" whereby the equation of "terrorist" with "Muslim" functions to "capture not only Arab Muslims, but Arab Christians, Muslim non-Arabs (such as Pakistanis and Indonesians), non-Muslim South Asians (Sikhs, Hindus), and even Latinos and African Americans, depending on how closely

they approach the phenotypic stereotype of the terrorist. 'Looking,' not 'Muslim,' is the operative word in 'Muslim-looking.'" Ahmad, "Rage Shared by Law," 1278–1279. See also Grewal, *Transnational America*, 197, 208–210. For more on how U.S. orientalist racial formations have been extended and transformed via September 11th rhetoric, see Brandzel and Desai, "Racism without Recognition."

4. While most scholarship on the violence of racial profiling operations focuses on how these actions target men of color, some argue that this scholarly focus on men of color obscures how state operations have targeted women of color as well. For more on this point, see Ritchie, "Law Enforcement Violence."

5. According to the South Asian American Leaders of Tomorrow (SAALT), there were 645 attacks in the week following September 11th. See their report, "American Backlash: Terrorists Bring War Home in More Ways than One," at http://www.saalt.org/biasreport.pdf. The Asian American Legal and Defense Fund (AALDEF) documented and compiled a partial list of 90 incidents in the month after September 11th. See their report, http://www.aaldef.org/images/101101list.pdf. The National Asian Pacific American Legal Consortium reported over 250 bias-motivated crimes against Asian and Pacific Americans in the three months following September 11th (out of a total of 507 reports for the year). See their report, "Backlash," at http://www.napalc.org/files/2001_Audit.pdf. According to the American-Arab Anti-Discrimination Committee (ADC), there were over 700 incidents against Arab Americans, or those perceived to be Arab Americans, within the first nine weeks following September 11th. See "Hate Crimes Report" at http://www.adc.org/hatecrimes/executive.htm. The FBI reported 481 attacks against people of Middle Eastern descent, Muslims, and South Asian Sikhs during 2001, up from just 28 in 2000. See Federal Bureau of Investigation, Uniform Crime Reporting Program, "Hate Crime Statistics 2001," Nov. 25, 2002, http://www.fbi.gov/ucr/01hate.pdf (all sites accessed March 15, 2005).

6. See Ahmad, "Rage Shared by Law," 1266; Volpp, "Citizen and the Terrorist," 1581; and Asian American Legal and Defense Fund (AALDEF) report.

7. See Robert Hanashiro, "Hate Crimes Born out of Tragedy Create Victims," *USA Today*, Sept. 11, 2002, available at http://www.usatoday.com/news/sept11/2002-09-1-mesa_x.htm, and Robert Pierre, "Victims of Hate, Now Feeling Forgotten," *Washington Post*, Sept. 14, 2002, reprinted at http://www.saja.org/dissect/vasudevpatelwp.html (both accessed March 15, 2005).

8. See especially Ahmad, "Rage Shared by Law."

9. Ibid., 1323.

10. For more on this point, see Reddy, *Freedom with Violence*.

11. Jordan, *Civil Wars*, 48.

12. Methodologically speaking, I read the debates and scholarship on hate crime legislation allegorically. By this I mean that I trace these discourses as forms of knowledge production that solidify social categories, differential levels of vulnerability, and the limits on what can be intelligibly said about the state's role in violence. There are, however, limits to this approach, with the most important being that as much as this

chapter engages with violence, it does not even begin to account for the lived experiences and the materialities of this violence. It is also important to remind readers that this chapter is focused only on federal hate crime legislation, and does not include state and local hate crime laws. Moreover, while I work to offer an intersectional analysis of the racialized, settler colonial, gendered, and sexualized violence of citizenship, this chapter fails to discuss how dis/ability informs these debates. And last, for the sake of time and space, this chapter does not offer the historical contextualizations as to how settler colonialism and slavery set the foundations for the violence of U.S. citizenship, hate violence, and police brutality. These are important gaps and they mark the limits of this study, limits that I hope other scholars can and will address in the future.

13. Streissguth, *Hate Crimes*, 3.

14. Some states and local municipalities recognize homelessness and age as protected categories under state/local hate crime laws. According to social science literature, undocumented immigrants are often presumed and subsumed under the category of "Hispanic," a problematic conflation that could potentially be exposed if legislators consider proposals for adding migrant documentation status to hate crime protections. For an example of social science advocacy and conflation of Hispanic/Immigrant, see Michele Stacey et al., "Demographic Change." In 2013, a year after the attacks on the Sikh Temple of Wisconsin (Oak Creek) in which six Sikhs were killed, the Department of Justice announced that it would add categories of "Sikhs, Hindus, Arabs, Buddhists, Mormons, Jehovah's Witnesses, and Orthodox Christians" to hate crime incident report forms. http://www.wpr.org/doj-announces-hate-crime-initiative-sikh-temple-shooting-memorial-service (accessed Dec. 4, 2014).

15. For an excellent discussion of the transitions from information gathering, to hate crime statistics, to the most recent focus on penalty enhancements, see Hanhardt, *Safe Space*.

16. *Hate Crime Statistics Act of 2009*, 28 U.S.C. § 534 (2009).

17. Christina Hanhardt argues, "as was the case in the field of criminology more generally, the antiviolence movement's own conception of evidence increasingly narrowed as the language of legislation shifted from mandating the collection of *information* to that of more *systemized data*." Hanhardt, *Safe Space*, 171 (emphasis in original).

18. Violent Crime Control and Enforcement Act of 1994, 108 Stat. 1796, 103rd Cong. (Sept. 13, 1994). This law also included sentence enhancements for crimes against the elderly, though these were positioned separately from the hate crime provisions.

19. Ibid.

20. The commerce clause can also be invoked if the weapon used for the crime traveled across state or national borders, or if the crime interferes with commercial or economic activities.

21. Sprinkle, *Unfinished Lives*, xvii.

22. Smith, "Unmasking the State," 230.

23. Rosga, "Deadly Words," 244.

24. Gelman and Lawrence, "Agreeing to Agree," 433.

25. Maroney, "Struggle against Hate Crime," 569.

26. Some examples of organizations that have furthered community-minded justice alternatives include: INCITE! Women of Color Against Violence http://www.incite -national.org/; Audre Lorde Project's Safe OUTside the System Collective http://alp .org/community/sos; Community United Against Violence http://www.cuav.org/ (all sites accessed June 29, 2012).

27. Spade, *Normal Life*, 36, 40.

28. Thomas, "Beyond the Privacy Principle," 1440, 1485–1486.

29. Ibid., 1490–1491 (my emphasis).

30. *United States v. Classic*, 313 U.S. 299, 326 (May 26, 1941).

31. See, for example, U.S. Department of Justice, Bureau of Justice Statistics, "Arrest-Related Deaths," http://www.bjs.gov/index.cfm?ty=tp&tid=82; FBI, Uniform Crime Reports, "Expanded Homicide Data," http://www.fbi.gov/about-us/cjis/ucr/crime -in-the-u.s/2011/crime-in-the-u.s.-2011/offenses-known-to-law-enforcement/ expanded/expanded-homicide-data; and Centers for Disease Control and Prevention, "National Vital Statistics Program," http://www.cdc.gov/nchs/nvss.htm (all sites accessed June 29, 2012).

32. See, for example, the site on "color of law" crimes, http://www.fbi.gov/about-us/ investigate/civilrights/color_of_law/, and "hate crimes," http://www.fbi.gov/about-us/ investigate/civilrights/hate_crimes/ (both accessed June 29, 2012).

33. Reddy, *Freedom with Violence*, 223–224.

34. Franklin, "Good Intentions," 80, 88.

35. Perry, *In the Name of Hate*. See also Perry, *Hate and Bias Crime*.

36. Franklin, "Good Intentions," 88.

37. Rosga, "Policing the State."

38. Ibid., 169.

39. Spalek, *Communities, Identities and Crime*, 27.

40. In 2012, these two guidelines were merged, and now the training manual and data collection guidelines are in the "Hate Crime Data Collection Guidelines and Training Manual." U.S. Dep't Of Justice, Fed. Bureau of Investigation, Hate Crime Data Collection Guidelines and Training Manual" (2012), available at http://www .fbi.gov/about-us/cjis/ucr/data-collection-manual (accessed June 29, 2012).

41. In his testimony before the House Judiciary Committee, scholar Jack McDevitt argued that one of the benefits of hate crime legislation is that it provides an opportunity for academics to train police about race in society. *Local Law Enforcement Hate Crimes Prevention Act of 2007: Hearing on H.R. 1592 Before the Subcomm. on Crime, Terrorism, and Homeland Security of the H. Comm. on the Judiciary*, 110th Cong. 83 (2007) [hereinafter *Hearing on H.R. 1592*] (statement of Jack McDevitt, associate dean, Northeastern University).

42. U.S. Dep't Of Justice, Fed. Bureau of Investigation, Hate Crime Data Collection Guidelines (1999), available at http://acic.org/crimeStatistics/Documents/Hate%20

Crime%20Data%20Collection%20Guidelines.pdf. See also U.S. Dep't Of Justice, Fed. Bureau of Investigation, Training Guide For Hate Crime Data Collection (1996), available at http://acic.org/crimeStatistics/Documents/Hate%20Crime%20Data%20 Collection%20Training%20Guide.pdf (both sites accessed June 29, 2012).

43. U.S. Dep't Of Justice, Fed. Bureau of Investigation, "Hate Crime Data Collection Guidelines and Training Manual" (2012): 17–18.

44. Ibid.

45. It should be noted that the 2012 training manual actually omitted the learning module on "Social Psychology of Prejudice," which is where the examples listed in this chapter were found. The revised manual includes only two of the three learning modules that were included up until this point: the learning module on "Bias-Motivated Crime: Definitions and Procedures" and "Case Study Exercises of Possible Bias-Related Crimes." One might speculate that as hate crime legislation has become more commonplace, and wider-encompassing in the categories of inclusion, the authors of the training manual might think this information is no longer necessary, as if prejudice and bias are now "understood" in this supposedly multicultural United States.

46. Rosga, "Deadly Words," 228.

47. Senator Sessions, for example, accused Attorney General Holder of relying upon subjective data as offered by community organizations, as opposed to the supposedly objective data by government agencies. As Sessions stated, "one of the studies heavily relied on by the Attorney General in support of this bill is a 2008 report published by the National Coalition of Anti-Violence Programs, which is composed primarily of lesbian, gay, bisexual, and transgender groups. They have every right to do those studies and present them, but it is a coalition clearly with a vested interest in the legislation, and it should be examined carefully." 111 Cong. Rec. S7675 (daily ed. July 20, 2009) (statement of Sen. Jeff Sessions).

48. *Matthew Shepard Hate Crimes Prevention Act of 2009: Hearing on S. 11-464 Before the S. Comm. on the Judiciary*, 111th Cong. 40 (2009) [hereinafter *Hearings on S. 11-464*] (statement of Gail Heriot, Comm'r on the U.S. Commission on Civil Rights).

49. Id., 58.

50. Caroline Wolf Harlow, Bureau of Justice Statistics, Hate Crime Reported by Victims and Police (NCJ 209911, Nov. 2005). www.bjs.gov/content/pub/pdf/hcrvp .pdf (accessed June 29, 2012).

51. Lynn Langton and Michael Planty, Bureau of Justice Statistics, Hate Crimes, 2003–2009 6 (NCJ 234085, June 2011), www.bjs.gov/content/pub/pdf/hc0309.pdf (accessed June 29, 2012).

52. William J. Krouse, Cong. Research Serv., RL33403, Hate Crime Legislation (Nov. 29, 2010).

53. Id., 14.

54. Id.

55. For a discussion about the pitfalls and usefulness of law for left politics, see Brown and Halley, *Left Legalism/Left Critique*. For a discussion of the paradox of legal

subjection, see Brown, *States of Injury* and "Suffering the Paradoxes of Rights." And for responses to Brown, see Balfour, "Reparations after Identity Politics"; Bramen, "Why the Academic Left."

56. Rosga, "Policing the State," 149.

57. Hwang, "Interrelationship between Anti-Asian Violence," 49.

58. Rosga, "Deadly Words," 243.

59. This was modified to "Person with Disability" in later incarnations.

60. *Hate Crime Data Collection Guidelines*, 1999, 3.

61. Id., 5.

62. Id., 4.

63. http://www.whitehouse.gov/omb/fedreg_1997standards (accessed June 29, 2012). Importantly, in disaggregating "Ethnicity" from "National Origin," hate crimes involving "national origins" are no longer being tracked, statistically, at the federal level. Within the contexts of hate crime legislation, "Ethnicity" appears to be simplified into "Hispanic and Latino" or "not-Hispanic or Latino." And while "national origin" was constrained by being tracked through the merged category of "Ethnicity/National Origin"—not to mention the presumed equivalence of Ethnicity = Hispanic—one could speculate that the category of national origins might have the most potential to work against and thwart whitenormative, colonialnormative citizenship in the United States.

64. Tuck and Yang, "Decolonization Is Not a Metaphor," 22.

65. Perry also points out that hate crimes against Natives have different qualities in that they tend to be related to struggles over resources and land. For more on these points, see Perry, *Silent Victims*, and "Normative Violence."

66. Steven W. Perry, Bureau of Justice Statistics, American Indians and Crime: A BJS Statistical Profile, 1992–2002 (NCJ 203097, Dec. 2004). http://www.justice.gov/sites/default/files/otj/docs/american_indians_and_crime.pdf (accessed June 29, 2012).

67. The egregious missteps and presumptions of this report are echoed throughout federal materials on crime and victimization in "Indian Country." And the tentacles of the federal government have been increasingly fortified through the Tribal Law and Order Act of 2010 (Pub. L. 111-211, H.R. 725, 124 Stat. 2258, enacted July 29, 2010), which includes provisions on establishing a tribal data collection system. For more information, see Liza Minno Bloom, "Whose 'Shared Humanity'? The Tribal law and Order Act (2010), Barack Obama, and the Politics of Multiculturalism in Settler Colonial States," MA Thesis, University of New Mexico, 2011.

68. For a detailed discussion about various LGBT rights organizations (such as the National Gay and Lesbian Task Force) and their involvement in pushing for hate crime legislation, see Hanhardt, *Safe Space*.

69. 101 Cong. Rec. S. 419 (daily ed. Feb. 8, 1990) (statement Sen. Helms) "Hate Crimes Statistics Act" *Congressional Record* (Feb. 8, 1990).

70. *Hate Crime Statistics Act* (1990). 101 Cong. Amend. 1251 proposed Feb. 8, 1990.

71. *Hate Crime Statistics Act* (1990). 101 Cong. Amend. 1250 proposed Feb. 8, 1990.

72. *Hate Crime Statistics Act* (1990), Pub. L. No. 101-275 § 104 Stat. 140. (1990) (amended 1990).

73. *Hearings on S. 11-464*, supra note 48 at 66, 75 (written response Att'y Gen. Holder).

74. 111 Cong. Rec. H4907 (daily ed. April 28, 2009) (statement of Rep. Gohmert).

75. 111 Cong. Rec. H4911 (daily ed. April 28, 2009) (statement of Rep. King).

76. 111 Cong. Rec. H4906 (daily ed. April 28, 2009) (statement of Rep. King) .

77. 111 Cong. Rec. H4908 (daily ed. April 28, 2009) (statement of Rep. King).

78. 111 Cong. Rec. H4953 (daily ed. April 29, 2009) (statement of Rep. Frank).

79. "Hate Crime Data Collection Guidelines and Training Manual" (2012).

80. Puar, *Terrorist Assemblages*.

81. Jenness and Broad, *Hate Crimes*, 142–143.

82. VAWA (part of the *Violent Crime Control and Law Enforcement Act of 1994*, Pub. L. No. 103-322) provided criminal penalties if a violent crime was committed crossing state lines and federal funds for education and activism against gender violence. It also allowed for individuals to file federal civil law suits in cases of gender-based violence, but this was struck down by the Supreme Court in the 2000 case, *U.S. v. Morrison* [529 U.S. 598] based on the finding that the commerce clause did not permit civil redress under VAWA. In 2013, VAWA was renewed for the third time only after an extensive fight with conservative legislators, a fight which started in 2011. We can see this refusal or downright reluctance to support the law stemming from a combination of factors: recognizing violence via gender is especially difficult, as this chapter argues; the 2013 VAWA law included expanded protections for LGBT domestic violence victims; and, perhaps most controversially, the law grants Native nations the power to prosecute non-Native, U.S. citizens for cases on Native lands. See http://www.huffingtonpost.com/2013/03/07/obama-violence-against-women-act_n_2830158.html?utm_hp_ref=politics (accessed March 7, 2013).

83. For examples of scholarship tracing the inclusion of "gender" within hate crimes, see Hodge, *Gendered Hate*; Jenness and Broad, "Engendering Hate Crime Policy."

84. *Hearings on S. 11-464, supra* note 48 at 437 (statement of Brian Walsh).

85. *Hearings on S. 11-464, supra* note 48 at 26 (statement of Gail Heriot, Comm'r on the U.S. Commission on Civil Rights).

86. *Hearings on S. 11-464, supra* note 48 at 446, 447 (written testimony of Women's Advocacy Organizations).

87. *Hate Crimes Prevention Act of 1997: Hearing on H.R. 3081 Before the H. Comm. on the Judiciary*, 105th Cong., 2nd Sess., 1 (1998).

88. Id., 2 (my emphasis).

89. *Hearing on H.R. 1592, supra* note 41 at 121. (Rep. Maxine Waters).

90. *Hearings on S. 11-464, supra* note 48 at 70 (question by Sen. Jeff Sessions in written testimony of Att'y Gen. Holder).

91. 111 Cong. Rec. S7673 (daily ed. July 20, 2009) (statement of Sen. Sessions).

92. *Hearings on S. 111-464, supra* note 48 at 74 (question by Sen. Jeff Sessions in written testimony of Att'y Gen. Holder).

93. *Hearing on H.R. 1592, supra* note 41 at 3 (statement of Rep. Gohmert).

94. *Hearings on S. 11-464, supra* note 48 at 25 (statement of Gail Heriot, Comm'r on the U.S. Commission on Civil Rights).

95. 111 Cong. Rec. H4908 (daily ed. April 28, 2009) (statement of Rep. Michelle Bachman).

96. *Hearings on S. 11-464, supra* note 48 at 37–38 (statement of Gail Heriot, Comm'r on the U.S. Commission on Civil Rights).

97. Craig, "Retaliation, Fear, or Rage," 65 (my emphasis).

98. Ibid.

99. Spalek, *Communities, Identities and Crime*, 23.

100. Ibid.

101. For more on this argument, see Brandzel and Desai, "Race, Violence, and Terror."

102. Levin and McDevitt, *Hate Crimes Revisited*, 7.

103. *Hearings on S. 11-464, supra* note 48 at 71 (written response Att'y Gen. Holder). See "Attack outside of Catholic church part of 'wave of intimidation,' says Yes on 8," *Catholic News Agency*, Oct. 15, 2008. http://www.catholicnewsagency.com/news/ attack_outside_of_catholic_church_part_of_wave_of_intimidation_says_yes_on _8/ (accessed June 29, 2012).

104. Id. For more information, see Andy Balaskovitz, "Bash Back! Resolved," *Lansing City Pulse*, July 20, 2011, http://www.lansingcitypulse.com/lansing/article-6100-bash -back_-resolved.html (accessed June 29, 2012).

105. *Hearings on S. 11-464, supra* note 48 at 72 (written response Att'y Gen. Holder).

106. Rosga, "Bias before the Law," 30.

## Chapter 2. Intersectionalities Lost and Found

1. *United States v. Windsor, Executor of the Estate of Spyer, et al.*, 570 U.S. ___ (2013), 133 S. Ct. 2675 (2013); *Hollingsworth et al. v. Perry et al.*, 570 U.S. ___ (2013), 133 S. Ct. 2652 (2013).

2. Some examples of these arguments include Jasmyne A. Cannick, "Even Though It's Legal, I Still Can't Marry My Girlfriend," *Advocate*, July 8, 2013, http://www.advocate .com/commentary/2013/07/08/op-ed-even-though-it%E2%80%99s-legal-i-still -can%E2%80%99t-marry-my-girlfriend; "Some Gay-Rights Activists Say Focus on Marriage Has Undercut Advocacy on AIDS and Other Issues," *Washington Post*, July 18, 2013, http://m.washingtonpost.com/national/some-gay-rights-activists -say-focus-on-marriage-has-undercut-advocacy-on-aids-and-other-issues/ 2013/07/18/630c16fa-efd8–11e2–8c36–0e868255a989_story.html; Lynne Huffer, "Bigotry Didn't Die with DOMA, Neither Should Radical Queer Politics," *Huffington Post*, July 6, 2013, http://www.huffingtonpost.com/lynne-huffer/bigotry -didnt-die-with-do_b_3541661.html; Kimberly Dark, "Why Gay Marriage May Not Be the Best Thing for Queer Families," *Huffington Post*, July 2, 2013, http://www

.huffingtonpost.com/kimberly-dark/why-gay-marriage-may-not-be-the-best
-thing-for-queer-families_b_3526764.html?utm_hp_ref=fb&src=sp&comm_ref
=false#sb=4944182b=facebook (all sites accessed July 25, 2013).

3. *Shelby County v. Holder*, 570 U.S. ___ (2013), 133 S. Ct. 2612 (2013); *Adoptive Couple v. Baby Girl*, 570 U.S. ___ (2013), 133 S. Ct. 2552 (2013); *Fisher v. University of Texas*, 570 U.S. ___ (2013), 133 S. Ct. 2411 (2013). Some examples of arguments comparing same-sex marriage decisions to other Supreme Court decisions include Stephen Markley, "One Step Forward, Another Step Back," *RedEye*, July 7, 2013, http://www.redeyechicago .com/news/ct-red-0708-gay-rights-americas-poor-20130707,0,7703356.story; Dana-Ain Davis and Christa Craven, "Equity at the Peril of Normativity: A Feminist Anthropological Take on Race, Marriage and Justice," *Feminist Wire*, June 26, 2013, http://thefeministwire.com/2013/06/equity-at-the-peril-of-normativity-a-feminist -anthropological-take-on-race-marriage-justice/; Mary Lyndon Shanley, "Ongoing Struggle for Recognition," *Boston Review*, June 27, 2013, http://www.bostonreview.net/ mary-lyndon-shanley-same-sex-marriage-equality-lgbqt-supreme-court; Verónica Bayetti Flores, "Reproductive Justice, Marriage Equality, and Undocumented Youth: The Racial Politics of Movement Success," *Feministing*, July 3, 2013, http://feministing .com/2013/07/03/reproductive-justice-marriage-equality-and-undocumented -youth-the-racial-politics-of-movement-success/; Mia McKenzie, "Calling In a Queer Debt: On DOMA, the VRA and the Perfect Opportunity," Black Girl Dangerous (blog), June 27, 2013, http://blackgirldangerous.org/new-blog/2013/6/27/calling-in-a -queer-debt; Dee Rees, "Divisive Moment or an Unparalleled Moment for Coming Together," *Huffington Post*, June 27, 2013, http://www.huffingtonpost.com/dee-rees/ voting-rights-act_b_3510722.html (all sites accessed July 25, 2013).

4. Kai M. Green and Treva Ellison, "Dispatch from the 'Very House of Difference': Anti-Black Racism and the Expansion of Sexual Citizenship—OR—We Need to Do So Much Better at Loving Each Other," *Feminist Wire*, July 4, 2013, http://thefeministwire .com/2013/07/dispatch-from-the-very-house-of-difference-anti-black-racism-and -the-expansion-of-sexual-citizenship-or-we-need-to-do-so-much-better-at-loving -each-other/ (accessed July 25, 2013).

5. In fact, as this book went to press, the U.S. Supreme Court ruled (in a 5–4 decision) that the right to marry is a fundamental right found within the nexus of the due process and equal protection clauses of the Fourteenth Amendment in *Obergefell v. Hodges*, 576 U.S. ___ (2015).

6. George W. Bush, "President Calls for Constitutional Amendment Protecting Marriage," *Office of the Press Secretary*, Speech, White House Press Conference, Washington, D.C., Feb. 24, 2004.

7. See "Alliance for Marriage" at www.allianceformarriage.org (accessed July 20, 2004).

8. Brandzel, "Queering Citizenship?"

9. Cott, "Giving Character," 108, 121. See also Cott, "Marriage and Women's Citizenship," and *Public Vows*.

10. *Adams v. Palmer*, 51 Me. 480, 485 (1863).

11. Maynard v. Hill, 125 U.S. 190, 205 (1888).

12. For more on settler heteronormativity as a tool of colonialism, see Morgensen, "Settler Homonationalism," and *Spaces between Us*; Rifkin, *When Did Indians Become Straight?*

13. 25 Stat. 392, vol. 1, 38 (ch. 818, sec. 2) (1888).

14. Pateman, *Sexual Contract*.

15. See Cott, "Marriage and Women's Citizenship," and *Public Vows*; Kerber, *No Constitutional Right*; Stanley, *From Bondage to Contract*.

16. Cott, "Marriage and Women's Citizenship"; Kerber, *No Constitutional Right*.

17. Act of Feb. 10, 1855, ch. 71 § 10 Stat. 604 (1855) (prior to Nationality Act of 1940). The 1885 law required that the wife meet the racial prerequisite of "free white person" from the Naturalization Law of 1790 in order to be eligible for U.S. citizenship. After 1870, the racial prerequisite included persons of "African descent." The racial prerequisites remained in effect until the 1952 Immigration Act (also known as the McCarran-Walter Act). For more information on the racial prerequisites, see Haney-López, *White by Law*.

18. Expatriation Act of 1907, ch. 2534, 34 Stat. 1228 (1907).

19. Cable Act of 1922, ch. 411, 42 Stat. 1021 (1922); Equal Nationality Bill of 1934, ch. 344, 48 Stat. 797 (1934). See Bredbenner, *Nationality of Her Own*; Cott, "Marriage and Women's Citizenship."

20. For more on interracial marriage bans in the United States, see Hodes, *Sex, Love, Race*; Pascoe, *What Comes Naturally*.

21. Cott, "Marriage and Women's Citizenship," 1461.

22. As quoted in Berger, "Red," 627.

23. African American women were also prosecuted, but less often. The legal charges ranged from bigamy, adultery, and fornication to less egregious infractions of marital and intimacy practices. See Franke, "Becoming a Citizen."

24. The Personal Responsibility and Work Opportunity Reconciliation Act of 1996, Pub. L. 104-193 § 110 Stat. 2105 (1996).

25. Alexander, "Not Just (Any)Body," 6.

26. Rifkin, *When Did Indians Become Straight?* and "Native Nationality."

27. Rifkin makes a very similar and nuanced argument about the appeal toward "civilization" in former Senator Rick Santorum's defense of heterosexual marriage. See Rifkin, *When Did Indians Become Straight?* 3–5.

28. Ibid., 5.

29. While earlier forms of the Equal Rights Amendment (ERA) were proposed in 1923, the ERA was finally passed by Congress and went to state legislatures for ratification in 1972. It has still not been ratified. State versions of the ERA were adopted in twenty-one states, including some that did not ratify the federal version. In Section 1, the ERA calls for "Equality of rights under the law shall not be denied or abridged by the United States or by any state on account of sex."

30. *Baker v. Nelson*, 191 N.W.2d 185 (Minn. 1971). The U.S. Supreme Court dismissed the appeal (*Baker v. Nelson*, 409 U.S. 810 [1972]).

31. *Baker*, 191 N.W.2d at 186.

32. *Jones v. Hallahan*, 501 S.W.2d 588 (Ky. 1973).

33. Id., 589.

34. *Singer v. Hara*, 522 P.2d 1187, 1188 (Wash. Ct. App. 1974).

35. For an excellent discussion of how and when courts deploy social science literature, see Pascoe, *What Comes Naturally*.

36. Maryland Laws, 1973, chap. 213, quoted in Pascoe, "Sex, Gender," 86.

37. *Baehr v. Lewin*, 852 P. 2d 44 (Hawaii 1993).

38. "Scrutiny" refers to the standards of review. "Strict scrutiny" means that it must satisfy the most stringent standards of review in order to be found constitutionally viable. Some categories of identity have been associated with various levels of scrutiny, from the highest level of "strict" to the minimum level of "rational." For example, while racial categories are often given strict scrutiny, gender-related categories are more often measured against an intermediate level of scrutiny, often on the basis that there are "real" differences between the two legally recognized genders, male and female, while race is understood as socially constructed. "Strict Scrutiny," *Legal Information Institute*, https://www.law.cornell.edu/wex/strict_scrutiny (accessed April 17, 2015).

39. *Baehr*, 852 P. 2d at 52, n.11.

40. Bartlett, "Recent Legislation," 581, 582.

41. Hawai'i Office of Elections, 1998 General Election Summary Report (Nov. 4, 1998); Haw. Const. Art. 1 §23.

42. Importantly, I do not include a discussion of same-sex marriage laws within Native nations, but only focus on how U.S. same-sex marriage debates reinforce settler colonial logics. However, scholars such as Joanne Barker, Jennifer Nez Denetdale, Qwo-Li Driskill, Chris Finley, and Daniel Heath Justice have been concerned with the ways in which arguments against same-sex marriage within Native nations have relied upon the adoption of U.S. setter-state norms, even while doing so in the name of (and battle over) Native "traditions." See Barker, *Native Acts*; Denetdale, "Chairmen, Presidents, and Princesses," and "Securing Navajo National Boundaries"; Driskill, "Asegi Ayetl"; Finley, "Decolonizing the Queer Native Body"; Justice, "Notes toward a Theory."

43. Defense of Marriage Act, Pub. L. No. 104-199, 110 Stat. 2419 (1996). It is not a coincidence that the same Congress that passed DOMA also passed the 1996 Welfare Reform Act (titled the Personal Responsibility and Work Opportunity Act) as well as the Illegal Immigration Reform and Immigrant Responsibility Act, thereby promoting and policing the proper marriages of some while disallowing the possibility of marriage for others.

44. Often referred to as the "choice of law" provision, this second part has been hotly debated by legal theorists attempting to decide whether it is redundant (since states can already refuse to recognize other states' laws) or a violation of the full faith and credit clause of the U.S. Constitution (since the intent of this clause is to ensure

that an individual's rights do not end at state borders). For examples of the legal debate, see Bix, "State of the Union"; Feather, "Defense of Marriage Acts"; Koppelman, "Dumb and DOMA"; Resenberger, "Sex Marriages."

45. 142 Cong. Rec. S10068 (daily ed. Sept. 9, 1996) (statement of Sen. Helms).

46. For more information on transgender law and rights, see Currah et al., *Transgender Rights*; Currah, "Transgender Rights Imaginary"; Currah and Minter, "Unprincipled Exclusions"; Spade, "Resisting Medicine, Re/Modeling Gender," and *Normal Life*.

47. Currah, "Queer Theory," 185.

48. In a 1976 case, *M.T. v. J.T.* (355 A.2d 204 [N.J. App. 1976]) a husband attempted to evade spousal support after he left his wife, claiming that she was born a man and therefore he did not owe her support. The court declared that she was a female and therefore he owed her support. *In re Estate of Gardiner* (42 P.3d 120 [Kan. 2002]) the deceased's son contested J'Noel Ball's sex/gender identity and, therefore, the validity of the marriage, in order to be the beneficiary of his father's very considerable estate. The court found J'Noel Ball was not female. Other transgender marriage cases have involved issues such as child custody; see, for example, the various trajectories of *Kantaras v. Kantaras* (898 So.2d 80 [Fla. 2005]). For more on transgender marriage law, see Robson, "Mere Switch?" and "Reinscribing Normality?"

49. *Littleton v. Prange*, 9 S.W.3d 223 (Tex. App. 1999).

50. Id., 224.

51. Id., 231.

52. Id.

53. Id.

54. *Littleton v. Prange*, 531 U.S. 872 (2000).

55. *Baker v. State of Vermont*, 744 A.2d 864 (Vt. 1999).

56. The Fourteenth Amendment (1868) granted citizenship to "all persons born or naturalized in the United States" and declares that no state can "deprive any person of life, liberty, or property, without due process of law; nor deny to any person within its jurisdiction the equal protection of the laws."

57. Civil Unions Act of 1999, Vt. Pub. L. No. 91-97 § 1, 1999.

58. *Goodridge v. Department of Public Health*, 798 N.E.2d 941 (Mass. 2003).

59. Id.

60. *Goodridge*, 798 N.E.2d at 964.

61. Id., 965.

62. Eng, *Feeling of Kinship*, 40; Halley, "'Like Race' Arguments," 40; Snorton, "Marriage Mimesis," 2; Somerville, "Queer Loving," 336; Reddy, "Time for Rights?" 2849.

63. Eng, *Feeling of Kinship*, 40.

64. *Goodridge*, 798 N.E.2d at 954.

65. Id.

66. Foucault, "Governmentality," 100.

67. *Goodridge*, 798 N.E.2d at 948.

68. Id., 966.

69. Id., 958.

70. While many bans on same-sex marriage and civil unions were passed throughout the states in 2004 (coincident with the presidential election of Barack Obama), a large number were also put in place between 2005–2008.

71. *United States v. Windsor, Executor of the Estate of Spyer, et al.*, 570 U.S. ___ (2013), 133 S. Ct. 2675 (2013); *Hollingsworth et al. v. Perry et al.*, 570 U.S. ___ (2013), 133 S. Ct. 2652 (2013).

72. *Windsor*, 570 U.S. at 2679 (2013).

73. The Fifth Amendment offers numerous protections in regards to criminal and civil cases and includes the declaration that no citizen shall "be deprived of life, liberty, or property, without due process of law; nor shall private property be taken for public use, without just compensation."

74. Id., 2694.

75. Id., 2706–2707.

76. Id., 2691, citing *Sosna v. Iowa*, 419 U. S. 393, 404 (1975).

77. One could easily begin *Perry*'s trajectory a bit earlier, starting with *In Re Marriage Cases* (183 P.3d 384 [Cal. 2008]). In the case, the California State Supreme Court declared that Proposition 22 (a voter referendum with the same phrasing as Proposition 8 but through a statute rather than state constitutional amendment) was unconstitutional for withholding the status of marriage from same-sex couples. The decision certainly attributed to the fuel behind the passage of Proposition 8, which was upheld in *Strauss v. Horton*, 207 P.3d 48 (2009).

78. *Perry v. Schwarzenegger*, 704 F. Supp. 2d 921 (N.D. Cal. 2010). The district court case was a cultural phenomenon from the beginning, and the trial was a media sensation (a reenactment is available online at http://marriagetrial.com/) (accessed July 25, 2013). The challengers brought in an impressive array of witnesses to contest the most common arguments on behalf of exclusive opposite-sex only marriage, including historians Nancy Cott and George Chauncey. Judge Walker's decision, with over eighty "findings of fact," was an extensive effort to lay the groundwork for the legalization of same-sex marriage.

79. *Perry v. Brown*, 671 F. 3d 1052, 1063–1064 (9th Cir. 2012).

80. The standing issue also surfaced in *Windsor* because the Obama administration and the U.S. Attorney General's office refused to participate in defending DOMA. Therefore, the Bipartisan Legal Advisory Group (BLAG) of the House of Representatives defended the law.

81. Spade, "Under the Cover," 80.

82. *Perry*, 671 F. 3d at 1078.

83. Id.

84. Id.

85. Rubin, "Thinking Sex," 281. For more on the connection between Gayle Rubin's arguments and same-sex marriage, see Willse and Spade, "Freedom in a Regulatory State," 314.

86. Franke, "Domesticated Liberty," and "Sexuality and Marriage"; Spade, "Under the Cover"; Vaid, "'Now You Get?'"; Willse and Spade, "Freedom in a Regulatory State."

87. Agathangelou et al., "Intimate Investments"; Kandaswamy, "State Austerity"; Snorton, "Marriage Mimesis"; Spade, "Under the Cover"; Vaid, "'Now You Get?'"; Willse and Spade, "Freedom in a Regulatory State."

88. Agathangelou et al., "Intimate Investments"; Franke, "Sexuality and Marriage"; Puar, *Terrorist Assemblages*; Puar and Rai, "Monster, Terrorist, Fag"; Spade, "Under the Cover."

89. Agathangelou et al., "Intimate Investments," 130. Other scholars that connect the prison industrial complex with "marriage equality" include Arkles, "Marriage and Mass Incarceration"; Ritchie, "Pertinence of Perry."

90. Barker, *Native Acts*, 196.

91. For more on the relationship between queerness and Indigeneity, see Driskill et al., *Queer Indigenous Studies*; Morgensen, "Settler Homonationalism"; Rifkin, *When Did Indians Become Straight?*; Schneider, "Oklahobo."

92. Morgensen, "Settler Homonationalism," 123. See also Morgensen, *Spaces between Us*.

93. For more on this argument, see Puar, "Circuits of Queer Mobility."

94. Trask, *From a Native Daughter*, 146.

95. Urvashi Vaid, Lisa Duggan, Tamara Metz, and Amber Hollibaugh, "What's Next for the LGBT Movement," *Nation*, June 27, 2013, http://www.thenation.com/blog/175015/whats-next-lgbt-movement#axzz2XSJiGkuI (accessed July 25, 2013).

96. Vaid, "'Now You Get?'" 106.

97. Ibid.

98. Franke, "Domesticated Liberty," 1425–1426.

99. Vaid, "'Now You Get?'" 106.

100. Willse and Spade, "Freedom in a Regulatory State," 311, 317.

101. For some examples, see Benshoff, *Monsters in the Closet*; Haefele-Thomas, *Queer Others in Victorian Gothic*; Haggerty, *Queer Gothic*; Halberstam, *Skin Shows*.

102. For more information on these organizations and their tactics, see Bérubé and Escoffier, "Queer/Nation"; Bower, "Queer Acts"; Chee, "Queer Nationalism"; Duggan, "Making It Perfectly Queer"; Rand, "Disunited Nation," and "Appetite for Activism"; Slagle, "In Defense of Queer Nation." See also the rich online archives available at http://lesbianavengers.com, http://www.actuporalhistory.org/, and http://actupny.org/ (all accessed July 25, 2013).

103. Berlant and Freeman, "Queer Nationality," 205.

104. Ibid., 207, 206.

105. Ibid., 206. See also Bérubé and Escoffier, "Queer/Nation"; "Guide to the San Francisco Street Patrol Records Collection, Online Archive of California," http://www.oac.cdlib.org/findaid/ark:/13030/kt2s2025pb/ (accessed July 25, 2013).

106. Rand, "Appetite for Activism," 123.

107. Berlant and Freeman, "Queer Nationality," 200; See also the leaflet, "Queers Read This!" (June 1990) at http://www.actupny.org/documents/QueersReadThis.pdf (accessed Aug. 30, 2013).

108. "Queers Read This!" 1.

109. Hanhardt, *Safe Space*.

110. Puar and Rai, "Monster, Terrorist, Fag," 117. See also Rai, "Of Monsters," and "Promise of Monsters."

111. Puar and Rai, "Monster, Terrorist, Fag," 138–139.

112. Morgensen, "Settler Homonationalism," 124.

113. Puar, *Terrorist Assemblages*. Please see the Preface for more on the linkages between queer inclusion and the queering of racialized terrorists.

114. "Queers Read This!" 1.

## Chapter 3. Legal Detours of U.S. Empire

1. "Interior Considers Procedures to Reestablish a Government-to-Government Relationship with the Native Hawaiian Community," *U.S. Department of the Interior Press Release*, June 18, 2014, http://www.doi.gov/ohr/reorg/index.cfm (accessed December 20, 2014).

2. Barker, *Native Acts*, 6.

3. According to Jodi Byrd's astute analysis, this discourse (Kanaka Maoli refusing "Indianness") also surfaced in earlier public debates and hearings on the Native Hawaiian Government Reorganization Act ("Akaka Bill"). See Byrd, *Transit of Empire*, 157.

4. *Department of the Interior*, "Public Meeting regarding whether the Federal Government should reestablish a government-to-government relationship with the Native Hawaiian community," 14–15, July 5, 2014.

5. *Department of the Interior*, "Public Meeting regarding whether the Federal Government should reestablish a government-to-government relationship with the Native Hawaiian community," 6, June 26, 2014.

6. *Department of the Interior*, "Public Meeting regarding whether the Federal Government should reestablish a government-to-government relationship with the Native Hawaiian community," 28, Hawaii State Capitol, June 23, 2014.

7. Byrd, *Transit of Empire*, xiii, 157–158.

8. Just a few of the many examples of work that address modes of decolonization are Alfred, *Peace, Power, Righteousness*, and *Wasáse*; Deloria, *Custer Died for Your Sins*; Smith, *Decolonizing Methodologies*; Wilson and Yellow Bird, *For Indigenous Eyes Only*. There are also useful resources at http://unsettlingamerica.wordpress.com/ (accessed Dec. 23, 2014).

9. Byrd, *Transit of Empire*, 53.

10. By marking Hawai'i as both colonized and occupied, I am following the lead of Noelani Goodyear-Ka'ōpua who refers to Kanaka Maoli resistance in the plural, rather than a singular, in order to reflect its diverse strategies and tactics. For more on the exciting variability of Kanaka resistance, see Goodyear-Ka'ōpua et al., *Nation Rising*; Kauanui, "Multiplicity of Hawaiian Sovereignty Claims."

11. Goodyear-Ka'ōpua, "Kuleana Lāhui," 132.

12. A small sampling of the scholarship on and from Kanaka Maoli sovereignty activists and organizations includes American Friends Service Committee, *He Alo Ā He Alo = Face to Face*; Hasager and Friedman, *Hawai'i*; Laenui, *Collection of Papers*; MacKenzie, *Native Hawaiian Rights Handbook*; Trask, *From a Native Daughter*; Trask, "Ka Lāhui Hawai'i"; and internet databases and organizations such as Agency of Public Affairs for the Reinstated Hawaiian Government, http://hawaii-gov.net/; "Free Hawai'i—Online Voice for the Kingdom of Hawai'i," http://www.freehawaii.org; Hawai'i—Independent & Sovereign, http://www.hawaii-nation.org; "Hawaiian Perspectives: Potpourri of Topics & Media on Hawaiian Issues," *Hawaiian Perspectives* (formerly: *Institute for the Advancement of Hawaiian Affairs*), http://www.hawaiianperspectives.org/; Ka Lāhui Hawai'i, https://kalahuihawaii.wordpress.com/; Kingdom of Hawai'i, http://www.pixi.com/~kingdom; Sovereign Hawaiian Government, http://www.sovereignhawaii.com; Office of Hawaiian Affairs, http://www.oha.org (all sites accessed June 3, 2013).

13. There are, of course, varieties within these strands as well. For example, some deoccupation activists argue for the international recognition of the Hawaiian Kingdom as a multiethnic nation-state, while others refer to it as an Indigenous nation. And even within arguments for a multiethnic independent nation, there are important differences. For an example, see MANA: Movement for Aloha No ka Aina, http://www.manainfo.com/home.html, versus David Keanu Sai's arguments for the multiethnic Hawaiian Kingdom, http://www.hawaiiankingdom.org/ (both sites accessed Dec. 23, 2014).

14. Hall, "'Hawaiian at Heart'"; Halualani, *In the Name of Hawaiians*.

15. Perhaps the easiest example of such a deployment is the antisovereignty organization, "Aloha For All," that works to disrupt all efforts toward revitalization of Kanaka Maoli heritage, culture, spaces, and identities. For more information, see "Aloha 4 All," http://www.aloha4all.org (accessed June 3, 2013). Also, for a deeper analysis of this organization, see Kauanui, "Colonialism in Equality," 645.

16. The "Rainbow" not only serves to represent the racial composite of Hawai'i, but also marks a (mythic) representation of its progressive politics, especially in regard to issues of sexuality. The reference to Hawai'i as a "true ethnic mosaic" comes from "Hawaii's Official Tourism Site," Hawaii Tourism Authority, http://www.gohawaii.com (accessed Nov. 2, 2011).

17. The critique of the "colorblindness" doctrine is one of the most important tenets of critical race theory. See, for example, Crenshaw et al., *Critical Race Theory*; Delgado, *Critical Race Theory*. For an intersectional queer analysis of colorblindness, see Eng, *Feeling of Kinship*.

18. Christine Donnelly, "Rice: It's about Protecting the Constitution, Not 'Racist,'" *Honolulu Star-Bulletin*, Feb. 23, 2000, http://starbulletin.com/2000/02/23/news/story3.html; Robert M. Rees, "Race Matters," *Honolulu Weekly*, April 28, 1999, http://www.honoluluweekly.com/archives (both sites accessed Nov. 2, 2011).

19. As a reminder, the Fourteenth Amendment (1868) granted citizenship to "all persons born or naturalized in the United States" and declares that no state can "de-

prive any person of life, liberty, or property, without due process of law; nor deny to any person within its jurisdiction the equal protection of the laws." The Fifteenth Amendment (1870) grants the right to vote regardless of "race, color, or previous condition of servitude."

20. Note the so-called "ceded lands" is a violent misnaming, and are more properly understood as "seized" or "stolen." For more on this point, see Imada, *Aloha America*, 260–261.

21. It is also worth mentioning that the attorneys in this case have directly furthered other anti-intersectional legal cases. For example, the State of Hawai'i's legal representative before the Supreme Court was none other than John Roberts, who then later became Chief Justice of the Supreme Court when nominated by President George Bush after Justice Rehnquist retired. It is painful to consider the ways in which the Roberts Court has furthered the injustices of the colorblindness doctrine and the erosion of Native sovereignty that began with the Rehnquist Court. Moreover, Rice's legal representative was none other than Theodore B. Olsen, who later became famous for joining forces with attorney David Bois (his opposing counsel in *Bush v. Gore*) to oppose California's Proposition 8 anti–same-sex marriage law, as described in Chapter Two.

22. The subheading is inspired by Osorio's *Dismembering Lāhui*.

23. Goodyear-Ka'ōpua et al., *Nation Rising*.

24. Osorio, *Dismembering Lāhui*.

25. Merry, *Colonizing Hawai'i*.

26. Kauanui, *Hawaiian Blood*.

27. Trask, *From a Native Daughter*, 114.

28. Buck, *Paradise Remade*, 1, 14.

29. Merry, *Colonizing Hawai'i*, 25.

30. For example, Osorio describes his book, *Dismembering Lāhui*, as a *mo'olelo*, that is, a tale, legend, story, folktale, account, and history that is not owned by Kanaka Maoli, but rather owns them. See *Dismembering Lāhui*, ix. For more examples of mo'olelo, see Beamer, *No Mākou Ka Mana*; ho'omanawanui, *Voices of Fire*; Osorio, "'What Kine Hawaiian Are You?'"

31. Silva, *Aloha Betrayed*.

32. Goodyear-Ka'ōpua, "Hawai'i," 60–61.

33. Osorio, "Kū'ē and Kū'oko'a," 221. See also Osorio, "'What Kine Hawaiian Are You?'" 361.

34. Deloria, "Indian Law and the Reach of History," 12.

35. Osorio, "Kū'ē and Kū'oko'a," 234.

36. *Rice v. Cayetano*, 528 U.S. 495, 499–500 (2000).

37. Id., 527–528.

38. White, "Historical Emplotment."

39. Importantly, while many scholars read legal cases via rhetorical and discursive analyses, scholars rarely read the form, narrative, and structure of law. An example of a similar method to the one I am deploying here is Cheyfitz, "Savage Law."

40. See, for example, Aikau, *Chosen People, a Promised Land*; Coffman, *Island Edge of America*; Kameʻeleihiwa, *Native Land and Foreign Desires*; Merry, *Colonizing Hawaiʻi*; Osorio, *Dismembering Lāhui*; Silva, *Aloha Betrayed*; Young, *Rethinking the Native Hawaiian Past*; as well as the vast digital resources available at "Annexation of Hawaii: A Collection of Documents," *University of Hawaiʻi at Mānoa Library* http://libweb.hawaii.edu/digicoll/annexation/annexation.html (accessed June 3, 2013).

41. Importantly, this narrative (or portions of it) is reproduced in conservative scholarship on the case, the brief for the Petitioner (Harold Rice), and the amicus brief by the Pacific Legal Foundation on behalf of the petitioner. Brief of Petitioner, Harold Rice; Brief of Amicus Curiae, Pacific Legal Foundation, *Rice v. Cayetano*, 528 U.S. 495 (2000) (No. 98-818); See also Deichert, "Rice v. Cayetano," Hanifin, "Rice Is Right"; Sullivan, "Recognizing the Fifth Leg."

42. This is a familiar maneuver in colonialist, U.S. exceptionalist rhetoric. See, for example, Vicente L. Rafael's analysis of how "wave immigration theory" is deployed in the service of racializing Philippine history during the Spanish-American-Philippine War in "White Love."

43. *Rice v. Cayetano*, 528 U.S. 495, 501 (2000).

44. Id.

45. Id.

46. Id., 504.

47. Brief of Petitioner at 2, *Rice v. Cayetano*, 528 U.S. 495 (2000) (No. 98-818); *Rice v. Cayetano*, 528 U.S. at 505.

48. *Rice v. Cayetano*, 528 U.S. at 504.

49. Id.

50. Id.

51. Id., 505 (citing Res. 55, 55th Cong., 30 Stat. 750 [1898]).

52. Id., 507.

53. Id.

54. Id., 508.

55. Id., 509–510.

56. Id., 524.

57. Streeby, "Empire," 97.

58. Apology Resolution, Pub. L. No.103-150, 107 Stat. 1510 (1993). For full text of the law, see http://en.wikisource.org/wiki/Public_Law_103-150 (accessed June 3, 2013). *Rice v. Cayetano*, 528 U.S. 495 (2000) (Stevens, J., dissenting). The briefs that deploy this narrative include the brief for the Respondent (the State of Hawaiʻi), and the amicus briefs by the United States, the State of California et al., and the Alaska Federation of Natives and Cook Inlet Region, Inc., *Rice v. Cayetano*, 528 U.S. 495 (2000) (No. 98-818). The scholarship that utilizes this emplotment includes Chestnut, "Matters of Trust"; Costello, "Rice v. Cayetano"; Heffner, "Between Assimilation and Revolt"; O'Malley, "Irreconcilable Rights"; Spruill, "Fate of Native Hawaiians"; Zissu, "What Hath Captain Cook Wrought?" For an example of an

article that demonstrates this trajectory before the *Rice* decision, see Van Dyke, "Political Status."

59. Apology Resolution, Pub. L. No. 103-150, 107 Stat. 1510 (1993).

60. Id.

61. Id.

62. The Apology Resolution is cited by many Kanaka Maoli activists, and these activists use the resolution to their advantage. For an example of using the resolution to try to stop the State of Hawai'i from selling some of the Hawaiian Kingdom Crown and Government Lands, see Kauanui, "Sorry State."

63. Heffner, "Between Assimilation and Revolt," 594.

64. Ibid.

65. O'Malley, "Irreconcilable Rights," 505.

66. Apology Resolution, Pub. L. No. 103-150, 107 Stat. 1510 (1993).

67. Brief for the Respondent at 5, *Rice v. Cayetano*, 528 U.S. 495 (2000) (No. 98-818).

68. I do not mean to underestimate the importance of documenting the events of 1893 in Hawai'i, as this date is extremely significant to decolonization/deoccupation activists. I am interested, however, in marking a series of dates in which the U.S. legalized its operations of settler colonialism/occupation.

69. *Rice*, 528 U.S. at 534.

70. Id.

71. Id., 534.

72. For more on these liberal strategies of recognition, see Povinelli, *Cunning of Recognition*.

73. *Rice*, 528 U.S. at 534–535.

74. Kirby and Coleborne, *Law, History, Colonialism*, 2.

75. Brief of Amicus Curiae Office of Hawaiian Affairs et al.; State Council of Hawaiian Homestead Association et al.; Kamehameha Schools Bishop Estate Trust; Hawai'i Congressional Delegation; and National Congress of American Indians; *Rice v. Cayetano*, 528 U.S. 495 (2000) (No. 98-818).

76. Importantly, many Kanaka Maoli activists and scholars have been quite critical of some of the organizations that ended up filing amicus briefs on behalf of the State of Hawai'i, such as the Office of Hawaiian Affairs and the Bishop Estate.

77. Brief of Amicus Curiae, State Council of Hawaiian Homestead Association at 5, *Rice v. Cayetano*, 528 U.S. 495 (2000) (No. 98-818).

78. Brief of Amicus Curiae, Kamehameha Schools at 7, *Rice v. Cayetano*, 528 U.S. 495 (2000) (No. 98-818).

79. Brief of Amicus Curiae, State Council of Hawaiian Homestead Associations at 3 and 7, *Rice v. Cayetano*, 528 U.S. 495 (2000) (No. 98-818).

80. Brief of Amicus Curiae, Office of Hawaiian Affairs at 5, *Rice v. Cayetano*, 528 U.S. 495 (2000) (No. 98-818).

81. Brief of Amicus Curiae, Kamehameha Schools at 11–16, *Rice v. Cayetano*, 528 U.S. 495 (2000) (No. 98-818).

82. Brief of Amicus Curiae, Kamehameha Schools at 16, *Rice v. Cayetano*, 528 U.S. 495 (2000) (No. 98-818).

83. Brief of Amicus Curiae, State Council of Hawaiian Homestead Associations at 9, *Rice v. Cayetano*, 528 U.S. 495 (2000) (No. 98-818).

84. Brief of Amicus Curiae, State Council of Hawaiian Homestead Associations at 8–9 FN27, *Rice v. Cayetano*, 528 U.S. 495 (2000) (No. 98-818).

85. Brief of Amicus Curiae, Kamehameha Schools at 12, *Rice v. Cayetano*, 528 U.S. 495 (2000) (No. 98-818).

86. Brief of Amicus Curiae, Office of Hawaiian Affairs at 8, *Rice v. Cayetano*, 528 U.S. 495 (2000) (No. 98-818).

87. For more on this point, see Barker, *Native Acts*; Kauanui, *Hawaiian Blood*; Wilkins, *American Indian Sovereignty*; Williams, *American Indian in Western Legal Thought*, and *Like a Loaded Weapon*.

88. Brief of Amicus Curiae, National Congress of American Indians at 3, *Rice v. Cayetano*, 528 U.S. 495 (2000) (No. 98-818).

89. Brief of Amicus Curiae, Hawai'i Congressional Delegation at 1, *Rice v. Cayetano*, 528 U.S. 495 (2000) (No. 98-818).

90. Brief of Amicus Curiae, Hawai'i Congressional Delegation at 6, *Rice v. Cayetano*, 528 U.S. 495 (2000) (No. 98-818).

91. Id.

92. The "political status" was recognized by the U.S. Supreme Court's in *Morton v. Mancari*, 417 U.S. 535 (1974) when the Court found that Bureau of Indian Affair's hiring preference for Native Americans is not racial, but political in nature.

93. Lindsey, "Akaka Bill," 713 (emphasis added).

94. *Rice*, 528 U.S. at 512.

95. Id.

96. Id., 513.

97. Id., 514.

98. Zissu, "What Hath," 678.

99. *Rice*, 528 U.S. at 523–524.

100. Id., 528.

101. Eng, *Feeling of Kinship*, 40.

102. Iijima, "Race over Rice," 92.

103. For some examples of legal scholarship concerned with the opposition of Indigeneity and race, see Berger, "Red"; Goldberg, "Descent into Race"; Krakoff, "Inextricably Political"; Rolnick, "Promise of Mancari."

104. See, for example, Barker, *Native Acts*, and "Recognition"; Byrd, *Transit of Empire*; Kauanui, *Hawaiian Blood*, and "Colonialism in Equality"; Rifkin, *When Did Indians Become Straight?*; Simpson, "On the Logic of Discernment," and *Mohawk Interruptus*.

105. Barker, *Native Acts*, 81.

106. Rifkin, *When Did Indians Become Straight?* 36.

107. Byrd, *Transit of Empire*, xxiii.

108. Simpson, "On the Logic of Discernment," 483–484.

109. Kauanui, *Hawaiian Blood*, 10; See also Barker, "Recognition," 148.

110. Kauanui, *Hawaiian Blood*, 8, 68.

111. Merry, *Colonizing Hawai'i*, 136, and "Law and Identity," 126.

112. Kauanui, *Hawaiian Blood*; Merry, *Colonizing Hawai'i*; Okihiro, *Cane Fires*.

113. Fujikane, "Foregrounding Native Nationalisms," and "Asian American Critique"; Fujikane and Okamura, *Asian Settler Colonialism*; King, "Competition, Complicity, and (Potential) Alliance"; Saranillio, "Colliding Histories," "Colonial Amnesia," "Kewaikaliko's Benocide," and "Why Asian Settler Colonialism Matters."

114. Fujikane and Okamura, *Asian Settler Colonialism*, 4.

115. Trask, "Settlers of Color," 2.

116. For a critique of the "Asian settlers of color" framing, see Takagi, "Faith, Race and Nationalism."

117. Fujikane, "Foregrounding Native Nationalisms," 84.

118. For more on these debates, see Amadahy and Lawrence, "Indigenous Peoples and Black People"; Kauanui and Wolfe, "Settler Colonialism Then and Now"; Lawrence and Dua, "Decolonizing Antiracism"; Morgensen, "White Settlers and Indigenous Solidarity"; Phung, "Are People of Colour?"; Sharma and Wright, "Decolonizing Resistance, Challenging Colonial States"; Stanley et al., "Intervention"; Veracini, "Natives Settlers Migrants."

119. Trask, *From a Native Daughter*, 25–26.

120. Kauanui, "Colonialism in Equality," 636.

121. Deloria, *Custer Died for Your Sins*; Deloria and Lytle, *Nations Within*; Kauanui, "Colonialism in Equality"; Trask, *From a Native Daughter*. For an argument on behalf of civil rights within Native governance, see Barker, *Native Acts*.

122. Singh, *Black Is a Country*, 3. See also Melamed, *Represent and Destroy*.

123. Tuck and Yang, "Decolonization Is Not a Metaphor," 28.

124. *Rice v. Cayetano*, 941 F. Supp 1529, 1534 n. 1 (1996).

125. *Kakalia v. Cayetano*, No. 96-00616-CV (D. Haw. July 18, 1996). Longtime sovereignty activists included Clara Kakalia, Billie Beamer, Lela Hubbard, and the "non-Hawaiian" ally, Stephen Kobata. For more on the Kakalia plaintiffs, see Robert M. Rees, "Race Matters," *Honolulu Weekly*, April 28, 1999, http://www.honoluluweekly.com/archives (accessed Nov. 2, 2011); Tracie Ku'uipo Cummings, "Hawaiian Sovereignty and Nationalism: History, Perspectives, Movements," MA Thesis, University of Hawai'i, 2004, 85, http://scholarspace.manoa.hawaii.edu/bitstream/handle/10125/11780/uhm_ma_3163_r.pdf?sequence=2; Mary Vorsino, "Activist Fought for Hawaiian Recognition," *Honolulu Star Bulletin*, Nov. 5, 2004, http://archives.starbulletin.com/2004/11/05/news/story11.html; Pat Omandam, "Ae or A'ole: The Native Hawaiian Sovereignty Vote," *Honolulu Star Bulletin*, July 10, 1996, http://archives.starbulletin.com/96/07/10/news/index.html; Pat Omandam, "Non-Hawaiians Back Hawaiians on Rights, Self-determination," *Honolulu Star Bulletin*, March 9, 2000, http://archives.starbulletin.com/2000/03/09/news/story2.html; and Pat Omandam, "OHA Keeps

Going as Beamer Would Want," *Honolulu Star Bulletin*, Jan. 26, 1998, http://archives.starbulletin.com/98/01/26/news/story2.html (all sites accessed Nov. 2, 2011).

126. Robert M. Rees, "Race Matters," *Honolulu Weekly*, April 28, 1999, http://www.honoluluweekly.com/archives (accessed Nov. 2, 2011).

127. As a reminder, a "strict scrutiny" requirement means that it must satisfy the most stringent standards of review in order to be found constitutionally viable. Some categories of identity have been associated with various levels of scrutiny, from the highest level of "strict" to the minimum level of "rational." For example, while racial categories are often given strict scrutiny, gender-related categories are more often measured against an intermediate level of scrutiny, often on the basis that there are "real" differences between the two legally recognized genders, male and female, while race is understood as socially constructed. "Strict Scrutiny," *Legal Information Institute*, https://www.law.cornell.edu/wex/strict_scrutiny (accessed April 17, 2015).

128. *Rice*, 941 F. Supp. at 1552.

129. Id., 1547.

130. Id., 1548.

131. Id., 1545.

132. Act 195 recognized Native Hawaiians as the Indigenous peoples of Hawai'i and created a Native Hawaiian Roll Commission (Kana'iolowalu) to register Native Hawaiians and certify that the registered meet the legal state definitions, Act 195, sec. 1, Sess. L. Haw. 2011. Kauanui refers to this law as possibly "the first documented evidence of collective acquiescence to the U.S. government or its subsidiaries." Kauanui, "Resisting the Akaka Bill," 314. For more analyses of the Kana'iolowalu, see Goodyear-Ka'ōpua et al., *Nation Rising*; Goodyear-Ka'ōpua, "Hawai'i."

## Conclusion

1. Freeman, Introduction, 165.

2. See, for example, Ellison, "Citizenship, Space and Time"; McCallum, "Timezone Endgame"; Shapiro, "National Times and Other Times."

3. Povinelli, "Governance of the Prior," 23. See also *Economies of Abandonment*.

4. Povinelli, "Governance of the Prior," 28.

5. Grosz, *Time Travels*, 4.

6. *Fisher v. University of Texas at Austin*, 133 S.Ct. 2411 (2013).

7. For more on the relationship between affirmative action and whiteness as property, see Harris, "Whiteness as Property."

8. On remand to the Fifth Circuit Court of Appeals, a 2–1 decision found in favor of the University of Texas, arguing that their admissions programs met the tests as laid out by the Supreme Court. *Fisher v. University of Texas*, No. 09-50822 12–14 (5th Cir. 2014). As this book went to press, the Supreme Court agreed to hear Abigail Fisher's appeal during the 2015–2016 term, which does not bode well for affirmative action programs.

9. *Fisher v. University of Texas at Austin*, 133 S.Ct. at 2428 (2013) (Thomas, J., concurring).

10. Id., 2423 (Thomas, J., concurring, citing *Wygant v. Jackson Bd. of Ed.*, 476 U.S. at 276 (1986). He is, actually, misconstruing the finding in *Wygant*. The majority decision, in criticizing the argument that the school district should hire more faculty of color in order to be role models for youth of color, actually reads, "Societal discrimination, without more, is too amorphous a basis for imposing a racially classified remedy."

11. *Shelby County v. Holder*, 570 U.S. ___ (2013).

12. *Shelby County v. Holder*, No. 12-399, slip op. at 20 (Supreme Court SC, June 25, 2013).

13. Id.

14. Id., 18 (Ginsberg, J., dissenting).

15. Id., 21.

16. *Adoptive Couple v. Baby Girl*, 570 U.S. ___ (2013).

17. Wolfe, "Land, Labor and Difference," 887.

18. *Adoptive Couple v. Baby Girl*, No. 12-399, slip op. at 1 (Supreme Court SC, June 25, 2013).

19. Cherokee Nation Tribal Citizenship, http://www.cherokee.org/Services/Tribal Citizenship/Citizenship.aspx (accessed Dec. 29, 2014).

20. *Adoptive Couple v. Baby Girl*, No. 12-399, slip op. at 16 (Supreme Court SC, June 25, 2013).

21. Alyosha Goldstein's insightful analysis of the *Adoptive Couple v. Baby Girl* case makes a similar point. See Goldstein, "Possessive Investment," 1078–1079.

22. See, for example, Bruyneel, *Third Space of Sovereignty*; Byrd, *Transit of Empire*; Povinelli, "Governance of the Prior," and *Economies of Abandonment*. Postcolonial scholars have also described the production of temporal subjectivities in the epistemological projects of colonialisms and anticolonial nationalisms. See, for example, Bhabha, *Location of Culture*; Fanon, *Wretched of the Earth*; McClintock, *Imperial Leather*.

23. Byrd, *Transit of Empire*, 6.

24. *Adoptive Couple v. Baby Girl*, No. 12-399, slip op. at 17 (Supreme Court SC, June 25, 2013).

25. Id., 24 (Sotomayor, J., dissenting). For more on this threat, see Krakoff, "Law, Violence."

26. As Addie Rolnick argues, "*Rice* stands as a cautionary tale of what could happen if indigenous groups fail to cast these laws as purely political." Rolnick, "Promise of Mancari," 1027.

27. Krakoff, "Inextricably Political," 1118. See also Goldberg, "Descent into Race."

28. *United States v. Windsor, Executor of the Estate of Spyer, et al.*, No. 12-307, slip op. at 4, 22 (Supreme Court SC June 26, 2013).

29. Id., 22, 21.

30. *Brown v. Board of Education*, 347 U.S. 483 (1954).

31. Some pundits and legal scholars made this connection clear by describing *Windsor* as "this generation's *Brown v. Board of Education*." See, for example, John Colhane, "*U.S. v. Windsor* Must Be This Generation's *Brown v. Board of Education*, Not Its *Roe v. Wade*," *Slate* online March 6, 2014, http://www.slate.com/blogs/outward/2014/06/state_anti_gay_segregation_bills_demonstrate_the_importance_of_u_s_v_windsor.html (accessed Dec. 29, 2014). Other scholars described *Brown* and *Windsor* as progressive decisions that were ahead of their time. See, for example, Klarman, "Windsor and Brown."

32. Halberstam, *In a Queer Time and Place*, 2.

33. Edelman, *No Future*, 3. See also Lauren Berlant's brilliant analysis of the use of the white child as future, as well as José Muñoz's critique of Edelman's whitenormative analysis. Berlant, *Queen of America*; Muñoz, *Cruising Utopia*.

34. Thank you so much to Wendy Kozol for pointing out this dynamic to me.

35. Dillon, "'It's Here, It's That Time,'" 41, 49.

36. The "death-bound" subject comes from JanMohamed, *Death-Bound-Subject*.

37. Lorde, *Sister Outsider*, 111, 112, 119.

38. Tuck and Yang, "Decolonization Is Not a Metaphor," 28.

# Bibliography

Agathangelou, Anna M., Daniel M. Bassichis, and Tamara L. Spira. "Intimate Investments: Homonormativity, Global Lockdown, and Seductions of Empire." *Radical History Review* 100 (2008): 120–143.

Ahmad, Muneer I. "A Rage Shared by Law: Post–September 11 Racial Violence as Crimes of Passion." *California Law Review* 92, no. 5 (2004): 1261–1327.

Aikau, Hokulani K. *A Chosen People, a Promised Land: Mormonism and Race in Hawai'i.* Minneapolis: University of Minnesota Press, 2012.

Alarcón, Norma. "The Theoretical Subject(s) of 'This Bridge Called My Back' and Anglo-American Feminism." In *Making Face, Making Soul = Haciendo Caras: Creative and Critical Perspectives by Feminists of Color*, edited by Gloria Anzaldúa, 27–37. San Francisco: Aunt Lute Foundation Books, 1990.

Alexander, M. Jacqui. "Erotic Autonomy as a Politics of Decolonization: An Anatomy of Feminist and State Practice in the Bahamas Tourist Economy." In *Feminist Genealogies, Colonial Legacies, Democratic Futures*, edited by M. Jacqui Alexander and Chandra Talpade Mohanty, 63–100. New York: Routledge, 1997.

———. "Not Just (Any) Body Can Be a Citizen: The Politics of Law, Sexuality, and Postcoloniality in Trinidad and Tobago and the Bahamas." *Feminist Review*, no. 48 (1994): 5–23.

———. *Pedagogies of Crossing: Meditations on Feminism, Sexual Politics, Memory, and the Sacred.* Durham: Duke University Press, 2006.

Alexander-Flyod, Nikol G. "Disappearing Acts: Reclaiming Intersectionality in the Social Sciences in a Post-Black Feminist Era." *Feminist Formations* 24, no. 1 (2012): 1–25.

Alfred, Taiaiake. *Peace, Power, Righteousness: An Indigenous Manifesto.* Don Mills: Oxford University Press, 1999.

————. *Wasáise: Indigenous Pathways of Action and Freedom*. Ontario: Broadview Press, 2005.

Amadahy, Zainab, and Bonita Lawrence. "Indigenous Peoples and Black People in Canada: Settlers or Allies?" In *Breaching the Colonial Contract: Anti-Colonialism in the U.S. and Canada*, edited by Arlo Kempf, 105–136. Dordrecht: Springer, 2010.

Anzaldúa, Gloria. *Borderlands: The New Mestiza = La Frontera*, 1st ed. San Francisco: Spinsters/Aunt Lute, 1987.

Arkles, Gabriel. "Marriage and Mass Incarceration." *New York University Review of Law & Social Change* 37 (2013): 13–22.

Baines, Donna, and Nandita Sharma. "Migrant Workers as Non-Citizens: The Case against Citizenship as a Social Policy Concept." *Studies in Political Economy* 69 (2002): 75–107.

Balfour, Lawrie. "Reparations after Identity Politics." *Political Theory* 33, no. 6 (December 2005): 786–811.

Barker, Joanne. *Native Acts: Law, Recognition, and Cultural Authenticity*. Durham: Duke University Press, 2011.

————. "Recognition," *Journal of Indigenous Nations Studies* and *American Studies* (special joint issue) 46, no. 3/4 (2005): 117–145.

Bartlett, Philip L., II. "Recent Legislation: Same-Sex Marriage." *Harvard Journal on Legislation* 36 (1999): 581–590.

Beamer, Kamanamaikalani. *No Mākou Ka Mana: Liberating the Nation*. Honolulu: Kamehameha Publishing, 2014.

Bell, David, and Jon Binnie. *The Sexual Citizen: Queer Politics and Beyond*. Malden: Polity Press, 2000.

Benshoff, Harry M. *Monsters in the Closet: Homosexuality and the Horror Film*. Manchester: Manchester University Press, 1997.

Berger, Bethany R. "Red: Racism and the American Indian." *UCLA Law Review* 56 (2009): 592–657.

Berger, Michele Tracy, and Kathleen Guidroz. *The Intersectional Approach: Transforming the Academy through Race, Class, and Gender.* Chapel Hill: University of North Carolina Press, 2009.

Berlant, Lauren. *Cruel Optimism.* Durham: Duke University Press, 2011.

————. *The Queen of America Goes to Washington City: Essays on Sex and Citizenship*. Durham: Duke University Press, 1997.

————. "Slow Death (Sovereignty, Obesity, Lateral Agency)." *Critical Inquiry* 33 (Summer 2007): 754–780.

Berlant, Lauren, and Elizabeth Freeman. "Queer Nationality." In *Fear of a Queer Planet: Queer Politics and Social Theory*, edited by Michael Warner, 193–229. Minneapolis: University of Minnesota Press, 1993.

Bérubé, Allan, and Jeffery Escoffier. "Queer/Nation." *OUT/Look: National Lesbian and Gay Quarterly* 11 (1991).

Bhabha, Homi K. *The Location of Culture*. London: Routledge, 1994.

Bilge, Sirma. "Beyond Subordination vs. Resistance: An Intersectional Approach to the Agency of Veiled Muslim Women." *Journal of Intercultural Studies* 31, no. 1 (2010): 9–28.

Bilge, Sirma, and Ann Denis. "Introduction: Women, Intersectionality and Diasporas." *Journal of Intercultural Studies* 31, no. 1 (2010): 1–8.

Bix, Brian. "State of the Union: The States' Interest in the Marital Status of Their Citizens." *University of Miami Law Review* 55 (2000).

Bosniak, Linda. *The Citizen and the Alien: Dilemmas of Contemporary Membership*. Princeton: Princeton University Press, 2006.

———. "Universal Citizenship and the Problem of Alienage." *Northwestern University Law Review* 94 (2000): 963–982.

———. "Varieties of Citizenship." *Fordham Law Review* 75 (2006–2007): 2449–2454.

Bouchard, Danielle. *A Community of Disagreement: Feminism in the University*. New York: Peter Lang, 2012.

———. "Women's Studies' Guilt Complex: Interdisciplinarity, Globalism, and the University." *Journal of the Midwest Modern Language Association* 37, no. 1 (2004): 32–39.

Bower, Lisa C. "Queer Acts and the Politics of 'Direct Address': Rethinking Law, Culture, and Community." *Law & Society Review* 28, no. 5 (1994): 1009–1034.

Bramen, Carrie Tirado. "Why the Academic Left Hates Identity Politics." *Textual Practice* 16, no. 1 (2002): 1–11.

Brandzel, Amy L. "Haunted by Citizenship: Whitenormative Citizen-Subjects and the Uses of History in Women's Studies." *Feminist Studies* 37, no. 3 (2011): 504–533.

———. "Queering Citizenship? Same-Sex Marriage and the State." *GLQ* 11, no. 2 (2005): 171–204.

Brandzel, Amy L., and Jigna Desai. "Race, Violence, and Terror." *Journal of Asian American Studies* 11, no. 1 (2008): 61–85.

———. "Racism without Recognition: Toward a Model of Asian American Racialization." In *Asian Americans in Dixie: Race and Migration in the South*, edited by Khyati Y. Joshi and Jigna Desai, 77–106. Champaign: University of Illinois Press, 2013.

Bredbenner, Candice Lewis. *A Nationality of Her Own: Women, Marriage, and the Law of Citizenship*. Berkeley: University of California Press, 1998.

Brown, Michael P. *RePlacing Citizenship: AIDS Activism and Radical Democracy*. New York: Guildford Press, 1997.

Brown, Wendy. *States of Injury: Power and Freedom in Late Modernity*. Princeton: Princeton University Press, 1995.

———. "Suffering the Paradoxes of Rights." In *Left Legalism/Left Critique*, edited by Wendy Brown and Janet Halley, 420–434. Durham: Duke University Press, 2002.

Brown, Wendy, and Janet Halley, eds. *Left Legalism/Left Critique*. Durham: Duke University Press, 2002.

Bruyneel, Kevin. *The Third Space of Sovereignty: The Postcolonial Politics of U.S.-Indigenous Relations*. Minneapolis: University of Minnesota Press, 2007.

Buck, Elizabeth. *Paradise Remade: The Politics of Culture and History in Hawai'i*. Philadelphia: Temple University Press, 1993.

Butler, Judith. *Gender Trouble: Feminism and the Subversion of Identity*. New York: Routledge, 1990.

Byrd, Jodi A. *The Transit of Empire: Indigenous Critiques of Colonialism*. Minneapolis: University of Minnesota Press, 2011.

Cacho, Lisa Marie. "But Some of Us Are Wise: Academic Illegitimacy and the Affective Value of Ethnic Studies." *Black Scholar* 40, no. 4 (2010): 28–36.

———. *Social Death: Racialized Rightlessness and the Criminalization of the Unprotected*. New York: New York University Press, 2012.

Carastathis, Anna. "Basements and Intersections." *Hypatia* 28, no. 4 (2013): 698–715.

———. "The Invisibility of Privilege: A Critique of Intersectional Models of Identity." *Les Ateliers de l'Éthique*, no. 2 (2008): 23–38.

———. "Reinvigorating Intersectionality as a Provisional Concept." In *Why Race and Gender Still Matter: An Intersectional Approach*, edited by Namita Goswami, Maeve M. O'Donovan, and Lisa Yount, 59–70. London: Pickering and Chatto, 2014.

Carbado, Devon W., Kimberlé Crenshaw, and Vickie M. Mays. "Intersectionality: Mapping the Movements of a Theory." *Du Bois Review: Social Science Research on Race* 10, no. 2: (2013): 303–312.

Cattelino, Jessica R. *High Stakes: Florida Seminole Gaming and Sovereignty*. Durham: Duke University Press, 2008.

Cha-Jua, Sundiata Keita. "Obama, the Rise of the Hard Right, Arizona and Texas, and the Attack on Racialized Communities Studies." *Black Scholar* 40, no. 4 (2010): 2–6.

Chakrabarty, Dipesh. *Provincializing Europe: Postcolonial Thought and Historical Difference*. Princeton: Princeton University Press, 2000.

Chávez, Karma R. "Border (In)Securities: Normative and Differential Belonging in LGBTQ and Immigrant Rights Discourse." *Communication and Critical/Cultural Studies* 7, no. 2 (2010): 136–155.

———. "Exploring the Defeat of Arizona's Marriage Amendment and the Specter of the Immigrant as Queer." *Southern Communication Journal* 74, no. 3 (2009): 314–324.

———. *Queer Migration Politics: Activist Rhetoric and Coalitional Possibilities*. Urbana: University of Illinois Press, 2013.

Chee, Alexander. "Queer Nationalism." *OUT/Look: National Lesbian and Gay Quarterly* 11 (Winter 1991): 15–19.

Chestnut, Becky. "Matters of Trust: Unanswered Questions after Rice v. Cayetano." *Hawai'i Law Review* 23 (2000): 363–388.

Cheyfitz, Eric. "Savage Law: The Plot against American Indians in *Johnson and Graham's Lessee v. M'Intosh* and *The Pioneers*." In *Cultures of United States Imperialism*, edited by Amy Kaplan and Donald E. Pease, 109–128. Durham: Duke University Press, 1993.

Cho, Sumi, Kimberlé W. Crenshaw, and Leslie McCall. "Toward a Field of Intersectionality Studies: Theory, Applications, and Praxis." *Signs* 38, no. 4 (2013): 785–810.

Coffman, Tom. *The Island Edge of America: A Political History of Hawai'i*. Honolulu: University of Hawai'i Press, 2003.

Cohen, Cathy J. "Punks, Bulldaggers, and Welfare Queens: The Radical Potential of Queer Politics?" *GLQ* 3 (1997): 437–465.

Cole, David. "Against Citizenship as a Predicate for Basic Rights." *Fordham Law Review* 75 (2007): 2541–2548.

———. *Enemy Aliens: Double Standards and Constitutional Freedoms in the War on Terrorism.* New York: The New Press, 2003.

Collective Combahee River. *The Combahee River Collective Statement: Black Feminist Organizing in the Seventies and Eighties.* Albany: Kitchen Table Women of Color Press, 1986.

Collins, Patricia Hill. *Black Feminist Thought: Knowledge, Consciousness, and the Politics of Empowerment.* Boston: Unwin Hyman, 1990.

———. "Forward: Emerging Intersections—Building Knowledge and Transforming Institutions." In *Emerging Intersections: Race, Class, and Gender in Theory, Policy, and Practice,* edited by Bonnie Thornton and Ruth E. Zambrana Dill, vii–xiv. New Brunswick: Rutgers University Press, 2009.

Cook-Lynn, Elizabeth. *A Separate Country: Postcoloniality and American Indian Nations.* Lubbock: Texas Tech University Press, 2012.

Cossman, Brenda. *Sexual Citizens: The Legal and Cultural Regulation of Sex and Belonging.* Stanford: Stanford University Press, 2007.

Costello, Kimberly. "Rice v. Cayetano: Trouble in Paradise for Native Hawaiians Claiming Special Relationship Status." *North Carolina Law Review* 79 (2001): 812–853.

Cott, Nancy F. "Giving Character to Our Whole Civil Polity: Marriage and the Public Order in the Late Nineteenth Century." In *U.S. History as Women's History: New Feminist Essays,* edited by Linda K. Kerber, Alice Kessler-Harris, and Kathryn Kish Sklar, 107–124. Chapel Hill: University of North Carolina Press, 1995.

———. "Marriage and Women's Citizenship in the United States, 1830–1934." *American Historical Review* 103 (1998): 1440–1474.

———. *Public Vows: A History of Marriage and the Nation.* Cambridge: Harvard University Press, 2000.

Craig, Kelina M. "Retaliation, Fear, or Rage: An Investigation of African American and White Reactions to Racist Hate Crimes." In *Crimes of Hate: Selected Readings,* edited by Phyllis B. Gerstenfeld and Diana R. Grant, 58–68. Thousand Oaks: Sage Publications, 2004.

Crenshaw, Kimberlé W. "Demarginalizing the Intersection of Race and Sex: A Black Feminist Critique of Antidiscrimination Doctrine, Feminist Theory and Antiracist Politics." *University of Chicago Legal Forum* 140 (1989): 139–168.

———. "Mapping the Margins: Intersectionality, Identity Politics, and Violence against Women of Color." *Stanford Law Review* 43, no. 6 (1991): 1241–1300.

Crenshaw, Kimberlé, Neil Gotanda, Gary Peller, and Kendall Thomas, eds. *Critical Race Theory: The Key Writings That Formed the Movement.* New York: The New Press, 1995.

Cronin, Anne M. *Advertising and Consumer Citizenship: Gender, Images, and Rights.* London: Routledge, 2000.

Currah, Paisley. "Queer Theory, Lesbian and Gay Rights, and Transsexual Marriages." In *Sexual Identities, Queer Politics,* edited by Mark Blasius, 178–199. Princeton: Princeton University Press, 2001.

——. "The Transgender Rights Imaginary." *Georgetown Journal of Gender and Law* 4 (2003): 705–720.

Currah, Paisley, Richard M. Juang, and Shannon Price Minter, eds. *Transgender Rights*. Minneapolis: University of Minnesota Press, 2006.

Currah, Paisley, and Shannon Minter. "Unprincipled Exclusions: The Struggle to Achieve Judicial and Legislative Equality for Transgender People." *William and Mary Journal of Women and Law* 7 (2000): 37–66.

Davis, Kathy. "Intersectionality as Buzzword: A Sociology of Science Perspective on What Makes a Feminist Theory Successful." *Feminist Theory* 9, no. 1 (2008): 67–85.

De Genova, Nicholas. "The Production of Culprits: From Deportability to Detainability in the Aftermath of 'Homeland Security.'" *Citizenship Studies* 11, no. 5 (2007): 421–448.

——. "The Queer Politics of Migration: Reflections on 'Illegality' and Incorrigibility." *Studies in Social Justice* 4, no. 2 (2010): 101–126.

Deichert, Robert. "Rice v. Cayetano: The Fifteenth Amendment at a Crossroads." *Connecticut Law Review* 32 (2000): 1075–1126.

Delgado, Richard, ed. *Critical Race Theory: The Cutting Edge*. Philadelphia: Temple University Press, 1995.

Deloria, Philip Joseph. *Playing Indian*. New Haven: Yale University Press, 1998.

Deloria, Vine, Jr. *Custer Died for Your Sins: An Indian Manifesto*. New York: Macmillan Company, 1969.

——. "Indian Law and the Reach of History." *Journal of Contemporary Law* 4 (1977–1978): 1–13.

Deloria, Vine, Jr., and Clifford M. Lytle. *The Nations within: The Past and Future of American Indian Sovereignty*. New York: Pantheon Books, 1984.

Deloria, Vine, Jr., and David E. Wilkins. *The Legal Universe: Observations on the Foundations of American Law*. Golden: Fulcrum Publishing, 2011.

Denetdale, Jennifer Nez. "Chairmen, Presidents, and Princesses: The Navajo Nation, Gender, and the Politics of Tradition." *Wicazo Sa Review* 21, no. 1 (2006): 9–44.

——. "Securing Navajo National Boundaries: War, Patriotism, Tradition, and the Diné Marriage Act of 2005." *Wicazo Sa Review* 24, no. 2 (2009): 131–148.

Desai, Jigna. *Beyond Bollywood: The Cultural Politics of South Asian Diasporic Film*. New York: Routledge, 2004.

Dill, Bonnie Thornton, and Ruth E. Zambrana, eds. *Emerging Intersections: Race, Class, and Gender in Theory, Policy, and Practice*. New Brunswick: Rutgers University Press, 2009.

Dillon, Stephen. "'It's Here, It's That Time': Race, Queer Futurity, and the Temporality of Violence in *Born in Flames*." *Women & Performance* 23, no. 1 (2013): 38–51.

Dower, Nigel, and John Williams, eds. *Global Citizenship: A Critical Introduction*. New York: Routledge, 2002.

Driskill, Qwo-Li. "Asegi Ayetl: Cherokee Two-Spirit People Reimagining Nation." In *Queer Indigenous Studies: Critical Interventions in Theory, Politics, and Literature*, edited by Qwo-Li Driskill, Chris Finley, Brian Joseph Gilley, and Scott Lauria Morgensen, 97–112. Tucson: University of Arizona Press, 2011.

Duggan, Lisa. "Making It Perfectly Queer." In *Sex Wars: Sexual Dissent and Political Culture*, edited by Lisa Duggan and Nan D. Hunter, 155–172. New York: Routledge, 1995.

——. "The New Homonormativity; The Sexual Politics of Neoliberalism." In *Materializing Democracy: Toward a Revitalized Cultural Politics*, edited by Russ Castronovo and Dana Nelson, 175–194. Durham: Duke University Press, 2002.

——. "Queering the State." *Social Text* 39 (1994): 1–14.

——. *The Twilight of Equality: Neoliberalism, Cultural Politics, and the Attack on Democracy.* Boston: Beacon Press, 2004.

Edelman, Lee. *No Future: Queer Theory and the Death Drive.* Durham: Duke University Press, 2004.

Ehrenreich, Nancy. "Subordination and Symbiosis: Mechanisms of Mutual Support between Subordinating Systems." *UMKC Law Review* 71 (2002): 251–324.

Ellison, Nick. "Citizenship, Space and Time: Engagement, Identity and Belonging in a Connected World." *Thesis Eleven* 118, no. 1 (2013): 48–63.

Eng, David L. *The Feeling of Kinship: Queer Liberalism and the Racialization of Intimacy.* Durham: Duke University Press, 2010.

——. "Out Here and Over There: Queerness and Diaspora in Asian American Studies." *Social Text* 52–53 (1997): 31–52.

Eng, David L., Judith Halberstam, and Jose Muñoz. "Introduction to 'What's Queer about Queer Studies Now?'" *Social Text* 84–85 (Fall/Winter 2005): 1–17.

Erel, Umut, Jin Haritaworn, Encarnación Guitiérrez Rodriguez, and Christian Klesse. "On the Depoliticisation of Intersectionality Talk: Conceptualising Multiple Oppressions in Critical Sexuality Studies." In *Out of Place: Interrogating Silences in Queerness/Raciality*, edited by Adi Kuntsman and Esperanza Miyake, 271–298. New York: Raw Nerve Books, 2008.

Ettelbrick, Paula. "Since When Is Marriage a Path to Liberation?" In *Lesbians, Gay Men, and the Law*, edited by William Rubenstein, 401–406. New York: New Press, 1993.

Evans, David T. *Sexual Citizenship: The Material Construction of Sexualities.* London: Routledge, 1993.

Fanon, Frantz. *The Wretched of the Earth*, translated by Constance Farrington. New York: Grove Press, Inc., 1965.

Feather, Nancy J. "Defense of Marriage Acts: An Analysis under State Constitutional Law." *Temple Law Review* 70 (1997): 1017–1035.

Ferguson, Roderick A. *Aberrations in Black: Toward a Queer of Color Critique.* Minneapolis: University of Minnesota Press, 2004.

——. "Of Our Normative Strivings: African American Studies and the Histories of Sexuality." *Social Text* 84/85 (2005): 85–100.

Finley, Chris. "Decolonizing the Queer Native Body (and Recovering the Native Bull-Dyke): Bringing 'Sexy Back' and Out of Native Studies Closet." In *Queer Indigenous Studies: Critical Interventions in Theory, Politics, and Literature*, edited by Qwo-Li Driskill, Chris Finley, Brian Joseph Gilley, and Scott Lauria Morgensen, 31–42. Tucson: University of Arizona Press, 2011.

Foucault, Michel. *Abnormal: Lectures at the Collège De France, 1974–1975*. New York: Picador, 2003.

――. *The Archaeology of Knowledge and the Discourses on Language*. New York: Pantheon Books, 1972.

――. "Governmentality." In *The Foucault Effect: Studies in Governmentality: With Two Lectures by and an Interview with Michel Foucault*, edited by Graham Burchell, Colin Gordon, and Peter Miller, 87–104. Chicago: University of Chicago Press, 1991.

――. *The History of Sexuality*. New York: Pantheon Books, 1978.

――. "The Subject and Power." *Critical Inquiry* 8, no 4 (1982): 777–795.

Foucault, Michel, Mauro Bertani, Alessandro Fontana, François Ewald, and David Macey, eds. *Society Must Be Defended: Lectures at the Collège De France, 1975–76*, 1st ed. New York: Picador, 2003.

Foucault, Michel, Graham Burchell, Colin Gordon, and Peter Miller. *The Foucault Effect: Studies in Governmentality: With Two Lectures by and an Interview with Michel Foucault*. Chicago: University of Chicago Press, 1991.

Franke, Katherine M. "Becoming a Citizen: Reconstruction Era Regulation of African American Marriages." *Yale Journal of Law and the Humanities* 11 (1999): 251–309.

――. "The Domesticated Liberty of Lawrence v. Texas." *Columbia Law Review* 104 (2004): 1399–1426.

――. "Sexuality and Marriage: The Politics of Same-Sex Marriage Politics." *Columbia Journal of Gender and Law* 15 (2006): 236–248.

Franklin, Karen. "Good Intentions: The Enforcement of Hate Crime Penalty-Enhancement Statutes." In *Crimes of Hate: Selected Readings*, edited by Phyllis B. Gerstenfeld and Diana R. Grant, 79–92. Thousand Oaks: Sage Publications, 2004.

Freeman, Elizabeth. Introduction. *GLQ* 13, no. 2 (2007): 159–176.

――. "Marriage." In *Keywords for American Cultural Studies*, edited by Bruce Burgett and Glenn Hendler, 152–159. New York: New York University Press, 2007.

Fujikane, Candace. "Asian American Critique and Moana Nui 2011: Securing a Future beyond Empires, Militarized Capitalism and APEC." *Inter-Asia Cultural Studies* 13, no. 2 (2012): 189–210.

――. "Foregrounding Native Nationalisms: A Critique of Antinationalist Sentiment in Asian American Studies." In *Asian American Studies after Critical Mass*, edited by Kent Ono, 73–97. Malden, Mass.: Blackwell, 2004.

Fujikane, Candace, and Jonathan Y. Okamura, eds. *Asian Settler Colonialism: From Local Governance to the Habits of Everyday Life in Hawai'i*. Honolulu: University of Hawai'i Press, 2009.

Garry, Ann. "Intersectionality, Metaphors, and the Multiplicity of Gender." *Hypatia*, no. 4 (2011): 826–850.

Gelman, Susan B., and Frederick M. Lawrence. "Agreeing to Agree: A Proponent and Opponent of Hate Crime Laws Reach for Common Ground." *Harvard Journal on Legislation* 41 (2004): 420–448.

Gilmore, Ruth Wilson. *Golden Gulag: Prisons, Surplus, Crisis, and Opposition in Globalizing California*. Berkeley: University of California Press, 2006.

Goldberg, Carole. "Descent into Race." *UCLA Law Review* 49 (2002): 943–990.

Goldstein, Alyosha. "Possessive Investment: Indian Removals and the Affective Entitlements of Whiteness." *American Quarterly* 66, no. 4 (2014): 1077–1084.

Goodyear-Kaʻōpua, Noelani. "Hawaiʻi: An Occupied County." *Harvard International Review* 35, no. 3 (2014): 58–62.

———. "Kuleana Lāhui: Collective Responsibility for Hawaiian Nationhood in Activists' Praxis." *Affinities: A Journal of Radical Theory, Culture, and Action* 5, no. 1 (2011): 130–162.

Goodyear-Kaʻōpua, Noelani, Ikaika Hussey, and Erin Kahunawaikaʻala Wright, eds. *A Nation Rising: Hawaiian Movements for Life, Land, and Sovereignty*. Durham: Duke University Press, 2014.

Gotanda, Neil. "'Other Non-Whites' in American Legal History: A Review of *Justice at War*." *Columbia Law Review* 85 (1985): 1186–1192.

———. "Race, Citizenship, and the Search for Political Community among 'We the People': A Review Essay on *Citizenship without Consent*." *Oregon Law Review* 76 (1997): 233–260.

Grewal, Inderpal. *Transnational America: Feminisms, Diasporas, Neoliberalisms*. Durham: Duke University Press, 2005.

Grosz, Elizabeth A. *Time Travels: Feminism, Nature, Power*. Durham: Duke University Press, 2005.

Gutiérrez, Laura, Christina B. Hanhardt, Miranda Joseph, Adela C. Licona, and Sandra K. Soto. "Nativism, Normativity, and Neoliberalism in Arizona." *Transformations: The Journal of Inclusive Scholarship and Pedagogy* 21, no. 2 (2011): 123–148.

Haefele-Thomas, Ardel. *Queer Others in Victorian Gothic: Transgressing Monstrosity*. Cardiff: University of Wales Press, 2012.

Haggerty, George E. *Queer Gothic*. Urbana: University of Illinois Press, 2006.

Halberstam, Judith. *In a Queer Time and Place: Transgender Bodies, Subcultural Lives*. New York: New York University Press, 2005.

———. *Skin Shows: Gothic Horror and the Technology of Monsters*. Durham: Duke University Press, 1995.

Hall, Lisa Kahaleole. "'Hawaiian at Heart' and Other Fictions." *Contemporary Pacific* 17, no. 2 (2005): 404–413.

Halley, Janet E. "'Like Race' Arguments." In *What's Left of Theory? New Work on the Politics of Literary Theory*, edited by Judith Butler, John Guillory, and Kendall Thomas, 40–74. New York: Routledge, 2000.

Halualani, Rona Tamiko. *In the Name of Hawaiians: Native Identities and Cultural Politics*. Minneapolis: University of Minnesota Press, 2002.

Hancock, Ange-Marie. "Intersectionality as a Normative and Empirical Paradigm." *Politics & Gender* 3, no. 2 (2007): 248–254.

Haney-López, Ian F. *White by Law: The Legal Constructions of Race*. New York: New York University Press, 1996.

Hanhardt, Christina B. *Safe Space: Gay Neighborhood History and the Politics of Violence*. Durham: Duke University Press, 2013.

Hanifin, Patrick. *"Rice* Is Right." *Asian-Pacific Law & Policy Journal* 3, no. 2 (2002): 283–307.

Harris, Angela P. "Loving before and after the Law." *Fordham Law Review* 76 (2008): 2821–2847.

Harris, Cheryl I. "Whiteness as Property." *Harvard Law Review* 106 (1993): 1707–1791.

Hasager, Ulla, and Jonathan Friedman. *Hawai'i: Return to Nationhood.* Copenhagen: International Work Group for Indigenous Affairs, 1994.

Heffner, John. "Between Assimilation and Revolt: A Third Option for Hawaii as a Model for Minorities World-Wide." *Texas International Law Journal* 37 (2002): 591–622.

Hemmings, Clare. *Why Stories Matter: The Political Grammar of Feminist Theory.* Durham: Duke University Press, 2011.

Henderson, James Sákéj Youngblood. "Sui Generis and Treaty Citizenship." *Citizenship Studies* 6, no. 4 (2002): 415–441.

Hindess, Barry. "Citizenship for All." *Citizenship Studies* 8, no. 3 (2004): 305–315.

———. "Citizenship in the International Management of Populations." *American Behavioral Scientist* 43 (2000): 1486–1497.

Hodes, Martha Elizabeth, ed. *Sex, Love, Race: Crossing Boundaries in North American History.* New York: New York University Press, 1999.

Hodge, Jessica. *Gendered Hate: Exploring Gender in Hate Crime Law.* Boston: Northeastern University Press, 2011.

Hong, Grace Kyungwon, and Roderick A. Ferguson, eds. *Strange Affinities: The Gender and Sexual Politics of Comparative Racialization.* Durham: Duke University Press, 2011.

ho'omanawanui, ku'ualoha. *Voices of Fire: Reweaving the Literary Lei of Pele and Hi'iaka.* Minneapolis: University of Minnesota Press, 2014.

Hoxie, Frederick E. *The Final Promise: The Campaign to Assimilate the Indians, 1880–1920.* Lincoln: University of Nebraska Press, 1984.

Hunter, Nan D. "Marriage, Law, and Gender: A Feminist Inquiry." In *Sex Wars: Sexual Dissent and Political Culture,* edited by Lisa Duggan and Nan D. Hunter, 105–118. New York: Routledge, 1995.

Hutchinson, Darren Lenard. "Out yet Unseen: A Racial Critique of Gay and Lesbian Legal Theory and Political Discourse." *Connecticut Law Review* 29, no. 2 (1997): 561–646.

Hwang, Victor M. "The Interrelationship between Anti-Asian Violence and Asian America." In *Anti-Asian Violence in North America: Asian American and Asian Canadian Reflections on Hate, Healing and Resistance,* edited by Patricia Wong Hall and Victor M. Hwang, 43–66. Walnut Creek: AltaMira Press, 2001.

Iijima, Chris K. "Race over Rice: Binary Analytical Boxes and a Twenty-First Century Endorsement of Nineteenth Century Imperialism." *Rutgers Law Review* 53 (Fall 2000).

Imada, Adria L. *Aloha America: Hula Circuits through the U.S. Empire.* Durham: Duke University Press, 2012.

Isin, Engin F., and Greg M. Nielsen. *Acts of Citizenship.* London: Zed Books, 2008.

Isin, Engin F., and Peter Nyers, eds. *Routledge Handbook of Global Citizenship Studies.* New York: Routledge, 2014.

Isin, Engin F., and Bryan S. Turner. "Citizenship Studies: An Introduction." In *Handbook of Citizenship Studies,* edited by Engin F. Isin and Bryan S. Turner, 1–10. London, U.K.: Sage, 2002.

Iverson, Peter. *Carlos Montezuma and the Changing World of American Indians.* Albuquerque: University of New Mexico Press, 1982.

JanMohamed, Abdul R. *The Death-Bound-Subject: Richard Wright's Archaeology of Death.* Durham: Duke University Press, 2005.

Jenness, Valerie, and Kendal Broad. "Engendering Hate Crime Policy: Gender, the 'Dilemma of Difference,' and the Creation of Legal Subjects." *Journal of Hate Studies* 2, no. 1 (2002/2003): 73–97.

———. *Hate Crimes: New Social Movements and the Politics of Violence.* New York: Aldine De Gruyter, 1997.

Johnson, Kevin R. "Race, the Immigration Laws, and Domestic Race Relations: A 'Magic Mirror' into the Heart of Darkness." *Indiana Law Journal* 73 (1998): 1111–1160.

Jordan, June. *Civil Wars.* New York: Simon and Schuster, 1981.

Josephson, Jyl. "Citizenship, Same-Sex Marriage, and Feminist Critiques of Marriage." *Perspectives on Politics* 3, no.2 (2005): 269–284.

Jun, Helen Heran. *Race for Citizenship: Black Orientalism and Asian Uplift from Pre-Emancipation to Neoliberal America.* New York: New York University Press, 2011.

Justice, Daniel Heath. "Notes toward a Theory of Anomaly." *GLQ* 16, no.1–2 (2010): 207–242.

Kameʻeleihiwa, Lilikalā. *Native Land and Foreign Desires: Pehea Lā E Pono Ai? How Shall We Live in Harmony?* Honolulu: Bishop Museum Press, 1992.

Kandaswamy, Priya. "State Austerity and the Racial Politics of Same-Sex Marriage in the United States." *Sexualities: Studies in Culture and Society* 11, no. 6 (2008): 706–725.

Kaplan, Amy. *The Anarchy of Empire: The Making of U.S. Culture.* Cambridge: Harvard University Press, 2002.

Kaplan, Amy, and Donald E. Pease, eds. *Cultures of United States Imperialism.* Durham: Duke University Press, 1993.

Karst, Kenneth L. *Belonging to America: Equal Citizenship and the Constitution.* New Haven: Yale University Press, 1989.

———. "Citizenship, Law, and the American Nation." *Indiana Journal of Global Legal Studies* 7 (2000): 595–601.

Kauanui, J. Kēhaulani. "Colonialism in Equality: Hawaiian Sovereignty and the Question of U.S. Civil Rights." *South Atlantic Quarterly* 107, no. 4 (Fall 2008): 635–650.

———. *Hawaiian Blood: Colonialism and the Politics of Sovereignty and Indigeneity.* Durham: Duke University Press, 2008.

———. "The Multiplicity of Hawaiian Sovereignty Claims and the Struggle for Meaningful Autonomy." *Comparative American Studies* 3, no. 3 (2005): 283–299.

——. "Resisting the Akaka Bill." In *A Nation Rising: Hawaiian Movements for Life, Land, and Sovereignty*, edited by Noelani Goodyear-Kaʻōpua, Ikaika Hussey, and Erin Kahunawaikaʻala Wright, 312–330. Durham: Duke University Press, 2014.

——. "A Sorry State: Apology Politics and Legal Fictions in the Court of the Conqueror." In *Formations of United States Colonialism*, edited by Alyosha Goldstein, 110–136. Durham: Duke University Press, 2014.

Kauanui, J. Kēhaulani, and Patrick Wolfe. "Settler Colonialism Then and Now: A Conversation between J. Kēhaulani Kauanui and Patrick Wolfe." *Politica & Società* 2 (2012): 235–258.

Kerber, Linda K. *No Constitutional Right to Be Ladies: Women and the Obligations of Citizenship*. New York: Hill and Wang, 1998.

King, Lisa. "Competition, Complicity, and (Potential) Alliance: Native Hawaiian and Asian Immigrant Narratives at the Bishop Museum." *College Literature* 41, no. 1 (2014): 43–65.

Kirby, Diane, and Catharine Coleborne, eds. *Law, History, Colonialism: The Reach of Empire*. Manchester: Manchester University Press, 2010.

Klarman, Michael J. "Windsor and Brown: Marriage Equality and Racial Equality." *Harvard Law Review* 127, no. 1 (2013): 127–160.

Koppelman, Andrew. "Dumb and DOMA: Why the Defense of Marriage Act Is Unconstitutional." *Iowa Law Review* 83 (1997): 1–33.

Krakoff, Sarah. "Inextricably Political: Race, Membership, and Tribal Sovereignty." *Washington Law Review* 87 (2012): 1041–1132.

——. "Law, Violence, and the Neurotic Structure of American Indian Law." *Wake Forest Law Review* 49 (2014): 743–756.

Kunnie, Julian. "Apartheid in Arizona? HB 2281 and Arizona's Denial of Human Rights of Peoples of Color." *Black Scholar* 40, no. 4 (2010): 16–26.

Kwan, Peter. "Jeffrey Dahmer and the Co-Synthesis of Categories." *Hastings Law Journal* 48 (1997): 1257–1293.

Kymlicka, Will. *Multicultural Citizenship: A Liberal Theory of Minority Rights*. Oxford: Oxford University Press, 1995.

Kymlicka, Will, and Wayne Norman. "Return of the Citizen: A Survey of Recent Work on Citizenship Theory." In *Theorizing Citizenship*, edited by Ronald Beiner, 283–322. Albany: State University of New York Press, 1995.

Laenui, Pōkā. *Collection of Papers on Hawaiian Sovereignty and Self-Determination*. Waiʻanae: Institute for the Advancement of Hawaiian Affairs, 1992.

Lawrence, Bonita, and Enakshi Dua. "Decolonizing Antiracism." *Social Justice* 32, no. 4 (2005): 120–143.

Lee, Charles T. "Suicide Bombing as Acts of Deathly Citizenship? A Critical Double-Layered Inquiry." *Critical Studies on Terrorism* 2, no. 2 (August 2009): 147–163.

——. "Undocumented Workers' Subversive Citizenship Acts." *Peace Review: A Journal of Social Justice* 20, no. 3 (2008): 330–338.

Lee, Elizabeth, and Geraldine Pratt. "The Spectacular and The Mundane: Racialised State Violence, Filipino Migrant Workers, and Their Families." *Environment and Planning A* 44, no. 4 (2012): 889–904.

Levin, Jack, and Jack McDevitt. *Hate Crimes Revisited: America's War on Those Who Are Different*. Boulder: Westview Press, 2002.

Lewis, Gail. "Celebrating Intersectionality? Debates on a Multi-Faceted Concept in Gender Studies: Themes from a Conference." *European Journal of Women's Studies* 16, no. 3 (2009): 203–210.

Lind, Andrew W. *Hawaii's Japanese: An Experiment in Democracy*. Princeton: Princeton University Press, 1946.

Lindsey, R. Hōkūlei. "The Akaka Bill: Native Hawaiians, Legal Realities, and Politics as Usual." *University of Hawai'i Law Review* 24 (2002): 693–727.

Linklater, Andrew. "Cosmopolitan Citizenship." *Citizenship Studies* 2, no. 1 (1998): 23–41.

Lipsitz, George. "Learning from New Orleans: The Social Warrant of Hostile Privatism and Competitive Consumer Citizenship." *Cultural Anthropology* 21, no. 3 (2006): 451–468.

Lister, Ruth. *Citizenship: Feminist Perspectives*, 2nd ed. New York: New York University Press, 2003.

Lomawaima, Tsianina K. "The Mutuality of Citizenship and Sovereignty: The Society of American Indians and the Battle to Inherit America." *American Indian Quarterly* 37.3 (2013): 333–351.

Lorde, Audre. *Sister Outsider: Essays and Speeches*. Trumansburg, N.Y.: Crossing Press, 1984.

Lowe, Lisa. *Immigrant Acts: On Asian American Cultural Politics*. Durham: Duke University Press, 1996.

Luibhéid, Eithne. *Entry Denied: Controlling Sexuality at the Border*. Minneapolis: University of Minnesota Press, 2002.

Luna-Firebaugh, Eileen M. "The Border Crossed Us: Border Crossing Issues of the Indigenous Peoples of the Americas." *Wicazo Sa Review* 17, no. 1 (2002): 159–181.

Lyons, Scott Richard. *X-Marks: Native Signatures of Assent*. Minneapolis: University of Minnesota Press, 2010.

MacKenzie, Melody Kapilialoha. *Native Hawaiian Rights Handbook*. Honolulu: University of Hawai'i Press, 1991.

Maddox, Lucy. *Citizen Indians: Native American Intellectuals, Race, and Reform*. Ithaca: Cornell University Press, 2005.

Mandell, Daniel R. *Tribe, Race, History: Native Americans in Southern New England, 1780–1880*. Baltimore: John Hopkins University Press, 2008.

Maroney, Terry A. "The Struggle against Hate Crime: Movement at a Crossroads." *New York University Law Review* 75 (1998): 564–620.

May, Vivian. *Pursuing Intersectionality, Unsettling Dominant Imaginaries*. New York: Routledge, 2015.

Mbembé, Achille. "Necropolitics," translated by Libby Meintjes. *Public Culture* 15, no 1 (2003): 11–40.

McCall, Leslie. "The Complexity of Intersectionality." *Signs*, no. 3 (2005): 190–197.

McCallum, E. L. "The Timezone Endgame." *CR: The New Centennial Review* 1, no. 1 (2001): 141–73.

McClintock, Anne. *Imperial Leather: Race, Gender, and Sexuality in the Colonial Contest.* New York: Routledge, 1995.

McNevin, Anne. "Irregular Migrants, Neoliberal Geographies and Spatial Frontiers of 'The Political.'" *Review of International Studies* 33, no. 4 (2007): 655–674.

Melamed, Jodi. *Represent and Destroy: Rationalizing Violence in the New Racial Capitalism.* Minneapolis: University of Minnesota Press, 2011.

Merry, Sally Engle. *Colonizing Hawai'i: The Cultural Power of Law.* Princeton: Princeton University Press, 1999.

———. "Law and Identity in an American Colony." In *Law and Empire in the Pacific: Fiji and Hawai'i*, edited by Sally Engle Merry and Donald Brenneis, 123–152. Santa Fe: School of American Research Press, 2004.

Miller, Toby. "Introducing . . . Cultural Citizenship." *Social Text* 19, no. 4 (2001): 1–5.

Moraga, Cherríe, and Anzaldúa, Gloria. *This Bridge Called My Back: Writings by Radical Women of Color*, 1st ed. Watertown: Persephone Press, 1981.

Morgensen, Scott Lauria. "Settler Homonationalism: Theorizing Settler Colonialism with Queer Modernities." *GLQ* 16, no. 1–2 (2010): 105–131.

———. *Spaces between Us: Queer Settler Colonialism and Indigenous Decolonization.* Minneapolis: University of Minnesota Press, 2011.

———. "White Settlers and Indigenous Solidarity: Confronting White Supremacy, Answering Decolonial Alliances." *Decolonization: Indigeneity, Education & Society* (2014); https://decolonization.wordpress.com/2014/05/26/white-settlers-and-indigenous -solidarity-confronting-white-supremacy-answering-decolonial-alliances/ (accessed Dec. 15, 2014).

Muñoz, José Esteban. *Cruising Utopia: The Then and There of Queer Futurity.* New York: New York University Press, 2009.

Nash, Jennifer C. "'Home Truths' on Intersectionality." *Yale Journal of Law & Feminism* 23, no. 2 (2011): 445–470.

———. "Re-Thinking Intersectionality." *Feminist Review*, no. 89 (2008): 1–15.

Newman, Janet. "'But We Didn't Mean That': Feminist Projects and Governmental Appropriations." In *Beyond Citizenship? Feminism and the Transformation of Belonging*, edited by Sasha Roseneil, 89–111. London: Palgrave MacMillan, 2013.

Okihiro, Gary Y. *Cane Fires: The Anti-Japanese Movement in Hawaii, 1865–1945.* Philadelphia: Temple University Press, 1991.

Okin, Susan Moller. *Is Multiculturalism Bad for Women?* Princeton: Princeton University Press, 1999.

O'Malley, Eric Steven. "Irreconcilable Rights and the Question of Statehood." *Georgetown Law Journal* 89 (2001): 501–542.

Ong, Aihwa. *Buddha Is Hiding: Refugees, Citizenship, the New America*. Berkeley: University of California Press, 2003.

———. "Cultural Citizenship as Subject-Making: Immigrants Negotiate Racial and Cultural Boundaries in the United States." *Current Anthropology* 37, no. 5 (December 1996): 737–762.

———. *Flexible Citizenship: The Cultural Logics of Transnationality*. Durham: Duke University Press, 1999.

Osorio, Jonathan Kay Kamakawiwoʻole. *Dismembering Lāhui: A History of the Hawaiian Nation to 1887*. Honolulu: University of Hawaiʻi Press, 2002.

———. "Kūʻē and Kūʻokoʻa: History, Law, and Other Faiths." In *Law & Empire in the Pacific*, edited by Sally Engle Merry and Donald Brenneis, 213–238. Santa Fe: School of American Research Press, 2004.

———. "'What Kine Hawaiian Are You?': A Moʻolelo about Nationhood, Race, History, and the Contemporary Sovereignty Movement in Hawaiʻi." *Contemporary Pacific* 13, no. 2 (Fall 2001): 359–379.

Painter, Nell Irvin. *Sojourner Truth: A Life, a Symbol*. New York: W. W. Norton, 1997.

Pascoe, Peggy. "Sex, Gender, and Same-Sex Marriage." In *Is Academic Feminism Dead? Theory in Practice*, edited by Social Justice Group at the Center for Advanced Feminist Studies, 86–129. New York: New York University Press, 2000.

———. *What Comes Naturally: Miscegenation Law and the Making of Race in America*. Oxford: Oxford University Press, 2009.

Pateman, Carole. *The Sexual Contract*. Stanford: Stanford University Press, 1988.

Perry, Barbara. *In the Name of Hate: Understanding Hate Crimes*. New York: Routledge, 2001.

———. "Normative Violence: Everyday Racism in the Lives of Native Americans." In *Structured Inequality in the United States: Critical Discussions on the Continuing Significance of Race, Ethnicity, and Gender*, edited by Jr. Adalberto Aguirre and David V. Baker, 239–264. Upper Saddle River, N.J.: Pearson Prentice Hall, 2008.

———. *Policing Race and Place: Over- and Under-policing in Indian Country*. Maryland: Lexington Books, 2009.

———. *Silent Victims: Hate Crimes against Native Americans*. Tucson: University of Arizona Press, 2008.

———, ed. *Hate and Bias Crime: A Reader*. New York: Routledge, 2003.

Peterson, V. Spike. "Sexing Political Identities/Nationalism as Heterosexism." In *Women, States, and Nationalism: At Home in the Nation?* edited by Sita Ranchod-Nilsson and Mary Ann Tétreault, 54–79. London: Routledge, 2000.

Phung, Malissa. "Are People of Colour Settlers Too?" In *Cultivating Canada: Reconciliation through the Lens of Cultural Diversity*, edited by Ashok Mathur, Jonathan Dewar, and Mike DeGagné. Ottawa: Aboriginal Healing Foundation, 2011.

Plummer, Ken. "The Square of Intimate Citizenship: Some Preliminary Proposals." *Citizenship Studies* 5, no. 3 (2001): 237–253.

Polikoff, Nancy. "We Will Get What We Ask For: Why Legalizing Gay and Lesbian Marriage Will Not 'Dismantle the Legal Structure of Gender in Every Marriage.'" *Virginia Law Review* 79 (1993).

——. "Why Lesbians and Gay Men Should Read Martha Fineman." *American University Journal of Gender, Social Policy, and the Law* 8 (2000): 167–176.

Povinelli, Elizabeth. *The Cunning of Recognition: Indigenous Alterities and the Making of Australian Multiculturalism*. Durham: Duke University Press, 2002.

——. *Economies of Abandonment: Social Belonging and Endurance in Late Liberalism*. Durham: Duke University Press, 2011.

——. "The Governance of the Prior." *Interventions* 13, no. 1 (2011): 13–30.

Prins, Baukje. "Narrative Accounts of Origins: A Blind Spot in the Intersectional Approach?" *European Journal of Women's Studies* 13, no. 3 (2006): 277–290.

Puar, Jasbir K. "Circuits of Queer Mobility: Tourism, Travel, and Globalization." *GLQ* 8, no. 1/2 (2002): 101–137.

——. "'I Would Rather Be a Cyborg Than a Goddess': Becoming-Intersectional in Assemblage Theory." *philoSOPHIA: A Journal of Continental Feminism* 2, no. 1 (2012): 49–66.

——. *Terrorist Assemblages: Homonationalism in Queer Times*. Durham: Duke University Press, 2007.

Puar, Jasbir K., and Amit S. Rai. "Monster, Terrorist, Fag: The War on Terrorism and the Production of Docile Patriots." *Social Text* 72 (2002): 117–148.

Rafael, Vicente L. "White Love: Surveillance and Nationalist Resistance in the U.S. Colonization of the Philippines." In *Cultures of United States Imperialism*, edited by Amy Kaplan and Donald E. Pease, 185–218. Durham: Duke University Press, 1993.

Rai, Amit S. "Of Monsters." *Cultural Studies* 18, no. 4 (2004): 538–570.

——. "The Promise of Monsters: Terrorism, Monstrosity and Biopolitics." *International Studies in Philosophy* 37, no. 2 (2005): 81–93.

Ramirez, Renya K. *Native Hubs: Culture, Community, and Belonging in Silicon Valley and Beyond*. Durham: Duke University Press, 2007.

Rand, E. J. "An Appetite for Activism: The Lesbian Avengers and the Queer Politics of Visibility." *Women's Studies in Communication* 36, no. 2 (2013): 121–141.

——. "A Disunited Nation and a Legacy of Contradiction: Queer Nation's Construction of Identity." *Journal of Communication Inquiry* 28, no. 4 (2004): 288–306.

Rand, Erica. *The Ellis Island Snow Globe*. Durham: Duke University Press, 2005.

Rasmussen, Claire, and Michael P. Brown. "Radical Democratic Citizenship: Amidst Political Theory and Geography." In *Handbook of Citizenship Studies*, edited by Engin F. Isin and Bryan S. Turner, 175–190. London: Sage Publications, 2002.

Reddy, Chandan. *Freedom with Violence: Race, Sexuality, and the U.S. State*. Durham: Duke University Press, 2011.

——. "Time for Rights? Loving, Gay Marriage, and the Limits of Legal Justice." *Fordham Law Review* 76 (2008): 2849–2872.

Resenberger, Jeffrey L. "Sex Marriages and the Defense of Marriage Act: A Deviant View of an Experiment in Full Faith and Credit." *Creighton Law Review* 32 (1998): 409–456.

Rifkin, Mark. "Native Nationality in the Contemporary Queer: Tradition, Sexuality, and History in 'Drowning in Fire.'" *American Indian Quarterly* 4 (2008): 443–470.

——. *When Did Indians Become Straight? Kinship, the History of Sexuality, and Native Sovereignty*. New York: Oxford University Press, 2011.

Ritchie, Andrea. "Law Enforcement Violence against Women of Color." In *The Color of Violence: The Incite! Anthology*, edited by Incite! Women of Color against Violence, 138–156. Cambridge: South End Press, 2006.

——. "The Pertinence of Perry to Challenging the Continuing Criminalization of LGBT People." *New York University Review of Law & Social Change* 37 (2013): 63–71.

Roberts, Dorothy, and Sujatha Jesudason. "Movement Intersectionality: The Case of Race, Gender, Disability, and Genetic Technologies." *Du Bois Review: Social Science Research on Race* 10, no. 2 (2013): 313–328.

Robson, Ruthann. "A Mere Switch or a Fundamental Change? Theorizing Transgender Marriage." *Hypatia* 22, no. 1 (2007): 58–70.

——. "Reinscribing Normality? The Law and Politics of Transgender Marriage." In *Transgender Rights*, edited by Richard M. Juang, Paisley Currah, and Shannon Price Minter, 299–309. Minneapolis: University of Minnesota Press, 2006.

Rolnick, Addie C. "The Promise of Mancari: Indian Political Rights as Racial Remedy." *New York University Law Review* 86 (2011): 958–1045.

Rosaldo, Renato. "Cultural Citizenship and Educational Democracy." *Cultural Anthropology* 9, no. 3 (1994): 402–411.

Rosen, Deborah A. *American Indians and State Law: Sovereignty, Race, and Citizenship, 1790–1880*. Lincoln: University of Nebraska Press, 2007.

Rosga, AnnJanette. "Bias before the Law: The Rearticulation of Hate Crimes in Wisconsin v. Mitchell." *New York University Review of Law & Social Change* 25, no. 1 (1999): 29–63.

——. "Deadly Words: State Power and the Entanglement of Speech and Violence in Hate Crime." *Law and Critique* 12, no. 3 (2001): 223–252.

——. "Policing the State." *Georgetown Journal of Gender and the Law* 1 (1999): 145–170.

Rubin, Gayle. "Thinking Sex: Notes for a Radical Theory of the Politics of Sexuality." In *Pleasure and Danger: Exploring Female Sexuality*, edited by Carole S. Vance. Boston: Routledge & Kegan Paul, 1984.

Saito, Natsu Taylor. "Model Minority, Yellow Peril: Functions of Foreignness in the Construction of Asian American Legal Identity." *Asian Law Journal* 4 (1997): 71–95.

Saranillio, Dean Itsuji. "Colliding Histories: Hawai'i Statehood at the Intersection of Asians 'Ineligible to Citizenship' and Hawaiians 'Unfit for Self-Government.'" *Journal of Asian American Studies* 13, no. 3 (2010): 283–309.

——. "Colonial Amnesia: Rethinking Filipino 'American' Settler Empowerment in the U.S. Colony of Hawai'i." In *Positively No Filipinos Allowed: Building Communities and Discourse*, edited by Antonio T. Tiongson, Edgardo V. Gutierrez, and Ricardo V. Gutierrez, 124–144. Philadelphia: Temple University Press, 2006.

——. "Kewaikaliko's Benocide: Reversing the Imperial Gaze of Rice v. Cayetano and Its Legal Progeny." *American Quarterly* 62, no. 3 (2010): 457–476.

——. "Why Asian Settler Colonialism Matters: A Thought Piece on Critiques, Debates, and Indigenous Difference." *Settler Colonial Studies* 3, no. 3–4 (2013): 280–294.

Sassen, Saskia. "Towards a Post-National and Denationalized Citizenship." In *Handbook of Citizenship Studies*, edited by Engin F. Isin and Bryan S. Turner, 277–292. London: Sage Publications, 2002.

Schneider, Bethany. "Oklahobo: Following Craig Womack's American Indian and Queer Studies." *South Atlantic Quarterly* 106, no. 3 (2007): 599–613.

Shapiro, Michael. "National Times and Other Times: Re-Thinking Citizenship." *Cultural Studies* 14, no. 1 (2000): 79–98.

Sharma, Nandita, and Cynthia Wright. "Decolonizing Resistance, Challenging Colonial States." *Social Justice* 35, no. 3 (2008): 120–138.

Shildrick, Margrit. "Sexual Citizenship, Governance and Disability: From Foucault to Delueze." In *Beyond Citizenship: Feminism and the Transformation of Belonging*, edited by Sasha Roseneil, 138–159. New York: Palgrave MacMillan, 2013.

Silva, Noenoe. *Aloha Betrayed: Native Hawaiian Resistance to American Colonialism*. Durham: Duke University Press, 2004.

Simpson, Audra. "Captivating Eunice: Membership, Colonialism, and Gendered Citizenships of Grief." *Wicazo Sa Review* 24, no. 2 (2009): 107–124.

——. *Mohawk Interruptus: Political Life across the Borders of Settler States*. Durham: Duke University Press, 2014.

——. "On Ethnographic Refusal: Indigeneity, 'Voice' and Colonial Citizenship." *Junctures: The Journal for Thematic Dialogue* 9 (2007): 67–80.

——. "On the Logic of Discernment." *American Quarterly* 59, no. 2 (2007): 479–491.

Singh, Nikhil Pal. *Black Is a Country: Race and the Unfinished Struggle for Democracy*. Cambridge: Harvard University Press, 2004.

Slagle, R. Anthony. "In Defense of Queer Nation: From Identity Politics to a Politics of Difference." *Western Journal of Communication* 59, no. 2 (1995): 85–102.

Smith, Andrea. "Unmasking the State: Racial/Gender Terror and Hate Crimes." In *State of White Supremacy: Racism, Governance, and the United States*, edited by Moon-Kie Jung, João H. Costa Vargas, and Eduardo Bonilla-Silva, 229–242. Stanford: Stanford University Press, 2011.

Smith, Linda Tuhiwai. *Decolonizing Methodologies: Research and Indigenous Peoples*. New York: Zed Books, 1999.

Smith, Rogers M. *Civic Ideals: Conflicting Visions of Citizenship in U.S. History*. New Haven: Yale University Press, 1997.

Snorton, C. Riley. "Marriage Mimesis." *Journal of International & Intercultural Communication* 6, no. 2 (2013): 1–8.

Somers, Margaret R. *Genealogies of Citizenship: Markets, Statelessness, and the Right to Have Rights*. Cambridge: Cambridge University Press, 2008.

Somerville, Siobhan B. "Notes toward a Queer History of Naturalization." *American Quarterly* 57, no. 3 (2005): 659–675.

———. *Queering the Color Line: Race and the Invention of Homosexuality in American Culture.* Durham: Duke University Press, 2000.

———. "Queer Loving." *GLQ* 11, no. 3 (2005): 335–370.

Soto, Sandra K., and Miranda Joseph. "Neoliberalism and the Battle over Ethnic Studies in Arizona." *Thought & Action* 26 (2010).

Soysal, Yasemin Nuhoglu. "Toward a Postnational Model of Membership." In *The Citizenship Debates*, edited by Gershon Shafir, 189–217. Minneapolis: University of Minnesota Press, 1998.

Spade, Dean. *Normal Life: Administrative Violence, Critical Trans Politics, and the Limits of Law.* Brooklyn: South End Press, 2011.

———. "Resisting Medicine, Re/Modeling Gender." *Berkeley Women's Law Journal* 18 (2003): 15–37.

———. "Under the Cover of Gay Rights." *Review of Law & Social Change* 37, no. 1 (2013): 79–100.

Spalek, Basia. *Communities, Identities and Crime.* Bristol: The Policy Press, 2008.

Sparks, Holloway. "Dissident Citizenship: Democratic Theory, Political Courage, and Activist Women." *Hypatia* 12, no. 4 (Fall 1997): 74–110.

Spiro, Peter J. "The Citizenship Dilemma." *Stanford Law Review* 51 (1999): 597–639.

Sprinkle, Stephen. *Unfinished Lives: Reviving the Memories of LGBTQ Hate Crimes Victims.* Eugene, Ore.: Resource Publications, 2011.

Spruill, William E. "The Fate of Native Hawaiians: The Special Relationship Doctrine, the Problem of Strict Scrutiny, and Other Issues Raised by Rice v. Cayetano." *University of Richmond Law Review* 35 (2001): 149–189.

Stacey, Michele, Kristin Carbone-Lopez, and Richard Rosenfeld. "Demographic Change and Ethnically Motivated Crime: The Impact of Immigration on Anti-Hispanic Hate Crime in the United States." *Journal of Contemporary Criminal Justice* 27, no. 3 (2011): 278–298.

Stanley, Amy Dru. *From Bondage to Contract: Wage Labor, Marriage, and the Market in the Age of Slave Emancipation.* Cambridge: Cambridge University Press, 1998.

Stanley, Anna, Sedef Arat-Koç, Laurie K. Bertram, and Hayden King. "Intervention—Addressing the Indigenous-Immigration 'Parallax Gap.'" *Antipode* (2014); http://antipodefoundation.org/2014/06/18/addressing-the-indigenous-immigration-parallax-gap/ (accessed Dec. 15, 2014).

Staunæs, Dorthe. "Where Have All the Subjects Gone? Bringing Together the Concepts of Intersectionality and Subjectification." *Nora: Nordic Journal of Women's Studies* 11, no. 2 (2003): 101–110.

Stewart, Maria. "Lecture Delivered at Franklin Hall, Boston, September 21, 1832." In *Philosophy Born of Struggle: Anthology of Afro-American Philosophy from 1917*, edited by Leonard Harris. Dubuque: Kendall Hunt, 2000.

Stoler, Ann Laura. "Tense and Tender Ties: The Politics of Comparison in North American History and (Post) Colonial Studies." *Journal of American History* 88, no. 3 (2001): 829–865.

Streeby, Shelley. "Empire." In *Keywords for American Cultural Studies*, edited by Bruce Burgett and Glenn Hendler, 95–101. New York: New York University Press, 2007.

Streissguth, Tom. *Hate Crimes*. New York: Facts on File, 2003.

Stychin, Carl. *Governing Sexuality: The Changing Politics of Citizenship and Law Reform*. Oxford: Hart Publishing, 2003.

Sullivan, Paul M. "Recognizing the Fifth Leg: The Akaka Bill Proposal to Create a Native Hawaiian Government in the Wake of Rice v. Cayetano." *Asian-Pacific Law & Policy Journal* 3, no. 3 (2002): 308–351.

Takagi, Dana Y. "Faith, Race and Nationalism." *Journal of Asian American Studies* 7, no. 3 (2004): 271–288.

Thomas, Kendall. "Beyond the Privacy Principle." *Columbia Law Review* 92 (1992): 1431–1516.

Tomlinson, Barbara. "Colonizing Intersectionality: Replicating Racial Hierarchy in Feminist Academic Arguments." *Social Identities: Journal for the Study of Race, Nation and Culture* 19, no. 2 (2013): 254–272.

———. "To Tell the Truth and Not Get Trapped: Desire, Distance and Intersectionality at the Scene of Argument." *Signs*, no. 4 (2013): 993–1017.

Trask, Haunani-Kay. *From a Native Daughter: Colonialism and Sovereignty in Hawai'i*. Honolulu: University of Hawai'i Press, 1999.

———. "Settlers of Color and 'Immigrant' Hegemony: 'Locals' in Hawai'i." *Amerasia Journal* 26, no. 2 (2000): 1–24.

Trask, Mililani B. "Ka Lāhui Hawai'i: A Native Initiative for Sovereignty." *Turning the Tide: Journal of Anti-Racist Activism, Research & Education* 6, no. 5–6 (December 1993).

Trucios-Haynes, Enid F. "The Legacy of Racially Restrictive Immigration Laws and Policies and the Construction of the American National Identity." *Oregon Law Review* 76 (1997): 348–368.

Tuck, Eve, and K. Wayne Yang. "Decolonization Is Not a Metaphor." *Decolonization: Indigeneity, Education & Society* 1, no. 1 (2012): 1–40.

Tyler, Imogen, and Katarzyna Marciniak. "Immigrant Protest." *Citizenship Studies* 17, no. 2 (2013): 1–20.

Vaid, Urvashi. "'Now You Get What You Want, Do You Want More?'" *New York University Review of Law & Social Change* 37 (2013): 101–112.

Valdes, Francisco. "Sex and Race in Queer Legal Culture: Ruminations on Identities & Interconnectivities." *Southern California Review of Law & Women's Studies* 5, no. 25 (1995): 25–74.

Van Dyke, Jon M. "The Political Status of the Native Hawaiian People." *Yale Law & Policy Review* 17 (1998): 95–147.

Veracini, Lorenzo. "Natives Settlers Migrants." *Politica & Società*, no. 2 (2012): 187–204.

Volpp, Leti. "The Citizen and the Terrorist." *UCLA Law Review* 49, no. 5 (2002): 1575–1600.

———. "Divesting Citizenship: On Asian American History and the Loss of Citizenship through Marriage." *UCLA Law Review* 53 (2005): 405–483.

———. "Impossible Subjects: Illegal Aliens and Alien Citizens." *Michigan Law Review* 103 (2004): 1594–1630.

———. "'Obnoxious to Their Very Nature': Asian Americans and Constitutional Citizenship." *Asian Law Journal* 8 (2001): 71–87.

Walters, William. "Acts of Demonstration: Mapping the Territory of (Non-)Citizenship." In *Acts of Citizenship*, edited by Engin Isin and Greg M. Nielsen, 182–207. London: Zed Books, 2008.

Warner, Michael, ed. *Fear of a Queer Planet*. Minneapolis: University of Minnesota Press, 1993.

Weeks, Jeffrey. "The Sexual Citizen." *Theory, Culture, and Society* 15, no. 3–4 (1998): 35–52.

White, Hayden V. "Historical Emplotment and the Problem of Truth." In *Probing the Limits of Representation: Nazism and the "Final Solution,"* edited by Ralph Cohen, 37–53. Cambridge: Harvard University Press, 1992.

Whitlock, Katherine. *In a Time of Broken Bones: A Call To Dialogue on Hate Violence and the Limitations of Hate Crime Legislation*. Philadelphia: American Friends Service Committee, 2001.

Wiegman, Robyn. "Academic Feminism against Itself." *NWSA Journal* 14, no. 2 (2002): 18–34.

———. "Feminism's Apocalyptic Futures." *New Literary History* 31, no. 4 (2000): 805–825.

———. "The Vertigo of Critique: Rethinking Heteronormativity." *Object Lessons*. Durham: Duke University Press, 2012.

Wilkins, David E. *American Indian Politics and the American Political System*. Lanham, Md.: Rowman & Littlefield, 2002.

———. *American Indian Sovereignty and the U.S. Supreme Court: The Masking of Justice*. Austin: University of Texas Press, 1997.

Williams, Robert A. *The American Indian in Western Legal Thought: The Discourses of Conquest*. New York: Oxford University Press, 1990.

———. *Like a Loaded Weapon: The Rehnquist Court, Indian Rights, and the Legal History of Racism in America*. Minneapolis: University of Minnesota Press, 2005.

Willse, Craig, and Dean Spade. "Freedom in a Regulatory State: Lawrence, Marriage and Biopolitics." *Widener Law Review* 11, no. 2 (2004): 309–329.

Wilson, Waziyatawin Angela, and Michael Yellow Bird. *For Indigenous Eyes Only: A Decolonization Handbook*. Santa Fe: School of American Research, 2005.

Wolfe, Patrick. "Land, Labor and Difference: Elementary Structures of Race." *American Historical Review* 106, no. 3 (2001): 886–905.

Young, Iris Marion. "Polity and Group Difference: A Critique of the Ideal of Universal Citizenship." *Ethics* 99, no. 2 (1989): 250–274.

Young, Kanalu G. Terry. *Rethinking the Native Hawaiian Past*. New York: Garland Publishing, 1998.

Yuval-Davis, Nira. "Women, Citizenship, and Difference." *Feminist Review*, no. 57 (1997): 4–27.

Yuval-Davis, Nira, and Prina Werbner, eds. *Women, Citizenship, and Difference*. New York: Zed Press, 1999.

Zack, Naomi. *Inclusive Feminism: A Third Wave Theory of Women's Commonality*. Lanham, Md.: Rowman & Littlefield Publishers, Inc., 2005.

Zissu, Erik M. "What Hath Captain Cook Wrought? Bloodlines, The Fifteenth Amendment, and Racial Democracy in the Pacific." *University of Pittsburgh Law Review* 63 (2002): 677–702.

# Index

**AMY L. BRANDZEL** is an assistant professor of American studies and women studies at the University of New Mexico.

## DISSIDENT FEMINISMS

The University of Illinois Press
is a founding member of the
Association of American University Presses.

University of Illinois Press
1325 South Oak Street
Champaign, IL 61820-6903
www.press.uillinois.edu